The Decalogue
through the Centuries

The Decalogue
through the Centuries

*From the Hebrew Scriptures
to Benedict XVI*

EDITED BY
JEFFREY P. GREENMAN
AND TIMOTHY LARSEN

WJK WESTMINSTER
JOHN KNOX PRESS
LOUISVILLE · KENTUCKY

© 2012 Westminster John Knox Press

First edition
Published by Westminster John Knox Press
Louisville, Kentucky

12 13 14 15 16 17 18 19 20 21—10 9 8 7 6 5 4 3 2 1

Unless otherwise indicated, Scripture quotations are from the New Revised Standard Version of the Bible, copyright © 1989 by the Division of Christian Education of the National Council of the Churches of Christ in the U.S.A., and are used by permission. Scripture quotations marked RSV are from the Revised Standard Version of the Bible, copyright © 1946, 1952, 1971, and 1973 by the Division of Christian Education of the National Council of the Churches of Christ in the U.S.A., and are used by permission. Scripture quotations marked AT are the author's own translation.

Chapter 1 was originally published as "Reading the Decalogue Right to Left: The Ten Principles of Covenant Relationship in the Hebrew Bible," in *How I Love Your Torah, O Lord! Studies in the Book of Deuteronomy* (Eugene, OR: Cascade, 2011). Used by permission of Wipf and Stock Publishers. www.wipfandstock.com. Chapter 4 has been excerpted and revised from Matthew Levering, *Jewish-Christian Dialogue and the Life of Wisdom: Engagements with the Theology of David Novak* (New York: Continuum, 2011). Used by permission of Continuum. Excerpts in chapter 7 from the Sermons on Deuteronomy, vol. 26, in John Calvin, *John Calvin's Sermons on the Ten Commandments*, ed. and trans. Benjamin W. Farley (Grand Rapids, MI: Baker Books, a division of Baker Publishing Group, 1980) are used by permission of Baker Publishing Group. Excerpts in chapter 7 from John Calvin, *Institutes of the Christian Religion* 4.10.15, ed. John T. McNeill, trans. Ford Lewis Battles (Philadelphia: Westminster, 1960) are reprinted by permission of Westminster John Knox Press. An earlier version of chapter 11 was published as Timothy Larsen, "Christina Rossetti, the Decalogue, and Biblical Interpretation," *Zeitschrift für Neuere Theologiegeschichte* 16, no. 1 (2009): 21–36 and is reprinted by permission of De Gruyter. www.degruyter.com. Excerpts in chapter 13 from John Paul II, *The Splendor of Truth: Veritatis Splendor, Encyclical Letter* (Boston: St. Paul Books & Media, 1993) are copyright 1993 by Libreria Editrice Vaticana and are reprinted by permission. Excerpts in chapter 13 from John Paul II, *Man and Woman He Created Them: A Theology of the Body* (Boston: Pauline Books and Media, 2006) are copyright 2006 by Libreria Editrice Vaticana and are reprinted by permission. Excerpts in chapter 13 from Joseph Ratzinger's "The Church's Teaching Authority-Faith-Morals," in *Principles of Christian Morality*, trans. Graham Harrison (Ignatius Press, 1986) are reprinted by permission of Ignatius Press. Excerpts in chapter 13 from Joseph Ratzinger's "Handing on the Faith and the Sources of Faith," in *Handing on the Faith in an Age of Disbelief*, trans. Michael J. Miller (Ignatius Press, 2006) are reprinted by permission of Ignatius Press.

Book design by Sharon Adams
Cover design by Mark Abrams

Library of Congress Cataloging-in-Publication Data

The Decalogue through the centuries : from the Hebrew scriptures to Benedict XVI / edited by Jeffrey P. Greenman & Timothy Larsen.
    pages cm
    Includes bibliographical references and index.
    ISBN 978-0-664-23490-4 (pbk.)
    1. Ten commandments—Criticism, interpretation, etc.—History.   I. Greenman, Jeffrey P., editor of compilation.   II. Larsen, Timothy, 1967– editor of compilation.
    BV4655.D358   2012
    241.5'209–dc23
                                                                                    2012015854

To Timothy George—

theologian, educator, and ecumenical leader

Contents

Contributors

Daniel I. Block is the Knoedler Professor of Old Testament at Wheaton College.

Craig A. Evans is the Payzant Distinguished Professor of New Testament at Acadia Divinity College.

Jeffrey P. Greenman is Associate Dean of Biblical and Theological Studies and Professor of Christian Ethics at Wheaton College.

George Hunsinger is the Hazel Thompson McCord Professor of Systematic Theology at Princeton Theological Seminary.

Timothy Larsen is the Carolyn and Fred McManis Professor of Christian Thought at Wheaton College.

Matthew Levering is Professor of Theology at the University of Dayton.

D. Stephen Long is Professor of Theology at Marquette University.

William E. May is the Michael J. McGivney Professor of Moral Theology Emeritus at the Pontifical John Paul II Institute for Studies on Marriage and Family at The Catholic University of America.

David Novak is the J. Richard and Dorothy Shiff Chair of Jewish Studies at the University of Toronto.

Alison G. Salvesen is University Research Lecturer in the Faculty of Oriental Studies at the University of Oxford.

Susan E. Schreiner is Professor of the History of Christianity and Theology at the University of Chicago Divinity School.

Carl R. Trueman is Professor of Historical Theology and Church History at Westminster Theological Seminary.

Timothy J. Wengert is the Ministerium of Pennsylvania Professor at The Lutheran Theological Seminary at Philadelphia.

Introduction

TIMOTHY LARSEN

Everyone ought to know the Ten Commandments. This has been a widespread conviction for over a millennium. Accounts from the medieval period of what the church expected every Christian to know standardly include two units of Scripture: the Decalogue and the Lord's Prayer. Far from the Protestant Reformation overturning this, the Reformers simply complained that these requirements had not been carried out with sufficient determination, rigor, and comprehensiveness. Luther's catechism (both the large and the small one) begins with the Ten Commandments. If anything, the Decalogue has an even more prominent place in Reformed catechesis. The Shorter Westminster Catechism has 107 questions, and at its heart is the longest thematic section, that on the Ten Commandments (questions 41–81). Numerous catechisms—including the Anglican Catechism in the Book of Common Prayer and the most recent Catechism of the Catholic Church (1994)—require the faithful especially to give sustained, careful attention to two passages of Holy Writ: the Ten Commandments and the Lord's Prayer.

This emphasis has been so effective that more people understand a reference to the Ten Commandments than a reference to any other section of the Old Testament. Indeed, more self-identified Christians probably have a greater sense of recognition when it comes to the Ten Commandments than they do to many parts of the New Testament. When asked to identify something taught in the Epistles of Jude or Titus (or more than half of the books of the New Testament), the only response could well be a blank stare; but if asked about the Decalogue, they would be able to rattle off at least a few of the ten. This elevated status has meant that the Decalogue has a prominent place even in popular culture. It is striking that the classic Charlton Heston blockbuster of 1956, even though it covered a much wider dramatic sweep, not least the plagues of Egypt and the parting of the Red Sea, was given the alluring title for the movie-going public, *The Ten Commandments*. Likewise, when Indiana Jones wanted to impress upon his associates (and thereby the audience) the importance of the ark of the covenant, he defined it as "the chest the Hebrews used to carry around the Ten Commandments." Most of all, the Decalogue is the unit of Scripture that is most often displayed in public, civic space in the United States, and increasingly activists have focused on this one section from the Bible being accorded this special privilege.

One of the interesting facts that this collection of essays highlights, however, is that this looming eminence was surprisingly slow to develop. Daniel I. Block observes that the Prophets and other writings in the Hebrew Scriptures beyond the Pentateuch give surprisingly little attention to the Decalogue. David Novak, writing on the great medieval Jewish thinker, Maimonides, reminds us that Jewish teaching emphasizes that there are 613 perpetual, divine commandments given in the Torah and this must not be pared down to two handfuls worth. Likewise, Craig A. Evans observes that some of the Ten Commandments are never even explicitly mentioned in the New Testament. During the patristic period, however, as Alison Salvesen demonstrates, the Decalogue does emerge as a core resource for Christian ethical teaching. Nevertheless, even this transformation is less prominent and decisive than one might imagine. The original plan for this volume assumed that there would be a chapter on Augustine, but the experts on that leading Western church father whom we approached replied that there simply was not enough material on the Decalogue in the vast Augustinian corpus to generate a sufficiently full and rich chapter.

On the other hand, as Professor Block also concedes, there is a sense in which the genuine uniqueness of the Decalogue is inherent in its very dramatic location as words given directly by the Almighty, inscribed in stone on Mount Sinai, smashed, restored, and stored in the ark of the covenant. Undoubtedly these arresting scenes have had their part in fueling our heightened preoccupation with the Decalogue. One thinks, for example, of Rembrandt's *Moses Smashing the Tables of the Law* (c. 1659). Indeed, the physicality of the tables has undoubtedly been part of what has made displaying the Ten Commandments so inviting. It became standard practice, for example, to have the Decalogue inscribed in Anglican churches. This physicality, in turn, has had haunting imaginative possibilities. In Thomas Hardy's *Jude the Obscure*, for example, the portentousness of Jude's love affair with a married woman is signaled by his finding paid employment repairing the Decalogue in a church. Or here is Charles Dickens in *Dombey and Son* luridly describing an ill-advised wedding: "The sun is shining down, upon the golden letters of the ten commandments. Why does the Bride's eye read them, one by one? Which one of all the ten appears the plainest to her in the glare of light? False Gods; murder; theft; the honour that she owes her mother; —which is it that appears to leave the wall, and print itself in glowing letters, on her book!"

Beyond its dramatic utility in popular culture, the Decalogue has been and continues to be a rich site for theological, ethical, moral, and devotional reflection. This collection of essays explores these interactions across the centuries through a series of suggestive encounters with this spectacularly resonant text from God's Word. It is intended to be deliberately interdisciplinary in a way that will open up additional lines of thought for students and scholars in specific disciplines. Students of the Hebrew Scriptures ought to be intrigued about how this material is appropriated in the New Testament; biblical scholars ought to wonder how it has been interpreted in historical theology; historical theologians ought to attend to the context of church history; systematic theologians ought to revivify some of their standard moves by drinking *ad fontes* from the biblical sources of these lines of thought; ethicists and activists ought to care about how the theology of the first table undergirds their humanitarian concerns and constructive theologians ought to ponder the ethical implications of theological claims; philosophers ought to attend to devotional readings of the Decalogue, and worshipers ought to worship with their minds as well as their hearts; Jews ought to wonder about the extent to which Christians interpret the Decalogue in the same way that they do, and Christians ought to wonder how Jews have expounded the meaning of the Ten Words; the same can be said of Catholics and Protestants, Lutherans and Calvinists, and on and on.

While the preeminence of the Decalogue has been a gradual development, the history of the interpretation of the Ten Commandments is a very old story indeed—and a fascinating one. In fact, Block argues in his provocative opening essay that the first interpretative appropriation happens not beyond but actually within the Pentateuch, with the move from Exodus to Deuteronomy. This volume tracks such moves all the way to the present day in which the current pope, Benedict XVI, continues to emphasize, as William E. May demonstrates, that the Ten Commandments are moral absolutes that need to be resolutely championed in deliberate defiance of the relativistic spirit of the age.

This collection of essays has a cumulative effect. On the one hand, it is important to see the striking continuities in reading the Decalogue that have been maintained across time and place and religious identities. David Novak reminds us that Jews and Christians agree on the basic interpretation of most of the commandments. Even more intriguingly, his essay on Maimonides is similar to George Hunsinger's on Karl Barth: despite their very different chronological and confessional locations, Maimonides and Barth shared a preoccupation with the First Commandment as the font and basis of all the others (an insight that also recurs in other chapters including the one on Lancelot Andrewes). In this long history of interpretation there are also deliberate departures from hitherto reigning readings. Not least in this latter camp is Luther's sharp distinction between law and grace, which is explored here by Timothy Wengert. For Luther, the commandments serve the negative function of reminding us that we are sinners who cannot keep them. This break with the past, however, is immediately counter-corrected in Reformed theology—as Susan E. Schreiner's essay documents—through Calvin's teaching of the third use of the law. Nevertheless, reading affinities reemerge in surprising places. Carl Trueman reveals that the Reformed Puritan John Owen, for example, drew on both the natural law tradition of Thomas Aquinas (presented in chapter 4 by Matthew Levering) and on Luther's law-gospel dialectic. John Wesley, however, as D. Stephen Long observes, deliberately took an anti-Lutheran approach, emphasizing instead the identification of Christ with the Torah.

To take up a couple other threads, the place of the Decalogue in moral formation has a different flavor again when the accent is placed on the devotional rather than dogmatic uses of this material. This is highlighted in Jeffrey P. Greenman's exploration of Lancelot Andrewes's prayers and in Timothy Larsen's presentation of Christina Rossetti's *Letter and Spirit: Notes on the Commandments*. Many of these chapters also draw attention toward the wider historical context in which theologizing takes place. Alison Salvesen reminds us that a more Jewish reading of the Law by some early Christians might have been motivated by an attempt to escape state persecution and—far from state persecution ending with Constantine—George Hunsinger would have us not forget that denouncing idolatry had a specific import for theologians such as Karl Barth who were reflecting on the Ten Commandments during the Nazi regime. To take just one more example of this, Pope John Paul II's exposition of the Decalogue must be situated in the context of a range of social practices that accelerated considerably during his own lifetime, including promiscuity and abortion.

Indeed, a whole series of issues recur in multiple chapters of this volume in stimulating ways. To name just some of them: the relationship between the Decalogue and natural law; how the Ten Commandments should be interpreted in the light of the Sermon on the Mount; whether or not the giving of the commandments implies that we have the ability to fulfill them; the distinction between the ceremonial and the moral law; the meaning of the Sabbath commandment for Christians; the relationship between law and grace; the commandments as headings that are applicable much more widely than the specific prohibition cited; and the necessity to read the commandments positively as fostering the good works, spiritual practices, and virtues that are the opposite of each sin. This list is merely suggestive rather than exhaustive—as is, of course, our choice of subjects for the chapters: the reader is invited to continue the exploration within the volume by tracking additional continuities, discontinuities, and reappearing themes; and outside it into other interpreters of the Ten Words.

This volume originated with a conference titled, "Reading the Ten Commandments through the Centuries" which was sponsored by Wheaton College in Wheaton, Illinois, held November 6 through 8, 2008. That event was made possible through the financial provision of Wheaton College's annual McManis Lectures and under the auspices of Wheaton's Department of Biblical and Theological Studies. Additional funding was provided by the Center for Applied Christian Ethics at Wheaton College. Special thanks are due to Rebekah Canavan, who provided outstanding organization of the conference. We are also grateful to Todd M. Heckman for his assistance in preparing this volume for publication and to Ann Gerber for her technical support.

We have dedicated this book to Dr. Timothy George, Dean and Professor of Divinity at Beeson Divinity School at Samford University in Alabama. Timothy has provided exemplary leadership as an evangelical theologian, educator, and ecumenical statesman. This book reflects his scholarly interest in the history of Christian biblical interpretation and doctrine. We are also grateful for his dedicated service to Wheaton College as a member of the Board of Trustees from 1999 through 2005, and for his continued involvement as an Advisory Life Trustee.

Abbreviations

AB	Anchor Bible
Ant.	*Antiquities of the Jews*
BBR	*Bulletin for Biblical Research*
BC	*The Book of Concord.* Edited by Robert Kolb and Timothy J. Wengert. Minneapolis, 2000.
BZAW	Beihefte zur Zeitschrift für die alttestamentliche Wissenschaft
CBQ	*Catholic Biblical Quarterly*
CBQMS	Catholic Biblical Quarterly Monograph Series
CD	Cairo Damascus document
CD	*Church Dogmatics.* Edinburgh: T. & T. Clark, 1948.
CSCO	Corpus scriptorum christianorum orientalium. Edited by I. B. Chabot et al. Paris, 1903
ExT	*Expository Times*
GCS	Die griechische christliche Schriftsteller der ersten [drei] Jahrhunderte
ICC	International Critical Commentary
Int	*Interpretation*
ISBE	*International Standard Bible Encyclopedia.* Edited by G. W. Bromiley. 4 vols. Grand Rapids, 1979–88
JBTh	*Jahrbuch für biblische Theologie*
JCS	*Journal of Cuneiform Studies*

JETS	*Journal of the Evangelical Theological Society*
JSOTSup	Journal for the Study of the Old Testament: Supplement Series
Kt	Kaiser Traktate
LC	Large Catechism. Translated by James Schaaf
LW	*Luther's Works* (American edition). 55 vols. Philadelphia and St. Louis, 1955–86.
LXX	The Septuagint
LXX^B	Codex Vaticanus of LXX
MLE	*The Morall Law Expounded.* London, 1642.
NICOT	New International Commentary on the Old Testament
NIDOTTE	*New International Dictionary of Old Testament Theology & Exegesis.* Edited by Willem VanGemeren. 5 vols. Grand Rapids, 1997.
NIVAC	New International Version Application Commentary
NovT	*Novum Testamentum*
NovTSup	Novum Testamentum Supplements
NTS	*New Testament Studies*
OBT	Overtures to Biblical Theology
OTL	Old Testament Library
PCD	*A Pattern of Catechistical Doctrine and Minor Works of Lancelot Andrews.* Oxford, 1846.
PD	*The Private Devotions of Lancelot Andrews.* Translated and edited by F. E. Brightman. Gloucester, 1983.
QD	Quaestiones disputatae
RSV	Revised Standard Version
SBLWAW	Society of Biblical Literature Writings from the Ancient World
SBS	Stuttgarter Bibelstudien
SBT	Studies in Biblical Theology
SC	Sources chrétiennes. Paris: Cerf, 1943
SNTSMS	Society for New Testament Studies Monograph Series
SS	Studi semitici
TDOT	*Theological Dictionary for the Old Testament.* Edited by G. J. Botterweck and H. Ringgren. Translated by J. T. Willis, G. W. Bromiley, and D. E. Green. 8 vols. Grand Rapids, 1974–

TOB	"Theology of the Body" in *Man and Woman He Created Them: A Theology of the Body*. Introduction, translation, and index by Michael Waldstein. Boston, 2006.
WA	*Luthers Werke: Kritische Gesamtausgabe [Schriften]*, 73 vols. Weimar: H. Böhlau, 1883–2009.
WBC	Word Biblical Commentary
WMANT	Wissenschaftliche Monographien zum Alten und Neuen Testament
WTJ	Westminster Theological Journal
WUNT	Wissenschaftliche Untersuchungen zum Alten und Neuen Testament
ZAW	*Zeitschrift für die alttestamentliche Wissenschaft*

Chapter 1

The Decalogue
in the Hebrew Scriptures

DANIEL I. BLOCK

INTRODUCTION

In the opening statement of the 1968 English edition of his monograph, *The Ten Commandments in New Perspective*, Eduard Nielsen writes, "Of all the passages in the Old Testament the Decalogue, 'the ten commandments,' is presumably the best known to western civilization, and not least in countries which have a Lutheran tradition."[1] Many will concur with this opinion. My own roots are not Lutheran, but growing up in a Mennonite community in northern Saskatchewan, I certainly was an heir to this tradition.

How is it that this 3,000-year-old document has come to hold such sway in Christian circles when much of the rest of the Torah, especially the constitutional

This essay contains material published in chapter 2 ("Reading the Decalogue Right to Left: The Ten Principles of Covenant Relationship in the Hebrew Bible"), in my *How I Love Your Torah, O Lord! Studies in the Book of Deuteronomy* (Eugene, OR: Cascade, 2011). Used by permission of Wipf and Stock Publishers. www.wipfandstock.com.

1. Eduard Nielsen, *The Ten Commandments in New Perspective: A Traditio-historical Approach*, SBT 2nd series 7 (Naperville, IL: Allenson, 1968), 1. Compare the observation of James Barr in the forward to Nielsen's work: "The Ten Commandments constitute beyond doubt the best known and most influential single passage in the whole Old Testament" (vii).

material, is ignored at best and rejected at worst? Many interpret the Decalogue as a distinctive statement of moral truth universally applicable and permanently relevant. Martin Luther elevated it to the status of natural law.[2] Is this how the Scriptures, particularly the Hebrew Bible, want us to treat the Decalogue? Frank Crüsemann for one does not think so. Reflecting on the Decalogue in Christian theology, ethics and especially catechesis, he categorically rejects the notion that this document can be regarded as a summary or essential statement of the Torah, and it was never intended to play this role.[3] The purpose of this essay is to explore whether or not Crüsemann is right. I shall do so by investigating how the Decalogue is perceived within the Hebrew Bible itself.

But this is an extremely complex matter, and may be pursued from several angles. Some approach the issue by tracing the evolution of the text of the Decalogue. More than seventy-five years ago, Rudolf Kittel reduced the original text to ten short sentences.[4]

Others investigate the redaction history of the narratives in which the document is embedded. Many conclude that the Decalogue is a late composition created by Deuteronomistic theologians as a ten-article compendium of covenantal expectations resembling a catechism to be used in lay instruction, and which was secondarily inserted into the Sinai narratives of Exodus 19–24 and 32–34.[5]

However, such efforts are fraught with uncertainty and often yield inconsistent results. I shall explore the role of the Decalogue in ancient Israel by examining its place in the biblical documents as we have them. While many reject efforts to let biblical texts make their own case, the contents and structure of the Hebrew Bible represent an early stage in the history of the interpretation. My assignment is to examine this stage. I shall read the evidence with a sympathetic disposition, reading it from right to left and letting the present shapes of the

2. See further Werner H. Schmidt, *Die Zehn Gebote im Rahmen alttestamentlicher Ethik*, Erträge der Forschung 281 (Darmstadt: Wissenschaftliche Buchgesellschaft, 1993), 20–21.

3. Frank Crüsemann, *The Torah: Theology and Social History of Old Testament Law*, trans. Allan W. Mahnke (Minneapolis: Fortress, 1996), 352–53.

4. See Rudolf Kittel, *Geschichte des Volkes Israel*, 6th ed. (Stuttgart: Kohlhammer, 1932), 383–84. For variations of Kittel's reconstruction, see Eduard Nielsen, *Ten Commandments*, 78–86; Walter Harrelson, *The Ten Commandments and Human Rights*, rev. ed. (Macon, GA: Mercer University Press, 1997), 33–34; Moshe Greenberg, "Decalogue (The Ten Commandments)," in *Encyclopaedia Judaica*, 2nd ed. (Farmington Hills, MI: Thomson Gale, 2007), 5.524; Moshe Weinfeld, "The Decalogue: Its Significance, Uniqueness, and Place in Israel's Tradition," in *Religion and Law: Biblical-Judaic and Islamic Perspectives*, ed. Edwin B. Firmage, Bernard G. Weiss, and John W. Welch (Winona Lake, IN: Eisenbrauns, 1990), 12–15; idem, "The Uniqueness of the Decalogue and Its Place in Jewish Tradition," in *The Ten Commandments in History and Tradition*, ed. Ben-Zion Segal and Gershon Levi (Jerusalem: Magnes, 1990), 6–8.

5. For variations of these reconstructions of the history of the narratives see Werner Schmidt, *Die Zehn Gebote*, 25–34; Eckhart Otto, *Theologische Ethik des Alten Testaments*, Theologische Wissenschaft 3/2 (Stuttgart: Kohlhammer, 1994), 208–19; Rainer Albertz, *A History of Israelite Religion in the Old Testament Period*, OTL (Louisville: Westminster John Knox, 1994), 214–16; Lothar Perlitt, *Bundestheologie im Alten Testament*, WMANT 36 (Neukirchen-Vluyn: Neukirchener Verlag, 1969), 83–86; Frank Crüsemann, *The Torah*, 351–57; Anthony Phillips, "A Fresh Look at the Sinai Pericope," in *Essays on Biblical Law* (London: T. & T. Clark, 2002), 25–48.

texts and the shape of the canon as a whole make their own statements.[6] My presentation will seek to answer three questions:

1. How does the Pentateuch (Torah) speak about the Decalogue?
2. How does Moses reinterpret the Decalogue in Deuteronomy?
3. What evidence is there elsewhere in the Hebrew Bible for a special status for the Decalogue in Israelite thought and life?

When we have answered these questions we should have a better understanding of the nature and function of this document in its original canonical context and have a base for evaluating the history of the interpretation of this text.

1. DESIGNATIONS FOR THE DECALOGUE IN THE HEBREW BIBLE

One of the most obvious clues to the Hebrew Bible's understanding of the Decalogue is found in the expressions used to refer to it. In the Torah we find four such expressions.

1. The Decalogue as the Words of YHWH

Remarkably, the Hebrew Bible never refers to the Decalogue as "the commandments."[7] Exodus 20:1 introduces the document with *wayedabber 'elohim 'et kol haddebarim ha'elleh le'mor*, "Then God spoke all these words saying. . . ."[AT].[8] In the covenant ratification narratives Moses distinguishes the "words" (*haddebarim*) of the Decalogue from the "judgments" (*mishpatim*) of the "Book of the Covenant" (*seper habberit*).[9] YHWH uses this expression in 34:1, when he says that he will write on new tablets the "words" that were

---

6. Contra David Clines and Michael Fox, who write, "Indeed the willingness *not* to take a text at face value is the essence of critical scholarship." See Michael Fox, *Character and Ideology in the Book of Esther* (Columbia, SC: University of South Carolina Press, 1991), 148.

7. We often find the word *mitswot* in the context of YHWH's revelation (including within the Decalogue itself (Exod. 20:6; Deut. 5:10), but the word is used more generally of the rest of the Sinai revelation, often in association with the *mishpatim* ("judgments") and *huqqim* ("statutes"). In Exodus 24:12 the singular *mitswah* refers to "the command that I have written for your instruction" [AT]. See further below. If one must refer to the *mitswot* of the Decalogue as imperatives (which they are), there is no need to refer to the individual injunctions as "commandments," rather than "commands." The use of this archaic expression reflects and reinforces the faulty notion that the terms of the Decalogue are exceptional in genre or authority.

8. The verb *dibber*, "to speak," recurs in v. 22. The noun *debarim*, "words," referring to the Decalogue recurs in 24:3, 4, 8; 34:1, 27, 28.

9. Exodus 24:3, 4, 8. The term *mishpatim*, literally "judgments," derives from 21:1, and the "Book of the Covenant" (*seper habberit*) is generally recognized to consist of 20:22–23:19. So also Jean-Louis Ska, "From History Writing to Library Building: The End of History and the Birth of the Book," in *The Pentateuch as Torah: New Models for Understanding Its Promulgation and Acceptance*, ed. Gary N. Knoppers and Bernard M. Levinson (Winona Lake, IN: Eisenbrauns, 2007), 165–69.

written on the tablets that Moses smashed, and even more emphatically in 34:27–28: "Write these **words** (*debarim*); in accordance with these **words** I have made a covenant with you and with Israel . . . And he wrote on the tablets the **words** of the covenant, the ten **words**." This pattern continues in Deuteronomy where Moses recalls both the original revelatory event and the rewriting of the document on new tablets.[10]

The Hebrew word *dabar* bears a wide range of meanings: "word," "statement," "message," "object," "event." Especially when used with the cognate verb, *dibber*, "to speak," the emphasis is on communication. The preference for *debarim*, "words," in these narratives highlights the revelation of the Decalogue as a communicative, rather than a specifically legislative, event.

2. The Decalogue as the Ten Words

The phrase '*aseret haddebarim*, "ten words," occurs for the first time in Exodus 34:28 and twice more in Moses' recollection of the original events in Deuteronomy 4:13 and 10:4.[11] No matter how deeply entrenched is the tradition of rendering the phrase as "the ten commandments," here translators should follow the lead of LXX, which translates the expression literally as *deka logous*, "ten words," in Exodus 34:28 and Deuteronomy 10:4, and *deka rhēmata*, "ten declarations," in Deuteronomy 4:13. The phrase is best interpreted as shorthand for "the ten principles of covenant relationship."

This raises the question why the Decalogue should consist of ten declarations. Why not seven, the typological number of completeness,[12] or twelve, a typological number tightly associated with Israel?[13] Admittedly, ten also functions as a typological number in the Torah,[14] but it seems more likely that the

10. On the former, see Deuteronomy 4:10, 12, 36; 5:22, 28; 9:10. With reference to the latter, see Deuteronomy 10:2.

11. Like many others, Anthony Phillips insists the reference to "Ten Words" in Exodus 34:28 is a Deuteronomistic phrase inserted by late Pentateuchal editors. See "The Decalogue: Ancient Israel's Criminal Law," in *Essays on Biblical Law*, 10.

12. E.g., seven days of creation (Gen. 1; Exod. 20:11); seven pairs of clean animals and birds for sacrifice (Gen. 7:2–3); seven ewe lambs used in ritual (Gen. 21:28, 30), seven good and seven lean years (Gen. 41), etc.

13. Note the references to Jacob's twelve sons (Gen. 35:22; 42:13, 32), who become the twelve tribes of Israel (Gen. 49:28; Exod. 24:4), and will be represented at the covenant ratification ritual by twelve pillars (Exod. 24:4), twelve stones on the high priest's breastpiece (Exod. 28:21; 39:14), twelve staffs (Num. 17:2, 6), and by twelve men sent out to scout the land (Num. 13:2–16; Deut. 1:23). Cf. also the twelve springs of water at Elim (Exod. 15:27; Num. 33:9). Ishmael also became the ancestor of twelve princes (Gen. 17:20; 26:16).

14. The genealogies in Genesis 5 and 11 and Ruth 4 consist of ten generations; for the sake of ten righteous in Sodom God would have spared the city (Gen. 18:32); the number "ten" figures prominently in the design of the Tabernacle (Exod. 26:1, 16; 27:12; 36:8, 21; 38:12.); in the sacred rituals (Exod. 29:40; Lev. 5:11; 6:20; 16:29; 27:32; Num. 5:15; 15:4; 28:5, 13, 21, 29; 29:4, 7, 10, 15, 23); the tithe (Lev. 27:30–32; Num. 18:21, 24, 26; Deut. 12:17; 14:22–24, 28; 26:12, 14); and in proverbial intensifying usage (Gen. 31:7, 41; Lev. 26:26; Num. 14:22); etc. Eduard Nielsen seems to favor this interpretation in *Ten Commandments*, 6–10. Philo (*De decalogo* 20) suggests ten is the perfect number that contains all kinds of numbers, both even and odd; it is the sum of the categories.

reason for ten is mnemonic: to facilitate memorization and recitation.[15] If the number of principles intentionally corresponds to the fingers on one's hands, then the Decalogue was composed to function as a sort of catechism, summarizing the essence of covenant relationship.[16]

3. The Decalogue as Torah

The Pentateuch refers to the Decalogue as *torah* only once. In Exodus 24:12 YHWH invites Moses to the top of Sinai to receive written copies of the covenant document sealed in the foregoing ritual. But the construction of the clause is difficult, with three direct objects of the verb: *we'ettena leka et luhot ha'eben wehattorah wehammitswah 'aser katabti lehorotam*, translated literally "and I will give you the tablets of stone and the *torah* and the command (*hammitswah*) that I have written for their instruction" [AT]. Although most translations suggest the tablets contained the Torah and the Command, we should interpret the *waw* conjunctions epexegetically: "the tablets of stone, that is the Torah, that is the command that I have written for their instruction."[17] LXX renders *torah* as *nomos*, "law," here and virtually everywhere else,[18] even though this word does not mean "law." It is cognate to the last word in this sentence, the infinitive *lehorotam*, "for their instruction." In Deuteronomy the word occurs repeatedly with precisely the same semantic range as Greek *didache* or *didaskalia*, both of which mean "instruction, teaching," rather than law. The odd construction of Exodus 24:12 highlights the close identification of the revelation with the tablets, but it also declares the genre of the text of the tablets.

Though singular, the second expression, *hammitswah*, "the command," recognizes that the Decalogue does indeed consist largely of commands, but the following clause explains that these should not be interpreted like laws decreed by a king. The surrounding narrative (cf. 19:4–6), the form of the Decalogue, and the nature of the ten terms demonstrate that this document functions, not as a legal code, but as a statement of covenantal policy, as guidance for life, creating an ideal rather than decreeing law.[19] The commands are so general as to be virtually unenforceable through the judicial system. Their intention is to create a framework and ethos within which Israelites were to live.

---

15. So also Walter Harrelson, *Ten Commandments*, 9, 135.

16. Patrick D. Miller suggests the Decalogue functions something like the American constitution, providing the basis for later specification of the laws in the book of the covenant, the Holiness Code and the so-called Deuteronomic Code [*sic*]. See "The Place of the Decalogue in the Old Testament and Its Law," in *The Way of the Lord: Essays in Old Testament Theology* (Grand Rapids: Eerdmans, 2004), 3–16; idem, "The Sufficiency and Insufficiency of the Commandments," ibid, 23.

17. Though scholars tend to explain the complicated syntax as the result of a series of later expansions. Thus Brevard Childs, *The Book of Exodus: A Critical, Theological Commentary*, OTL (Philadelphia: Westminster, 1974), 499.

18. Of the 220 occurrences of *torah* LXX renders 202 as *nomos*.

19. Cf. Werner Schmidt (*Die Zehn Gebote*, 17–18), "Die Gebote stellen also im strengen Sinne keine Rechtssätze dar, dienen nicht der Gerichtsbarkeit, sondern sind eher Verhältnisregeln, Anweisungen für das Leben, mehr Ethos als Jus."

4. The Decalogue as the Foundational Covenant Document

The etymology of the Hebrew word *berit* continues to elude us. Nevertheless, its meaning is clear: it involves a solemn commitment between two parties, usually formally concluded with an oath. Covenants occur in two primary forms: parity covenants between persons/parties of equal status,[20] and suzerainty covenants involving a superior and a vassal.[21] In the Hebrew Bible *berit* is used of YHWH's covenants with the cosmos and its representative Noah (Gen. 9:8–17), with Abraham (Gen. 5:18; 17:1–14), and with David (2 Sam. 7; Ps. 89). It is also used with reference to the relationship that YHWH established with Israel at Sinai.[22] So tightly linked to the covenant is the Decalogue that its contents may be referred to as *dibre habberit*, "the words of the covenant" (Exod. 34:28) and even more directly *berito*, "his covenant" (Deut. 4:13),[23] and the written document itself as *luhot habberit*, "the tablets of the covenant" (Deut. 9:9, 11, 15). As the covenant document, the Decalogue provided Israel with concrete proof of the Divine Suzerain's immutable commitment to them and a constant reminder of their commitment to him. This document was stored in the Holy of Holies of the tabernacle in a specially designed container known as the "ark of the covenant of YHWH" (*'aron berit yhwh*),[24] or "the ark of the covenant of God (*'aron berit ha'elohim*),[25] or simply "the ark of the covenant" (*'aron habberit*),[26] because it contained the tablets that functioned as the primary symbol of the covenant (Deut. 10:1–8; 1 Kgs. 8:9).[27]

---

20. E.g., the covenant involving Jacob and Laban in Genesis 31:44–54.

21. E.g., the covenant involving Nebuchadnezzar and Zedekiah, Ezekiel 17:11–21. The bibliography on "covenant" is immense. For a helpful beginning, see Paul R. Williamson, "Covenant," in *Dictionary of the Old Testament: Pentateuch*, ed. T. Desmond Alexander and David W. Baker (Downers Grove, IL: InterVarsity, 2003), 155.

22. Since within the context of Jeremiah 31, the prophecy of the so-called "new covenant," is thoroughly parochial, announcing finally the fulfillment of the ideals represented by the covenant that YHWH made with Israel at Sinai and renewed on the plains of Moab (as reported in Deuteronomy), this should be understood as the "renewed covenant." We interpret the covenant made with Israel at Sinai to be essentially the same as the covenant made with Abraham, representing the fulfillment of YHWH's promise in Genesis 17:7, and a formal elaboration of its terms, especially in revealing the appropriate ethical responses to YHWH's grace in election and redemption and in providing for the maintenance of the covenant through the ritual.

23. Following Norbert Lohfink, Georg Braulik ("Deuteronomium 4,13 und der Horebbund," in *Für immer verbündet: Studien zur Bundestheologie der Bibel*, ed. Christoph Dohmen and Christian Freud, SBS 211 [Stuttgart: Katholisches Bibelwerk, 2007], 29–33) is correct in interpreting the *'asher* particle in Deuteronomy 4:13 as an explicative, rather than relative particle: YHWH declared to Israel his covenant; that is, he charged (*tsiwwah*) them to apply (*'asah*) the ten words. However, this does not negate the function of the Decalogue as the foundational covenant document. I am grateful to my doctoral student, Jerry Hwang, for drawing my attention to Braulik's discussion.

24. Numbers 10:33; 14:44; Deuteronomy 10:8; 31:9, 25, 26; Joshua 3:3, 11, 17; 4:7, 18; 6:8; 8:33; 1 Samuel 4:3–5; 1 Kings 3:15; 6:19; 8:1, 6; 1 Chronicles 15:25–29; 16:37; 17:1; 22:19; 28:2, 18; 2 Chronicles 5:2, 7; Jeremiah 3:16.

25. Judges 20:27; 1 Samuel 4:4; 15:24; 1 Chronicles 16:16.

26. Joshua 3:6, 8, 14; 4:9; 6:6.

27. On the ark, see now Ian Wilson, "Merely a Container? The Ark in Deuteronomy," in *Temple and Worship in Biblical Israel*, ed. John Day (London: T. & T. Clark, 2007), 212–49.

The frequent references to the Decalogue as 'edot/'edut reinforces its covenantal sense. Assuming a derivation from the same root as 'ud, "to testify,"
and 'ed, "witness," many translations continue to follow the ancient versions in
translating the word as "testimony."[28] However, this interpretation is misleading, because we usually think of "testimony" as the utterances of a witness in
a court of law or some less formal context.[29] The usage of the word as a vir-
tual synonym for berit and the etymological link with ade, the Akkadian word
for "covenant/treaty" and "loyalty oath,"[30] strengthen the case for interpreting
'edut as "pact,"[31] and the plural form 'edot as "contractual obligations, covenant
stipulations," to which one committed oneself through formal legal procedures,
including the oath. The word occurs three times in the phrase luhot ha'edut, "the
tablets of the pact" (Exod. 31:18; 32:15; 34:29), and more than a dozen times in
the phrase 'aron ha'edut, "the ark of the pact."[32]

Although the way the Decalogue is embedded in the narrative creates some
tension,[33] the events described in Exodus 19–24 constitute an elaborate covenant revelation and ratification ritual, beginning with the announcement in
Exodus 19:3b–5, and concluding with the covenant meal (24:9–11). When the

28. Thus LXX, Vulgate, the Targumim.

29. Stephen T. Hague (*NIDOTTE* 1.502) notes that "the translation of 'edut as 'testimony' is
reasonable, as long as we understand the testimony as *the law* that is the seal of the Lord's covenant
with Israel."

30. On the meaning and significance of ade, see Simo Parpola and Kazuko Watanabe, *Neo-
Assyrian Treaties and Loyalty Oaths*, SAA 2 (Helsinki: Helsinki University Press, 1988), xv–xxv.

31. Thus *TANAKH*. The plural form 'edot functions as a general designation for the stipulations of the covenant, which Deuteronomy 4:45 associates with *hahuqqim*, "the statutes," and
hammishpatim, "the ordinances." Cf. also Deuteronomy 6:17, 20; 1 Kings 2:3; 2 Kings 17:15;
23:3; 1 Chronicles 29:19; 2 Chronicles 34:31; Nehemiah 9:34; Jeremiah 44:23; Psalms 25:10;
78:56; 93:5; 99:7; 119:2–168 (22 times). Note also that what Moses calls the ark of the covenant
(of YHWH) ('aron berit YHWH, Deut. 10:8; 31:9, 25–26) is elsewhere referred to as the ark of the
'edut (Exod. 25:22; 26:33–34; 30:6, 26; 31:7; 39:35; 40:3, 5, 21; Num. 4:5; 7:89; 4:16). The present triad of terms recurs in Deuteronomy 6:20 with 'edah preceding the present pair. 'Edot appears
between mitswot and huqqim in 6:17. On the meaning and significance of 'edut, 'edot, see Horacio
Simian-Yofre, *TDOT* 10/514–15.

32. Exodus 25:22; 26:33, 34; 30:6, 26; 31:7; 39:35; 40:3, 5, 21; Numbers 4:5; 7:89; Joshua
4:16. In addition, we encounter expressions like mishkan ha'edut, "the tabernacle of the pact" (Exod.
38:21; Num. 1:50, 53; 10:11), ohel ha'edut, "the tent of the pact" (Num. 9:15; 17:22, 23; 18:2;
2 Chr. 24:6), and paroket ha'edut, "the veil of the pact" (Lev. 24:3). Frequently the expression
appears by itself functioning elliptically for 'aron ha'edut, "the ark of the pact," especially when used
with prepositions "before the pact" (Exod. 16:34; 27:21; 30:36; Num. 17:4), "over the pact" (Lev.
16:13), or for luhot ha'edut, "the tablets of the pact" (Exod. 25:21; 40:20) [All AT]. Two special
cases occur. In Isaiah 8:20 ha'edut appears alongside hattorah, probably serving as an alternative
designation for the Torah (i.e., Deuteronomy), and in 2 Kings 11:12 (= 2 Chr. 23:11), as part of
the investiture of Joash, Jehoiada the priest places on him the diadem (nezer) and the 'edut. Here the
expression may serve as a substitute for hattorah, "the Torah" (Moses' speeches in Deuteronomy)
which the king is to copy and read for himself all the days of his life (Deut. 17:18–19). See further
Mordechai Cogan and Hayim Tadmor, *II Kings: A New Translation with Introduction and Commentary*, AB 11 (n.p.: Doubleday, 1988), 128.

33. Chapter 19 ends with Moses descending the mountain and "saying to them [the people]"
(wayyo'mer 'alehem), but the content of his speech is dropped. Chapter 20 begins with God speaking, and the content of his speech clearly presented as the Decalogue. This disjunction apparently
serves the literary function of highlighting the role of YHWH and the Decalogue as divine speech.

ritual is completed YHWH invites Moses up the mountain to receive from him the official copy of the covenant (24:12–18).[34]

The identification of the Decalogue as a covenant document, rather than a legal code, helps to explain several other features. Structurally the Decalogue incorporates at least five of the primary elements of ancient Near Eastern covenant forms:

1. The preamble identifies the suzerain (Exod. 20:2a). The document opens with the divine Suzerain identifying himself by name and declaring the relational basis of the claims on Israel that will follow: *'anoki YHWH 'eloheka,* "I am YHWH your God" [AT].[35] This introduction compares with the opening lines of many Hittite treaties of roughly the same period.[36]

2. The historical prologue summarizes the history of the relationship (Exod. 20:2b). Whereas in most second-millennium Hittite and first-millennium BCE. Neo-Assyrian treaties the suzerain vassal relationship was established by the suzerain overwhelming the vassal,[37] YHWH's relationship with Israel had its roots in his triumph over those who held the nation in bondage. This sets the stage for the stipulations that follow, which clarify how Israel was to respond to YHWH's gracious actions on her behalf (cf. 19:4). Significantly, the principles of the Decalogue are not addressed to the world at large or to Israel in Egypt, but to a redeemed people as a summary of the appropriate response to grace already experienced. They are not presented as preconditions to Israel's redemption, and contrary to some of Martin Luther's statements, they certainly are not presented as "natural law."[38]

3. The stipulations summarize the divine Suzerain's expectations of his vassal. In examining the stipulations, several features stand out. First, the preamble and the first command are presented in a relational I-you form. Second, the stipulations are cast as apodictic (unconditional) as opposed to casuistic (conditional)

---

34. The official copy provided by the Suzerain is to be distinguished from the temporary copy prepared by Moses, and the official copy is used in the covenant ratification procedures. According to Exodus 24:1–8, following the direct revelation of the Decalogue to the people and apparently the revelation of the contents of the "book of the covenant" to Moses, Moses recounted (*sipper*) the words of YHWH (the Decalogue) and the *mishpatim* ("judgments") to the people (v. 3).

35. This is in fulfillment of YHWH's promise to Abraham in Genesis 17:7: "I will establish my covenant between me and you, and your offspring after you throughout their generations, for an everlasting covenant, to be God to you and to your offspring after you."

36. Cf. the opening of the treaty between Muwattalli II of Hatti and Alaksandu of Wikusa: "Thus says My Majesty, Muwattalli, Great King, [King] of Hatti, Beloved of the Storm-god of Lightning; son of Mursili, Great King, Hero." As translated by Gary Beckman, *Hittite Diplomatic Texts*, 2nd ed., SBLWAW 7 (Atlanta: Scholars Press, 1999), No. 13, §1.

37. Though some propagandistically highlight the overlord's grace toward the vassal. The introduction to treaty between Suppiluliuma I of Hatti and Huqqana of Hayasa bears a striking resemblance to the preamble to the Decalogue, highlighting the superior's benevolence to his vassal and beginning the stipulations with a call for exclusive allegiance to the overlord: "I have now elevated you, Huqqana, a lowly dog, and have treated you well. In Hattusa I have distinguished you among the men of Hayasa and have given you my sister in marriage. All of Hatti, the land of Hayasa, and the outlying and central lands have heard of you. Now you, Huqqana, recognize only My Majesty as overlord" (as translated by Gary Beckman, ibid, no. 3, §1–2).

38. See further Schmidt, *Die Zehn Gebote*, 20–21.

Table 1.   A Comparison of Conditional and Unconditional Law

Conditional Law (Casuistic)	Unconditional Law (Apodictic)
When an ox gores a man or woman to death, the ox shall be stoned, and its flesh shall not be eaten; but the owner of the ox shall be liable. (Exod. 21:28)	You shall have no other gods before me. (Exod. 20:3)
If you take your neighbor's cloak in pawn, you shall restore it before the sun goes down, for it may be your neighbor's only clothing; in what else shall that person sleep? (Exod. 22:26–27)	You shall not bear false witness against your neighbor. (Exod. 20:16)
Features	*Features*
Indicative mood	Imperative mood
In third (or second) person	In second person
Specific: based on actual cases, often with motive or exception clauses	General: without qualification or exception
Usually positive in form	Often negative in form
Begin with "If" or "When"	Begin with the verb (in the imperative)

commands. The former (apodictic) all transcend specific circumstances and most omit any reference to consequences, either good or bad.[39] The differences between these two kinds of commands are highlighted in Table 1.

Third, although the Decalogue has binding authority for all Israelites, strictly speaking it is addressed to individual adult male heads of households. All the main verbs and pronouns are cast in the second person masculine singular. Judging by the content of the ten principles, the addressee is a father with children (Exod. 20:5; Deut. 5:9); the head of a household, with authority over sons and daughters, male and female slaves, livestock, and aliens within the village (Exod. 5:9–10; Deut. 5:14); apparently has aged parents still living with him (Exod. 20:12; Deut. 5:16); is tempted to commit adultery (Exod. 20:14; Deut. 5:18), and to testify falsely against his neighbor in legal proceedings (Exod. 20:16; Deut. 5:20), and to covet his neighbor's wife and his property, including house and field (Exod. 20:17; Deut. 5:21). Frank Crüsemann describes the addressee as a middle-aged male householder, a member of the 'am ha'arets, that is, the empowered citizenry.[40]

But this raises the question, Whose interest does this document serve? In recent years it has become fashionable to argue the Decalogue was drafted to

39. The exceptions are the first command, which warns of the dire consequences of idolatry, and the fourth command, which presents honoring parents as a precondition to future blessing.

40. Frank Crüsemann, *Bewahrung der Freiheit: Das Thema des Dekalogs in sozialgeschichtlicher Perspektive*, Kaiser Traktate 78 (Munich: Kaiser, 1983), 28–35. For a helpful review of Crüsemann's work, see William Johnstone, "The Ten Commandments: Some Recent Interpretations," *ExT* 100 (1988–89): 455–57.

protect the interests of the rich and the powerful in Israel at the expense of the poor and marginalized. David Clines argues that the addressee must be an urban middle-aged male who threatens the status and security of wealthy male property owners.[41] But this can scarcely be the case. The addressee himself is deemed the potential threat to the community; he threatens the well-being of others. Accordingly, this document functions as Israel's Magna Carta,[42] perhaps the world's oldest bill of rights.[43] However, unlike modern bills of rights, the Decalogue is not interested in the addressees' rights, but seeks to protect the rights of members of the addressee's household and his neighbors by reining in his propensity to abuse them. Israel was indeed a covenant community that has been freed from the bondage of Egyptian slavery,[44] but the community was under the constant threat of individual Israelites, especially those with social and economic power, behaving like little pharaohs.[45] We may summarize briefly how each of the principles seeks to protect the right of someone else.[46]

1. YHWH has the right to exclusive allegiance—not only because he has triumphed over all gods (Exod. 12:12; Num. 33:4; Deut. 4:34–35, 39), but especially because he has graciously redeemed Israel, brought them to himself, and entered into covenant relationship with them (Exod. 19:4–6).

2. YHWH has the right to fair and honest representation. Bearing the name primarily means claiming YHWH as one's God and covenant Lord; to bear it falsely (*lashshaw*) means to claim this name but live as if one belongs to Baal or some other god.[47]

41. See especially David Clines, "The Ten Commandments, Reading from Left to Right," but also Cyril Rodd, *Glimpses of a Strange Land: Studies in Old Testament Ethics* (Edinburgh: T. & T. Clark, 2001), 87. For a radical feminist reading of the Decalogue, see Hagith Sivan, *Between Woman, Man and God: A New Interpretation of the Ten Commandments*, JSOTSup 401; Bible in the Twenty-first Century 4 (London: T & T Clark, 2004). However, see also Bernard S. Jackson's critical review of her work, "A Feminist Reading of the Decalogue(s)" in *Biblica* 87 (2006): 542–54. Jackson rightly concludes that her "privileging of the Decalogue" is a response "to a contemporary rather than an ancient agenda" (554).

42. Thus J. David Pleins, *The Social Visions of the Hebrew Bible: A Theological Introduction* (Louisville, KY: Westminster John Knox, 2001), 47.

43. See also Christopher J. H. Wright, "Ten Commandments," *ISBE*, rev. ed., 4.790.

44. Though I agree in general with those who treat this document as a "charter of human freedom" (Walter Harrelson, *The Ten Commandments*, 154–65; Johann. J. Stamm, *The Ten Commandments in Recent Research*, trans. Maurice E. Andrew [London: SCM Press, 1967], 112–14; especially Frank Crüsemann, *Bewahrung der Freiheit*), I view it from another angle with the view to seeing how it protects the next person's freedom.

45. Note the framing of the document with references to the "house of slaves" (*bet 'abadim*) in the preamble, and "your neighbor's house" (*bet re'eka*) in the last command—especially of the Deuteronomic version.

46. The discourse grammar of the text argues in favor of the Roman Catholic and Lutheran numbering.

47. Cf. Isaiah 44:1–5; 2 Peter 4:12–19. For a full development of this interpretation, see Daniel I. Block, *Deuteronomy*, NIVAC (Grand Rapids: Zondervan, 2012), 163; idem, "Bearing the Name of the LORD with Honor," *Bibliotheca Sacra* 168 (2011): 20–31; reprinted in Daniel I. Block, *How I Love Your Torah, O LORD! Studies in the Book of Deuteronomy* (Eugene, OR: Cascade Books, 2011) 61–72.

3. YHWH has the right to the Israelite's life and trust (Exodus version), and all the members of his household (including the livestock) have the right to humane treatment by the male head (Deuteronomy version).[48]

4. The addressee's parents have the right to his respect, which will mean more than piously verbalizing honor, but concretely caring for them in their old age and honoring them after death.

5. The addressee's family members and neighbors have the right to life.

6. The addressee's neighbors have the right to a pure marriage.

7. The addressee's neighbors have the right to their own property.[49]

8. The addressee's neighbors have the right to a true and honest reputation.

9. The addressee's neighbor and his wife have the right to freedom from fear of his intentions regarding them.

10. The addressee's neighbor has the right to freedom from fear of the addressee's intentions concerning his property.

In short, the Decalogue calls on the head of the household to be covenantally committed to YHWH, his household, and his neighbors so that he will resist seeking his own advantage and seek the interests of others. In so doing, the document views the householder's role, not primarily in terms of power and authority, but in terms of care and responsibility toward others. In this regard the Decalogue, the Book of the Covenant (Exod. 22:20, 25; 23:12), the Holiness Code (Lev. 19:9–10, 13–14, 29, 33–34) and the Deuteronomic Torah exhibit remarkable coherence, for they are all concerned about the well-being of those who are at the mercy of persons with power.[50] Indeed, Jesus distills all the commands to two, "You shall love the Lord your God with all your heart and with all your being and with all your resources"[51] [AT], and "You shall love your neighbor as yourself"[52] (see Figure 1).

4. The blessings and curses seek to motivate loyalty. Hittite and Neo-Assyrian treaties, as well as the Holiness Code (Lev. 26) and the Deuteronomic Torah (Deut. 28) gather the blessings and curses towards the end of the respective documents. Fragments of curses occur after the first and second principles (Exod.

48. While Deuteronomy clearly grounds the rhythm of Israel's life in their own experience, the Exodus version is less humanitarian, and its link with the rest of the Decalogue less certain.

49. Assuming *ganab* means more than "stealing a person," that is, robbing a person of his or her freedom (cf. Exod. 21:16), but also includes stealing in the broader sense.

50. Note the numerous contexts in which the plight of the widow, the fatherless and the alien are addressed: Deuteronomy 10:18; 14:29; 16:11, 14; 24:19–21; 26:12–13; 27:19.

51. The appropriate interpretation of the Hebrew word *me'od*, which underlies the Greek *tēs psychēs*, is "your strength," in Mark 12:30.

52. For a convincing discussion of *'ahab*, "love," as active and concrete demonstration of commitment to the well-being of the next person, rather than an abstract emotional expression, see A. Malamat, "'You Shall Love Your Neighbor as Yourself': A Case of Misinterpretation?" in *Die Hebräische Bibel und ihre zweifache Nachgeschichte: Festschrift für Rolf Rendtorff zum 65. Geburtstag*, ed. Erhard Blum, et al. (Neukirchen-Vluyn: Neukirchener Verlag, 1990), 111–15.

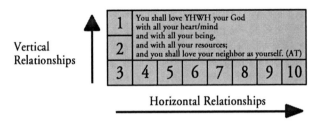

Vertical Relationships

Horizontal Relationships

Figure 1. Jesus' Understanding of the Decalogue

20:5, 7), and fragments of blessings occur at the end of the first and fourth principles (20:6, 12).

5. Provision for a covenant document promotes the fidelity of the parties to the covenant. The preparation of tablets inscribed with the covenant principles plays a significant role in both the Sinai narrative (Exodus 24:12–18) and in Moses' recollections of these events in Deuteronomy (4:9–14; 9:15–17; 10:1–5). These tablets were made of stone,[53] and inscribed by the divine suzerain, YHWH himself.[54] After Moses had smashed the original tablets, they were replaced with exact duplicates,[55] which provided concrete proof that YHWH had taken the Israelites back as his covenant people and that the terms of the renewed relationship were identical to the original covenant. Longstanding tradition has it that the first of the two tablets[56] contained those commands that deal with Israel's vertical relationship to God, and that the second dealt with horizontal relationships.[57] While devotionally and homiletically interesting, this interpretation is without exegetical or contextual foundation. The need for two stone tablets accords with ancient Near Eastern practice of providing each party to a covenant with a copy of the agreement.[58]

---

53. For John Calvin, the stone spoke of the permanence of the laws, in contrast to the transience of the ceremonies. *John Calvin's Sermons on the Ten Commandments*, ed. and trans. Benjamin W. Farley (Grand Rapids, MI: Baker, 1980), 249.

54. Exodus 24:12; 31:18; 32:16; 34:1, 28; Deuteronomy 4:13; 5:22; 9:10; 10:2, 4.

55. Exodus 34:28; Deuteronomy 10:1–4; cf. Exodus 32:19; Deuteronomy 9:15–17.

56. References to "two" tablets occur sixteen times in the Hebrew Bible: Exodus 31:18; 32:15; 34:1, 4a, 4b, 29; Deuteronomy 4:13; 5:22; 9:10, 11, 15, 17; 10:1, 3; 1 Kings 8:9; 2 Chronicles 5:10. To these should be added the plural references to the tablets without the numerical modifier: Exodus 24:12; 32:1, 19, 28, 29; Deuteronomy 9:9; 10:2, 4, 5.

57. John Calvin, *Institutes of the Christian Religion*, ed. John T. McNeill, Library of Christian Classics (London: S.C.M., 1961), 2.8.11 (pp. 376, 377). While New Testament scholars and theologians often use the language of "two tables," surprisingly the expression surfaces in Christopher Wright's *Old Testament Ethics for the People of God* (Downers Grove, IL: InterVarsity, 2004), 341. According to the *perashiyoth* (pericopes marked in the Hebrew text) the Masoretes seemed to think the "second table" begins with the Sabbath command, though most have thought that the "second table" opens with the command to honor parents. Since reverence for parents is regarded as a religious duty, many Jews count this command as the last in the "first table."

58. For a detailed study of this issue see Meredith G. Kline, "The Two Tables of the Covenant," *WTJ* 22 (1960): 138–46. Hittite custom had each party deposit a copy in the treaty in the temple of the deity, where they would be under the respective god's oversight, but from where they could be retrieved and read aloud at prescribed intervals. For an example see the treaty between Suppiluliuma I of Hatti and Shattiwaza of Mittani in Gary Beckman, *Hittite Diplomatic Texts*, 6A, §13, pp. 46–47.

While the Decalogue was not the only part of the Pentateuch associated with the covenant,[59] it was recognized as the original and official covenant document, announced to the people by YHWH himself and written by his own hand (Exod. 24:12; 31:18; Deut. 10:1–4). However, the Decalogue did not function as a law code to be administered in the courts; it was a foundational statement of principle, creating a worldview that begins by declaring YHWH's past grace in redeeming Israel from bondage, and then offers a "sampling of several important aspects of the new life of obedience within the covenant."[60] As Exodus 19:4 and the preamble to the Decalogue emphasize, Israel was not called primarily to conformity to a code of conduct, but to a relationship with their gracious redeemer.

2. THE REINTERPRETATION
OF THE DECALOGUE IN DEUTERONOMY

The presence of two versions of the Decalogue in the Pentateuch offers a rich opportunity for intertextual and synoptic study. Although many insist the Deuteronomic version antedates the Exodus version,[61] the authors of the Pentateuch intended for the Deuteronomic version to be read in light of the Exodus version.[62] The two versions begin identically, but beginning with the Sabbath command they diverge significantly.

The modifications involve deletion, addition of new features, rephrasing, and fundamental reworking of terms.

But how should we interpret these changes? Scholars have long observed the humanistic trajectory of Deuteronomy as a whole, especially when compared with corresponding regulations in the book of the covenant and the Holiness Code.[63] This trajectory is evident already in the Deuteronomic version of the Decalogue, particularly the Sabbath ordinance. First, anticipating later expressions of concern for the well-being of animals,[64] Moses specifies the ox and

59. We have already noted the content of the *seper habberit*, "book of the covenant," and its role in the covenant ratification procedure (Exod. 24:1–8). From the colophonic conclusion to the Holiness Code (Lev. 17–26) in Leviticus 26:46 it is evident that the divine speeches of Leviticus were also considered stipulations of the covenant. And Moses' second address in Deuteronomy (Deut. 4:44–26:19; 28:1–28:60 [Eng. 29:1]) is presented as a sermon on covenant relationship that was a part of a covenant renewal ceremony.

60. Thus Waldemar Janzen, *Old Testament Ethics: A Paradigmatic Approach* (Louisville, KY: Westminster John Knox, 1994), 92.

61. See Frank Crüsemann, *The Torah*, 352, 355; Bernhard Lang, "The Number Ten and the Antiquity of the Fathers: A New Interpretation of the Decalogue," *ZAW* 118 (2006): 218, following Frank-Lothar Hossfeld, *Der Dekalog*.

62. So also Moshe Weinfeld, *Deuteronomy 1–11: A New Translation with Introduction and Commentary*, AB 5 (New York: Doubleday, 1991), 243, et passim.

63. See Moshe Weinfeld, *Deuteronomy and the Deuteronomic School* (Winona Lake, IN: Eisenbrauns, 1992), 282–97; S. R. Driver, *A Critical and Exegetical Commentary on Deuteronomy*, ICC (Edinburgh: T. & T. Clark, 1902), 85.

64. Cf. 22:4, 6; 25:4.

Table 2. Synopsis of the Exodus and Deuteronomy Versions of the Decalogue

Bold font = variation in reading; *Italic font* = addition

	Exodus 20:2–17[AT]	Deuteronomy 5:6–21[AT]	
2	I am YHWH your God, who brought you out of the land of Egypt, out of the house of slavery.	I am YHWH your God, who brought you out of the land of Egypt, out of the house of slavery	6
3 – 6	You shall have no other gods before me. You shall not make for yourself a carved image, *or* any likeness of anything that is in heaven above, or that is in the earth beneath, or that is in the water under the earth. You shall not bow down to them or serve them, for I YHWH your God am a jealous God, visiting the iniquity of the fathers on the children to the third and the fourth generation of those who hate me, but showing steadfast love to thousands of those who love me and keep my commandments.	You shall have no other gods before me. You shall not make for yourself a carved image, any likeness of anything that is in heaven above, or that is on the earth beneath, or that is in the water under the earth. You shall not bow down to them or serve them, for I YHWH your God am a jealous God, visiting the iniquity of the fathers on the children to the third and the fourth generation of those who hate me, but showing steadfast love to thousands of those who love me and keep my commandments.	7 – 10
7	You shall not bear in vain the name of YHWH your God, for YHWH will not hold him guiltless who bears his name in vain.	You shall not bear in vain the name of YHWH your God, for YHWH will not hold him guiltless who bears his name in vain.	11
8 – 11	**Remember** the Sabbath day, to keep it holy. Six days you shall labor, and do all your work, but the seventh day is a Sabbath to YHWH your God. On it you shall not do any work, you, or your son, or your daughter, your male servant, or your female servant, or your livestock, or the sojourner who is within your gates.	**Observe** the Sabbath day, to keep it holy, *as YHWH your God commanded you.* Six days you shall labor and do all your work, but the seventh day is a Sabbath to YHWH your God. On it you shall not do any work, you, or your son, or your daughter *or* your male servant, or your female servant, *or your ox or your donkey* or *any of* your livestock, or the sojourner who is within your gates,	12 – 15

Table 2.   (*Continued*)

Bold font = variation in reading; *Italic font* = addition

	Exodus 20:2–17[AT]	Deuteronomy 5:6–21[AT]	
8 – 11	**For in six days YHWH made heaven and earth, the sea, and all that is in them, and rested the seventh day.** Therefore YHWH **blessed the Sabbath day and made it holy.**	**that your male servant and your female servant may rest as well as you. You shall remember that you were a slave in the land of Egypt, and YHWH your God brought you out from there with a mighty hand and an outstretched arm.** Therefore YHWH **your God commanded you to keep the Sabbath day.**	12 – 15
12	Honor your father and your mother, that your days may be long in the land that YHWH your God is giving you.	Honor your father and your mother, *as YHWH your God commanded you,* that your days may be long, *and that it may go well with you* in the land that YHWH your God is giving you.	16
13	You shall not murder.	You shall not murder.	17
14	You shall not commit adultery.	*And* you shall not commit adultery.	18
15	You shall not steal.	*And* you shall not steal.	19
16	You shall not bear **false** witness against your neighbor.	*And* you shall not bear **useless** witness against your neighbor.	20
17	You shall not covet your neighbor's **house;** you shall not **covet** your neighbor's **wife,** or his male servant, or his female servant, *or* his ox, or his donkey, or anything that belongs to your neighbor.	*And* you shall not covet your neighbor's **wife.** *And* you shall not **desire** your neighbor's **house,** *his field,* or his male servant, or his female servant, his ox, or his donkey, or anything that belongs to your neighbor.	21

the donkey, draft and pack animals respectively, as deserving of the Sabbath rest.[65] Second, beyond patterning human creative work after that of God the Creator, Deuteronomy portrays the Sabbath as a gift, offering all who toil an opportunity to refresh themselves. Third, instead of calling on Israelites to remember the Sabbath, it calls them to treasure the Sabbath by recalling the time when they labored for brutal Egyptian taskmasters, without Sabbath or

65. This insertion may reflect the influence of the last command and/or Exodus 23:12.

relief.[66] The seventh-day Sabbath celebrates YHWH's special creative work in rescuing them from bondage.[67]

The adjustments to the commands on coveting follow the same trajectory. While scholars have spent a great deal of time exploring the significance of the shift from *hamad*, "to covet," to *hit'awwah* "to desire," in Deuteronomy,[68] the substitution of one verb with another does not appear to be nearly as consequential as the transposition of "house" and "wife," and the elevation of the command against coveting one's neighbor's wife by casting it as a completely separate command.

The Exodus commands concerning coveting consist of two statements, each involving the identical negative command, *lo' tahmod*, "You shall not covet," followed by a direct object. The traditional Reformed numbering of the terms of the Decalogue treats the first statement as titular and the second as expositional, clarifying the meaning of *bayit*, "house," in part 1.[69] This is the *bet 'ab*, "the household of the father," the domestic realm over which he exercises leadership. However, the discourse grammar of the Decalogue as a whole and syntax of these two statements in particular[70] require distinguishing coveting the neighbor's real property (the house) from coveting the living creatures—including human beings and livestock—who make up the economic unit, the household.[71] Even so the Deuteronomic version goes in a different direction, isolating the neighbor's wife and then treating the rest as the property of the head of the household.[72]

---

66. The second address repeatedly buttresses ethical and spiritual appeals with reminders of the Israelites' slavery in Egypt. Cf. Deuteronomy 15:15; 16:12; 24:18, 22.

67. YHWH's deliverance of Israel as a special creative act and his cosmic creative actions are also prominent in Psalms 95 and 136.

68. Specifically whether the former forbids envious desire for what belongs to another person or prohibits taking specific actions to satisfy those desires, on which, see Marvin L. Chaney, "'Coveting Your Neighbor's House' in Social Context," in *The Ten Commandments: The Reciprocity of Faithfulness*, ed. William P. Brown, LTE (Louisville, KY: Westminster John Knox, 2004), 302–8; Alexander Rofe, "The Tenth Commandment in the Light of Four Deuteronomic Laws," in *The Ten Commandments in History and Tradition*, 45–54.

69. For similar listings, including everything associated with the family as an economic unit, see Genesis 12:5, 16; 26:14; Numbers 16:30, 32; Deuteronomy 11:6.

70. For a detailed discourse analysis of the Decalogue yielding similar results, see Jason DeRouchie, "Numbering the Decalogue: A Textlinguistic Reappraisal," paper presented to Midwest Regional Meeting of the Society of Biblical Literature (St. Paul, MN, April, 2007) and the Evangelical Theological Society (Washington, DC; November, 2006).

71. We should translate the last phrase in Exodus 20:17, *wekol 'aser lere'eka*, either as "or anyone else belonging to your neighbor," or "or any other [living] thing belonging to your neighbor."

72. To match the following pairs (his male and female servants; his ox and donkey), by adding "field" Deuteronomy restores a traditional pair of words. "House" and "field" appear together in Genesis 39:5; Leviticus 25:31; Nehemiah 5:3, 11; Isaiah 5:8; Jeremiah 6:12; 32:15; Micah 2:2. LXX and Nash Papyrus add this element in Exodus 20:17 as well, perhaps under the influence of Deuteronomy. The addition of "field" also restores the full complement of seven items, like the list of those who are to benefit from the Sabbath rest in Exodus 20:10. Cf. Umberto Cassuto, *A Commentary on the Book of Exodus*, trans. Israel Abrahams (Jerusalem: Magnes, 1967), 249. This move brings the prohibition on coveting remarkably close to the form of a similar prohibition in an Old Assyrian treaty text (1920–1840 BCE) from Kültepe (*Kaneš*) in Anatolia: "You shall not covet a fine house, a fine slave, a fine slave woman, a fine field, or a fine orchard belonging to any citizen of Assur, and you will not take (any of these) by force and hand them over to your own subjects/servants." Kt 00/k6:62–66, as translated by Veysel Donbaz, "An Old Assyrian Treaty from Kültepe," *JCS* 57 (2005): 65.

It seems best to interpret these changes in Deuteronomy as deliberate efforts to ensure the elevation of the wife in a family unit and to foreclose men's use of the Exodus version to justify treatment of wives as if they were mere property, along with the rest of the household possessions.[73] The Hebrew narratives are indeed rife with accounts of abusive men who treat women as property that may be disposed of at will for the sake of male honor and male ego,[74] confirming that in everyday life the Decalogue was largely ignored.

We have argued here that the Decalogue functioned as a bill of rights, seeking to protect my neighbor from my potential violation of his or her rights as a human being created as an image of God and as a member of the redeemed community in covenant relation with God and with one another. Although the principles of covenant relationship reflected in the Decalogue were determinative for the entire community, technically they addressed the heads of the households, perceiving them as the greatest threats to the well-being of society. This document recognizes that heads of households are particularly susceptible to abusing their position as a seat of power, rather than being inclined to practice good stewardship of an office that exists for the good of those in one's care.[75] In so doing the Decalogue establishes the trajectory of the rest of the book of Deuteronomy, which calls on all, especially leaders, to demonstrate love by looking out for the interests of others rather than guarding their own honor and status.[76]

3. THE STATUS OF THE DECALOGUE IN THE HEBREW BIBLE

Both the Sinai narratives and the speeches of Moses that make up Deuteronomy highlight the special place of the Decalogue in Israel's tradition. Of all the

73. References to the *bayit* as a designation for domain frame the Decalogue: in the preamble Egypt is a "house of slavery" (*bet 'abadim*); in the last command the "house" is the domain of the male head, whose style of leadership may be as oppressive as the bondage under Pharaoh. Hagith Sivan (*Between Woman, Man and God*, 220) interprets the transposition of "wife" and "house" in the last commands of the Decalogue as symbolic of "the interchangeability of woman with other items of property." Regarding the menial status of women in ancient Israel, Anthony Phillips speaks for many: "They had no legal status, being the personal property first of their fathers, and then of their husbands." *Ancient Israel's Criminal Law: A New Approach to the Decalogue* (Oxford: Blackwood; New York: Schocken, 1970), 70. For critical responses to this perspective see Daniel I. Block, "Marriage and Family in Ancient Israel," 61–72; Christopher J. H. Wright, *God's People in God's Land: Family, Land, and Property in the Old Testament* (Grand Rapids, MI: Eerdmans, 1990), 291–316.

74. See Phyllis Trible, *Texts of Terror: Literary-Feminist Readings of Biblical Narratives*, OBT (Philadelphia: Fortress, 1984). While Hagith Sivan (*Between Woman, Man and God*, 215) rightly recognizes that these modifications reflect "scales of desires," elevating women "as the most desirable objects of coveting," the Deuteronomic form is not intended to secure the welfare of men (216–17), but to curb a weakness in men and secure the rights of one's neighbor and his wife to a healthy and secure marital relationship.

75. Contra David Clines, "The Ten Commandments, Reading from Left to Right," 97–112.

76. For detailed discussion of this point see Daniel I. Block, "'You shall not covet your neighbor's wife': A Study in Deuteronomic Domestic Ideology," *JETS* 53 (2010): 449–74; reprinted in Daniel I. Block, *The Gospel according to Moses: Theological and Ethical Reflections on the Book of Deuteronomy* (Eugene, OR: Cascade, 2012), 137–68.

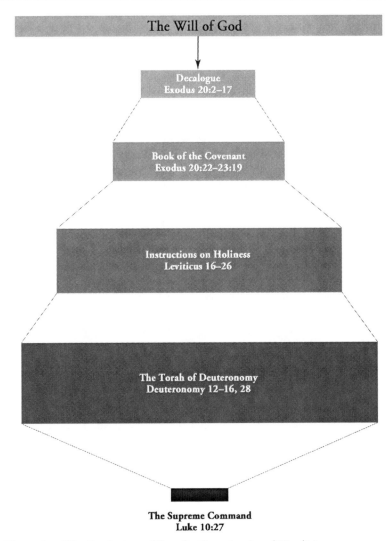

Figure 2.   The Evolution of Israel's Constitutional Tradition

divine revelation at Sinai and beyond, only the Decalogue was (1) spoken by YHWH directly to the people; (2) accompanied by the awe-inspiring appearance of the divine presence (Exod. 19:16–25; 20:18–21; Deut. 4:9–14, 36; 5:23–31); (3) written down by YHWH's own fingers (Exod. 31:18); (4) presented as a closed, self-contained unit (Deut. 5:22, "and he added no more"); (5) preserved in duplicate written form on durable tablets of stone; (6) stored in the ark of the covenant in the Holy of Holies of the tabernacle/temple; (7) referred to by its technical title: "The Ten Words"; and (8) repeated virtually verbatim by Moses in the context of his valedictory pastoral exposition of the *mishpatim* and *huqqim* (cf. Deut. 4:44–45, 5:1) on the plains of Moab. This document is the foundation of all the other documents that came to make up Israel's constitutional tradition: the book of the covenant, the Holiness Code, and the Deuteronomic Torah. The interrelationships among the major constitutional documents may be portrayed graphically as in Figure 2.

But did this mean that the Decalogue was elevated above and had greater authority than the rest of the law? Does this mean that, in contrast to the rest of the laws, which were temporally conditioned, the principles announced in the Decalogue were permanent and unalterable, as is commonly believed?[77] The weight of the evidence points in the opposite direction.[78] Simply because the Decalogue was special in its form, and in the manner of its revelation and preservation, does not mean it was more binding. This conclusion may be demonstrated both from within the Pentateuch and in the remainder of the Hebrew Bible.

1. The Pentateuchal Evidence

We have already noted that the Decalogue served as the foundational covenant document that would undergird all the subsequent revelation mediated through Moses and Moses' own exposition of the terms of the covenant in Deuteronomy. Evidence that each of these was regarded as authoritative and as binding as the Decalogue is clear.

The Book of the Covenant (Exod. 20:22–23:19)

Several relevant features of this document stand out. First, the narrator prefaces the document with "And YHWH said to Moses: 'Thus you shall say to the Israelites'" [AT], after which the contents of the speech are given. The book of the covenant represents the speech of God as much as the Decalogue. The only difference is that it is mediated speech, albeit by the divinely authorized mediator (Exod. 19:9; 20:18–21; Deut. 5:22–31). Second, like the beginning of the Decalogue, much of the document is cast in the first person, "I . . . you" form, that is, as YHWH's voice to the people.[79] Indeed, Exodus 20:22b suggests this is a continuation of the speech the people witnessed (*ra'ah*) YHWH give from heaven. Third, although many of the regulations are cast in third person casuistic form,[80] an equal number are cast in apodictic form much like the Decalogue (Exod. 22:18–23:19). Fourth, YHWH expressly urges the people to "Be on guard" (AT, Hebrew *shamar*) concerning all that he has said to them—assuming they have heard his voice (23:13). Fifth, in the ceremony involving the

---

77. See Norbert Lohfink, "Kennt das Alte Testament einen Unterschied von 'Gebot' und 'Gesetz'? Zur biblelteologischen Einstufung des Dekalogs," *JBTh* 4 (1989): 63–89.

78. So also Frank Crüsemann, *The Torah*, 351–57.

79. Exodus 20:22–26; 21:13–14; 22:23–25, 27, 29–31; 23:13–15, 18.

80. Exodus 21:1–22:17. (Exod. 22:25–27 is in second person casuistic form.)

ratification of the covenant, the book of the covenant played a more important role than the Decalogue.[81]

The Holiness Code (Lev. 17–26)

Similar features are found here. First, the entire section is cast as a series of divine speeches, each introduced with the divine speech formula, *wayedabber yhwh 'el mosheh le'mor*, "And YHWH spoke to Moses saying" [AT].[82] Second, the entire section is cast in the "I . . . you" form, as direct divine speech. Third, like the Decalogue much of this material is apodictic, rather than casuistic in form.[83] Fourth, the code is punctuated by divine exhortations to keep all the statutes and judgments as preconditions for the people's well-being,[84] by declarations that these statutes are timeless,[85] and by YHWH's self-identification, "I am YHWH [your God]" (AT; almost fifty times), as if to remind the people whose voice is behind what they hear Moses relay to them.[86] Fifth, the Holiness Code concludes with a lengthy list of blessings and curses that Israel will experience in the future, depending on their fidelity or infidelity to YHWH's revealed will (Lev. 26).

The Deuteronomic Torah (Deut. 4:1–40; 5:1–26:19; 28:1–69)

If one's disposition regarding the relative authority of these laws is to be determined by the texts themselves, then surely the authority of the Deuteronomic Torah exceeds them all. First, Moses expressly charged the people not to add to or delete any of the words that he commanded them (4:2). Second, the narrator declares that Moses' final pastoral instructions are entirely in accord with YHWH's command to him (1:3; 34:9). Third, notices of their timeless relevance punctuate the instructions.[87] Fourth, Moses declares that the people's well-being and their very life depend on fidelity to the Torah (6:24–25; 32:44–47); indeed in setting the Torah before them he gives them the choice of blessing or curse (11:26–28; 30:15–20). Fifth, by prefacing the exposition of the Sinai revelation with the Decalogue Moses declares the fundamental unity of his present utterances with the original covenant document. Sixth, both Moses (29:8, 18 [Eng. vv. 9, 19] and the narrator (28:69 [Eng. 29:1]) explicitly elevate the Torah that Moses has proclaimed to the level of the original covenant made at Sinai. Finally, the narrator attaches the following colophonic interpretation to Moses' lengthy

---

81. While both Decalogue and the book of the covenant were recounted and written down by Moses prior to the sacrifices and the sprinkling of the blood on the altar, prior to the sprinkling of the blood on the people Moses apparently read only the book of the covenant (24:1–8).

82. Leviticus 17:1; 18:1; 19:1; 20:1; 21:16; 22:1, 17, 26; 23:1, 9, 23, 26, 33; 24:1, 13; cf. also 25:1.

83. Leviticus 18, 19; 20:22–21:24; etc.

84. Leviticus 18:4–5, 26; 19:19, 37; 20:8, 22, 25:18; 26:3.

85. Leviticus 17:7; 23:14, 21, 31, 41; 24:3; cf. also Numbers 15:15; 18:23; 19:10; 21; cf. Leviticus 24:8, 9, 34.

86. Leviticus 18:2, 4, 5, 6, 21, 30; 19:3, 4, 10, 12, 14, 16, 18, 25, 28, 30, 31, 32, 34, 36, 37; 20:7, 8, 24; 21:12, 15, 23; 22:2, 3, 8, 9, 16, 30, 31, 32, 33; 23:22, 43; 24:22; 25:17, 55; 26:1, 2, 13, 44, 45.

87. Deuteronomy 5:29; 6:24; 11:1; 12:1, 28; 14:23; 18:5; 19:9; 23:3, 6.

second address: "These are the words of the covenant that YHWH commanded Moses to make (*karat*) with the people of Israel in the land of Moab, in addition to [the words of] the covenant that he had made with them at Horeb" (28:69 [Eng. 29:1]; AT).

The terms of this covenant were revealed in stages[88]and can be compared to the amendments of the U.S. Constitution. Already at Sinai, and then in later installments given during Israel's journey to the promised land, YHWH revealed his will in ever-greater detail. Moses' speeches in Deuteronomy represent the culmination of that revelatory process; and the covenant renewal ceremony that underlies the entire book represents the occasion when the Israelites committed themselves to the entire package—text and interpretation. The Decalogue was indeed a very special document, but it was no more or less binding on the people of Israel than any of the other constitutional documents. It symbolized the covenantal relationship that YHWH had established with his people and laid the foundations for the way in which the people were to think about that relationship both horizontally and vertically.

2. The Evidence of the Rest of the Hebrew Bible

What evidence does the rest of the Hebrew Bible provide for an elevated status of the Decalogue? The total absence of citations and scarcity of allusions to the Decalogue is striking.[89]

Moshe Weinfeld has discussed the links between the Decalogue and the rest of the Hebrew Bible in detail in two essays.[90] He begins by citing supposed allusions within the other law collections. He notes that Leviticus 19 opens with references to the fifth, fourth and first commands [*sic*; fourth, third, and first]: "You shall each revere your mother and father, and you shall keep my sabbaths: I am YHWH your God" (Lev. 19:3–4; AT).[91] However, it is difficult to prove that this text borrows from the Decalogue; it may just as well have been based on a general awareness of the importance of these three commands for maintaining a covenantal culture. If these commands are based on the Decalogue, why are they rearranged? Why does the first command use *yare* rather than *kibbed* for "honor"? Why does it reverse the order of "mother and father"? Why does

---

88. Despite the absence of any record of the detailed revelation, YHWH describes Abraham as having kept "My charge (*mishmeret*), my commands (*mitswot*), my statutes (*huqqot*) and my instructions (*torot*)"[AT]. These expressions echo those found in Numbers 18 and Deuteronomy, though it is unclear how specific Abraham's knowledge of the will of God was.

89. So also Cyril Rodd, *Glimpses of a Strange Land,* 82–85.

90. Moshe Weinfeld, "The Decalogue: Its Significance, Uniqueness, and Place in Israel's Tradition," in *Religion and Law: Biblical-Judaic and Islamic Perspectives,* ed. Edwin B. Firmage, Bernard G. Weiss, and John W. Welch, 18–26; idem, "The Uniqueness of the Decalogue and Its Place in Jewish Tradition," in *The Ten Commandments in History and Tradition,* eds. Ben-Zion Segal and Gershon Levi, 15–21.

91. These links are also cited by Gordon Wenham, *The Book of Leviticus,* NICOT (Grand Rapids, MI: Eerdmans, 1979), 264; and Walter C. Kaiser Jr., "Leviticus," in *The New Interpreter's Bible,* ed. Leander E. Keck, et al. (Nashville: Abingdon, 1994), 1131.

it speak of "sabbaths," which regularly refers to the high holy days of the cultic calendar, rather than "the Sabbath," that is, the last day of the week? Why does the prohibition on idolatry skip the first part of the command, and then employ language totally different from the decalogic statement? Indeed the language suggests it is influenced more by the golden calf incident than the Decalogue.[92] Moshe Weinfeld also points to the list of curses of Deuteronomy 27:15–26, but he recognizes that although references to idolatry, incest, murder, and dishonoring parents link the text curses to the Decalogue, the content, form, and style are quite different.

David Noel Freedman has proposed that the structure of the narratives from Exodus to 2 Kings reflects serially the violation of each of the first nine commands.[93] However, to make this work he uses data extremely selectively and is forced to rearrange the commands on stealing (Josh. 7), murder (Judg. 19), and adultery (2 Sam. 11–12) on the basis of Jeremiah 7:9. One could just as easily find illustrations of the violations of most of the other commands in each of these narratives.[94] Indeed, the aim of the Deuteronomistic historians in particular was to demonstrate that the fundamental problem with Israel was the abandonment of the spirit of the covenant, especially the demand for exclusive devotion to YHWH, not just violations of specific commands.

Series of commands are found in several other places in the Hebrew Bible. Ezekiel 18 provides a catalog of vices that distinguish righteous people from the wicked. Variations of the list occur three times (vv. 5–9, 10–13, 14–18).[95] The references to idolatry, adultery, and theft apparently link this list to the Decalogue. However, the sharp differences in the language used render a direct link unlikely. Although the lists in this chapter display a pronounced priestly stamp, I have argued elsewhere that some features may also have been inspired by what some call the royal "code of honor,"[96] perhaps a generally recognized if not codified standard of royal/administrative conduct.

In Job 31 the venerable saint Job presents his own code of honor before God, declaring his innocence (vv. 1–4) and averring that he has not cheated in his economic dealings (vv. 5–8), lusted after his neighbor's wife (vv. 9–12), abused his servants (vv. 13–15), withheld charity from the poor, the widow, and the fatherless (vv. 16–23), put his confidence in wealth or other gods instead of in God (vv. 24–28), been heartless toward his enemy or toward

---

92. The word *masseka*, "cast image," is regularly used of this calf. Cf. Exodus 32:4, 8; 34:17; Deuteronomy 9:12, 16; Nehemiah 9:18; Hosea 13:2.

93. David N. Freedman, *The Nine Commandments: Uncovering the Pattern of Crime and Punishment in the Hebrew Bible* (New York: Doubleday, 2000).

94. See also Cyril Rodd's critique, *Glimpses of a Strange Land*, 82.

95. For translation and discussion see Daniel I. Block, *The Book of Ezekiel Chapters 1–24*, NICOT (Grand Rapids, MI: Eerdmans, 1997), 564–79.

96. Daniel I. Block, *Ezekiel Chapters 1–24*, 568–69. See also Karl-Friedrich Pohlmann, *Ezechiel Studien: Zur Redaktionsgeschichte des Buches und zur Frage nach den ältesten Texten*, BZAW 202 (Berlin: de Gruyter, 1992), 225–31.

those outside his own household (vv. 29–34), or abused his land (vv. 38–40). We can find several thematic links with the Decalogue in Job's confession, and we recognize that he has caught its spirit, but again the tone is more Deuteronomic than decalogic.

Lists of commands also occur in Psalms 15 and 24, both of which are often interpreted as entrance liturgies. The latter seems to assume three commands. Those whose worship is acceptable to YHWH "have clean hands and pure hearts," they "do not lift up their souls to what is false," and they "do not swear deceitfully." But these statements are extremely vague and while the Psalm 24:4 speaks of lifting something to what is false, the expression refers to something else. [97] Psalm 15 is more concrete, but again specific links with the Decalogue are lacking. At best, the listing of commands in the Decalogue inspires other lists. The same is true of Isaiah 33:14b–16, which considers the qualifications for survival of YHWH's judgment. More likely candidates for direct decalogic influence are found in two prophetic texts, Hosea 4:2 and Jeremiah 7:9. In the former Hosea summarizes YHWH's case against Israel in the eighth century BCE:

1   YHWH has a case against the inhabitants of the land.
     There is no faithfulness (*'emet*) or loyalty (*hesed*),
     and no knowledge (*da'at*) of God in the land.
2   There is cursing and lying,
         murder, and stealing, and adultery break out;
         bloodshed follows bloodshed.
3   Therefore the land mourns,
     and all who live in it languish;
     together with the wild animals and the birds of the air,
     even the fish of the sea are perishing.

The vocabulary for murder, theft, and adultery are the same as in the Decalogue, but the order of the latter two is reversed.[98] The rest of the indictment has no connection at all to the Decalogue.

Jeremiah asks a telling question in Jeremiah 7:9–10: "Will you steal, murder, commit adultery, swear falsely, make offerings to Baal, and go after other gods

---

97. Compare the expressions:

| Exodus 20:7 | _lo' tissa' 'et shem yhwh 'eloheka lashshaw_ | You shall not lift the name of yhwh your God falsely. |
| Psalm 24:2 | _lo' nasa' lashshaw naphshi_ | He has not lifted his soul to falsehood |

For recent discussion highlighting the link between these texts, see Carmen Imes, "Psalm 24:4 and the Decalogue: A Mutually Illuminating Relationship?" a paper presented to the Evangelical Theological Society in San Francisco, November 17, 2011.

98. Meir Weiss ("The Decalogue in Prophetic Literature," in *The Ten Commandments in History and Tradition*, 71) argues that since these three crimes constitute a chiastic inversion of the arrangement in LXX[B] to Exodus 20, the prophet alludes to a variant tradition of "the Second Table" of the Decalogue. The reverse is more likely: LXX[B] is influenced by Hosea.

that you have not known, and then come and stand before me in this house, which is called by my name?" Again the vocabulary for theft, murder, and adultery is the same as in the Decalogue, but the order (theft, murder, adultery) differs from both Exodus 20 and Deuteronomy 5 (murder, adultery, theft).[99] More significantly, the context seems especially concerned with injustice against one's neighbors and exploitation of the poor, issues that in the Decalogue are latent at best. These charges may reflect the spirit of the Decalogue rather than specific commands, but those features may be more easily attributed to Deuteronomic rather than decalogic influence.

Although the Psalter deals with virtually all the spiritual and ethical issues raised in the commands of the Decalogue (except perhaps the Sabbath),[100] to say that the Psalter "supports the principles of the Decalogue"[101] is a far cry from establishing that the Decalogue itself inspired the psalmists. In most instances the links are closer to the Torah of Deuteronomy or the Holiness Code than to the Decalogue. Moshe Weinfeld argues that the tone of Psalms 50 and 81 resembles the admonitions in Jeremiah and Hosea, and that both psalms hint at festive covenant ceremonies, which he takes to be Shabuoth.[102] He suggests that prophets (Jeremiah and Hosea) and psalmists deliberately remonstrated the people on the festival celebrating the theophany on Sinai and the revelation of the law. The thematic link between the theophany on Zion described in Psalm 50:1–7 and climaxing in the declaration, "I am God, your God," and the Sinai theophany seems obvious. Supposedly the Ten Commandments would be read at these festivals, but the psalmists and prophets seized the opportunity to expose the hypocrisy of those who led in these recitations, but refused to live by the principles of the covenant.[103] However, Weinfeld overstates the case when he asserts that Psalm 50:7 quotes the opening of the Decalogue. The differences between the divine self-introductions are obvious when they are juxtaposed:

Exodus 20:2	*'anoki yhwh 'eloheka*	I am YHWH your God.
Psalm 50:7	*'elohim 'eloheka 'anoki*	God your God I am. [AT]

Verses 16–19 may allude to the Decalogue, though they seem also to be influenced by other constitutional documents:

99. Meir Weiss (ibid., 70–71) argues that Jeremiah's order chiastically inverts the decalogic tradition that underlies Jesus' statement in Luke 18:20, Paul's in Romans 13:9, the Nash Papyrus, and LXX[B]. But again the influence may have been in the opposite direction. Weiss' claim that 3:1–2 is based on the Decalogue (ibid., 72–81) is even less convincing.

100. Cf. Gordon J. Wenham, "The Ethics of the Psalms," in *Interpreting the Psalms: Issues and Approaches*, ed. David Firth and Philip S. Johnston (Downers Grove, IL: InterVarsity, 2005), 183.

101. Thus Gordon Wenham, ibid., 187.

102. Moshe Weinfeld, "The Uniqueness of the Decalogue," 21–27; "The Decalogue in Israel's Tradition," 28–32.

103. Moshe Weinfeld, "The Uniqueness of the Decalogue," 23.

16 But to the wicked God says:
    "What right have you to recite my statutes,
      or take my covenant on your lips?
17 For you hate discipline,
    and you cast my words behind you.
18 You make friends with a thief when you see one,
    and you keep company with adulterers.
19 You give your mouth free rein for evil,
    and your tongue frames deceit."

The references to theft, adultery, and falsehood in vv. 18–20 may derive from the Decalogue, but the vocabulary and style mute specific memory of the document.

Psalm 81 offers a more likely candidate for direct influence, especially v. 11 [Eng. 10], which seems to echo the preamble to the Decalogue:[104]

Exodus 20:2	*'anoki yhwh 'eloheka 'aser hotse'tika me'erets mitsrayim*
Psalms 81:11 [Eng. 10]	*'anoki yhwh 'eloheka hamma'aleka me'erets mitsrayim*
Exodus 20:2	I am YHWH your God who brought you out from the land of Egypt [AT].
Psalms 81:11 [Eng. 10]	I am YHWH your God who brought you up from the land of Egypt [AT].

But this link is not as sure as it appears on first sight. The change of verb from *hotsi'*, "to take out," to *he'elah*, "to bring up," is striking. Furthermore, apart from the form of the initial personal pronoun, the psalmist's statement bears a closer resemblance to Leviticus 11:45 than to Exodus 20:2.[105] It also recalls the third person version of the divine introduction formula in Deuteronomy 20:1.[106] Indeed the Shema in v. 9 [8], and the vocabulary around this verse link this psalm much more tightly to the Deuteronomic Torah than the Decalogue.[107]

CONCLUSION

By now it should be clear that apart from Deuteronomy 5 there is no evidence that the Decalogue was deemed to have exceptional authority in Israel. The

104. According to Werner Schmidt (*Die Zehn Gebote*, 33) this echo demonstrates that the Decalogue was a fixture in Israel's worship.

105. Leviticus 11:45 reads, *'ani yhwh hamma'aleh 'etkem me'erets mitsrayim*.

106. Deuteronomy 20:1 reads, *ki yhwh 'eloheka 'immak hamma'aleka me'erets mitsrayim*, "for YHWH your God is with you, who brought you up out of the land of Egypt" [AT].

107. Note the following "Deuteronomic" expressions: "to testify against" (*he'id be*, v. 9 [8]; cf. Deuteronomy 31:28); "strange god" (*'el zar*, v. 10 [9]; cf. *zarim*, Deuteronomy 32:16); "foreign god" (*'el nekar*, v. 10 [9]; cf. Deuteronomy 31:16); et passim in vv. 12–17 [11–16].

absence of any unequivocal citations of the Decalogue in the Hebrew Bible and the paucity of allusions to it present a striking contrast to the book of the covenant and the Holiness Code, echoes of which abound. If anything, the Decalogue is refracted through the lens of the Deuteronomic Torah in the remainder of the Hebrew Bible, and we have to ask whether the Decalogue itself or familiarity with the Deuteronomic instruction triggered the allusions. Indeed, if any single document incorporated into the Pentateuch was elevated above the rest in the thinking of the people and in its influence over the rest of the Hebrew Bible, it had to be the Deuteronomic Torah of Moses. According to the internal evidence of Deuteronomy, the instructions he proclaimed as Torah are identified with the commands (*mitswot*) and statutes (*huqqot*; 30:8–11; cf. 1:3) of YHWH and presented as commands authorized by YHWH himself;[108] they are canonical by definition (4:2); those who keep them will be declared righteous (6:25); obedience to them is the key to life and well-being not only for the people generally (11:1–32), but particularly for the king, whose primary function is to embody covenant righteousness as described in the Torah of Moses (17:14–20); they were transcribed by Moses' own hand (31:9); they were handed to the Levitical priests as the guardians of the Torah (31:9; 33:10); the written copy was placed beside the ark of the covenant as a witness to their commitments and equal in authority to that of the Decalogue (31:24–26); and only Deuteronomic Torah figures in the instructions for liturgical gatherings of the people: at the end of every seventh year, at the festival of Sukkoth, the entire Torah was to be read before all the people. No such instructions have been given for the Decalogue. The importance of this liturgy involving the Deuteronomic Torah is reflected in the formula for success in 31:12–13: read "that you may hear that you may fear [YHWH] that you may obey that you may live."

Read → Hear → Fear → Obey → Live

  This extraordinary status of the Deuteronomic Torah is evident throughout the Hebrew Bible. The Scriptures have a variety of names for the Deuteronomic Torah.[109] This book is the heart of the Torah, which priests were to teach,

108. Note the frequency of references to obedience to YHWH "as I command you." Variations occur in Deuteronomy 1:43; 4:2, 40; 6:2, 6; 7:11; 8:1, 11; 11:8, 13, 22, 27; 12:11, 28, 32; 15:5, 11, 15; 18:18; 19:7, 9; 24:18, 22; 27:1, 4, 10; 28:1, 13, 14, 15; 30:2, 8, 11, 16; 32:46.

109. *Seper torat mosheh*, "the book of the Torah of Moses" (Josh. 8:31, 32; 23:6; 2 Kgs. 14:6; Neh. 8:1); *seper mosheh*, "the book of Moses" (Neh. 13:1; 2 Chr. 25:4; 35:12); *torat mosheh*, "the Torah of Moses" (1 Kgs. 2:3; 2 Kgs. 23:25; 1 Chr. 23:18; 30:16; Ezra 3:2; 7:6; Dan. 9:11,13; Mal. 3:22); *seper torat YHWH beyad mosheh*, "the book of the Torah of YHWH by the hand of Moses" (2 Chr. 34:14, 15); and *dibre YHWH beyad mosheh*, "the words of YHWH by the hand of Moses" (2 Chr. 35:6). Compare the New Testament references to "the *nomos* of Moses" (Luke 2:22; 24:44; John 7:23; Acts 13:39; 15:5 [cf. "the manner of Moses" in v. 1]; 28:23; 1 Cor. 9:9; Heb. 10:28); "Moses" used as a substitute for "*ho nomos*," (Luke 16:29, 31; 24:27; John 5:45, 46; Acts 6:11; 21:21; 26:22; 2 Cor. 3:15); "the book of Moses" (Mark 12:26); Moses' "writings" (John 5:47); vaguer references to laws that Moses commanded (Matt. 8:4; 19:7, 8; 22:24; Mark 1:44; 7:10; 10:3, 4; Luke 5:14; John 8:5; Acts 6:14); statements like "Moses wrote" (Luke 20:28, referring to Deut.

and model,[110] which psalmists praised,[111] to which the prophets appealed,[112] by which faithful kings ruled,[113] and by which righteous citizens lived (Ps. 1). And herein lies the profound significance of the Decalogue, for in the Torah of Moses the covenantal seed that was planted by YHWH himself has come to full flower. Herein we discover the grace of God demonstrated in his election and redemption of Israel; grace demonstrated in his call to covenant relationship with himself; and grace demonstrated in the revelation of his will. And herein we discover how multicolored and multifaceted is the decalogic call to love YHWH with all one's inner being, one's entire person, and all one's resources and to love one's neighbor as oneself.

The other chapters in this volume show how quickly the spirit and function of the Decalogue and indeed all the constitutional material of the Pentateuch were lost.

25:5); "Moses says" (Rom. 10:5, 19); "customs that Moses delivered to us" (Acts 6:14) [all AT]. In the Gospels Jesus frequently refers to Moses as a recognized authority in Jewish tradition and as an authority behind his own teachings.

110. Deuteronomy 33:10; 2 Chronicles 15:3; 19:8; Malachi 2:6, 9; cf. Jeremiah 18:18; Ezekiel 7:26; Ezra 7:10.

111. Psalms 19:7–14; 119; etc.

112. Isaiah 1:10; 5:24; 8:20; 30:9; 51:7.

113. 1 Kings 2:2–4; 2 Kings 14:6; 22:11; 23:25.

Chapter 2

The Decalogue
in the New Testament

CRAIG A. EVANS

Most of the Ten Commandments are quoted or paraphrased in the writings that make up the New Testament. Those not quoted or paraphrased are alluded to or at least appear to be presupposed. Accordingly, it may be that all ten of these famous commandments appear in the New Testament in one form or another.[1]

INVENTORY

It will be helpful to tabulate the phenomena and then comment on some of the passages. First, let us identify those commandments that are quoted or paraphrased:

1. For classic examples of form and source-critical approaches to the origin and formation of the Decalogue in the Old Testament, see Eduard Nielsen, *The Ten Commandments in New Perspective*, SBT 2, no. 7 (London: SCM Press, 1968); Johann Jakob Stamm and Maurice Edward Andrew, *The Ten Commandments in Recent Research*, SBT 2, no. 2 (London: SCM Press, 1967). For more recent examples, which reflect the newer approaches to Old Testament narrative and Pentateuchal criticism, see David H. Aaron, *Etched in Stone: The Emergence of the Decalogue* (New York: T. & T. Clark, 2006); *Die Zehn Worte. Der Dekalog als Testfall der Pentateuchkritik*, ed. Christian Frevel, Michael Konkel, and Johannes Schnocks, QD 212 (Freiburg: Herder, 2005); Dominic Markl, *Der Dekalog als Verfassung des Gottesvolkes. Die Brennpunkte einer Rechtshermeneutik des Pentateuch in Exodus 19–24 und Deuteronomium 5*, Herders biblische Studien 49 (Freiburg: Herder, 2007).

Commandment 1 "You shall have no other gods before me"
(Exod. 20:3 RSV; cf. Deut. 5:7)

The First Commandment is not quoted or paraphrased in the New Testament. But there may be a few allusions to it. When tempted to worship Satan, Jesus responds, "You shall worship the Lord your God and him only shall you serve" (Matt. 4:10 RSV). Jesus has quoted Deuteronomy 6:13, a command that presupposes the First Commandment.[2] When Jesus responds to the question about the greatest commandment by citing Deuteronomy 6:4–5 and Leviticus 19:18, the scribe who had put the question to him agrees, saying, "You are right, Teacher; you have truly said that he is one, and there is no other but he . . . " (Mark 12:32 RSV). The words, "he is one," allude to Deuteronomy 6:4 ("the LORD our God is one LORD"), but the words, "there is no other but he" (*ouk estin allos plēn autou*), which approximate Deuteronomy 4:35 (*ouk estin eti plēn autou*), may also allude to Exodus 20:3 (*ouk esontai soi theoi heteroi plēn emou*).[3]

Monotheism is not an item of debate in the Jewish community of the New Testament era; it is presupposed and fiercely adhered to by all. It is only in encounters with Gentiles that polytheism and idolatry become issues. When in the book of Acts we hear someone say of Paul, "[T]his Paul has persuaded and turned away a considerable company of people, saying that gods made with hands are not gods" (19:26 RSV), we may be sure that Jewish and Christian readers would think of the declaration of Deuteronomy 6:4–5, which in turn is based on the First Commandment. Twice in his letters Paul reminds his Gentile converts that at one time, when they did not know God, they were in bondage to things that were not gods at all (Gal. 4:8; 1 Cor. 8:5–6). Again, although the First Commandment is not quoted, paraphrased, or even alluded to, it is presupposed.[4] The comment in James, that "God is one" (Jas. 2:19), alludes to Deuteronomy 6:4, but again probably presupposes the First Commandment.[5]

2. Reginald H. Fuller, "The Decalogue in the New Testament," *Int* 43 (1989): 243–55, here 248.

3. Some New Testament interpreters suspect that the words of the scribe comprise a post-Easter gloss, perhaps with polytheistic Gentiles in view. This view wrongly assumes that Jesus and his scribal contemporaries gave no thought to polytheistic Gentiles, many of whom lived in and nearby the land of Israel. On this question, see Robert Banks, *Jesus and the Law in the Synoptic Tradition* (SNTSMS 28; Cambridge: Cambridge University Press, 1975), 167 n. 1. Moreover, why would the evangelist Mark, or Christian tradents before him, portray a scribe in such a favorable light, when the tendency was just the opposite? On this important point, see Alyosius M. Ambrozic, *The Hidden Kingdom: A Redaction-Critical Study of the References to the Kingdom of God in Mark's Gospel*, CBQMS 2 (Washington, DC: Catholic Biblical Association, 1972), 177–81.

4. Fuller, "The Decalogue in the New Testament," 253. Fuller rightly suspects that Paul's words are "reminiscent" of the First Commandment, even if the main influence comes from the Shema (Deut. 6:4–5) itself.

5. For a reflection on the theological and ethical implications of the First Commandment, see James A. Diamond, "The Face of Ethical Encounter," and Calvin P. Van Reken, "Response," in Roger E. Van Harn, ed., *The Ten Commandments for Jews, Christians, and Others* (Grand Rapids: Eerdmans, 2007), 3–15 and 16–21, respectively.

Commandment 2 "You shall not make for yourself a graven image"
(Exod. 20:4–6; Deut. 5:8–10)

The New Testament does not quote or paraphrase the Second Commandment. However, it seems to be alluded to or presupposed in a few passages. The latter part of the commandment, where God describes herself as jealous and as "visiting the iniquity of the fathers upon the children" (Exod. 20:5b RSV; Deut. 5:9b), may be presupposed in the question of the disciples: "Rabbi, who sinned, this man or his parents, that he was born blind?" (John 9:2 RSV).[6] The assumption underlying this question is that God has judged the blind man, perhaps for a sin of his parents. A sin that can be visited upon one's descendants is serving or showing respect to an idol or to one of the gods of the Gentiles. Several passages in the New Testament speak disparagingly of idols or images (cf. Acts 15:20, 29; 21:25; Rom. 2:22; 1 Cor. 10:14; 12:2; 2 Cor. 6:16; 1 John 5:21; Rev. 9:20; 13:14; 14:9; etc.).[7] Although none of these passages quotes the Second Commandment, its prohibition of making images, including idols, is presupposed by all of them.[8]

Commandment 3 "You shall not take the name of the Lord your God in vain" (Exod. 20:7; Deut. 5:11)

The Third Commandment is not quoted or paraphrased in the New Testament, though it may be alluded to in the injunction in Ephesians: "Let no evil talk come out of your mouths . . . And do not grieve the Holy Spirit of God" (Eph. 4:29–30 RSV). One also thinks of Paul's assertion in 1 Corinthians: "Therefore I want you to understand that no one speaking by the Spirit of God ever says 'Jesus be cursed!'" (1 Cor. 12:3a RSV). The Third Commandment may be presupposed in the Pauline confession: "But God's firm foundation stands, bearing this seal: 'The Lord knows those who are his,' and, 'Let everyone who names the name of the Lord depart from iniquity'" (2 Tim. 2:19 RSV). Although the first quotation alludes to Numbers (16:5) and the second quotation may have been influenced by Numbers (16:26), the concatenation of the language, naming "the name of the Lord" and departing from iniquity, may have called to mind the warning not to take the name of the Lord in vain.[9]

6. George R. Beasley-Murray, *John*, WBC 36 (Dallas: Word, 1987), 154–55; Raymond E. Brown, *The Gospel according to John*, AB 29 and 29A (Garden City: Doubleday, 1966–70), 1:371. For a survey of the Jewish traditions linking physical defects to sin, see Craig S. Keener, *The Gospel of John: A Commentary* (Peabody, MA: Hendrickson, 2003), 1:777–78.

7. The Hebrew word "graven image" (*pesel*) in Exodus 20:4 and Deuteronomy 5:8 is rendered *eidōlon* ("idol") in the Septuagint. Accordingly, many of the New Testament's negative references to idols and idolatry would have called to mind the language of the Second Commandment as it was known to Greek speakers. Again, see Fuller, "The Decalogue in the New Testament," 253.

8. For a reflection on the theological and ethical implications of the Second Commandment, see Daniel Polish, "No other Gods," and Leanne Van Dyk, "Response," in Van Harn, ed., *The Ten Commandments*, 23–39 and 40–45, respectively.

9. For a reflection on the theological and ethical implications of the Third Commandment, see R. Kendall Soulen, "The Blessing of God's Name," and Rochelle L. Millen, "Response," in Van Harn, ed., *The Ten Commandments*, 47–61 and 62–67, respectively.

Commandment 4 "Remember the Sabbath day, to keep it holy" (Exod. 20:8–11; Deut. 5:12–15)

The Fourth Commandment is not quoted or paraphrased, but it is appealed to in several passages. Because the disciples of Jesus pick grain on the Sabbath, Pharisees ask Jesus why he permits them to do what is not lawful on this special day (Mark 2:23–28; Matt. 12:1–8; Luke 6:1–5).[10] Several times Jesus sparks controversy when he heals on the Sabbath (e.g., the man with the withered hand, in Mark 3:1–6 = Matt. 12:9–14 = Luke 6:6–11; the woman with the curved spine, in Luke 13:10–17; the man with dropsy, in Luke 14:1–6; the lame man at the pool of Bethesda, in John 5:1–18; and the blind man, instructed to wash in the pool of Siloam, in John 9:1–34).[11]

There are other passages where the Sabbath is observed, in keeping with Jewish law and custom. The validity of the Sabbath is apparently presupposed by the Matthean evangelist, who augments Jesus' hope that his followers will not have to flee Jerusalem "in winter" (Mark 13:18) by adding "or on a Sabbath" (Matt. 24:20). The evangelists apparently do not see respect for the Sabbath as inconsistent with Jesus' openness to deeds of kindness or mercy on that day. Respect for the Sabbath is seen in Luke 23:56, where the women who prepared spices to anoint Jesus' body "rest on the Sabbath according to the commandment."[12] Even the evangelist's comment that the disciples "returned to Jerusalem from the mount called Olivet, which is near Jerusalem, a Sabbath day's journey away" (Acts 1:12 RSV), probably reflects respect for the seventh day.[13]

Commandment 5 "Honor your father and your mother" (Exod. 20:12; Deut. 5:16)

Jesus quotes the Fifth Commandment explicitly on two occasions. In one story Jesus appeals to the commandment as part of his argument that the oral tradition of the scribes and Pharisees nullified God's Law (Mark 7:1–13 = Matt. 15:1–9). In the second Jesus cites the Fifth Commandment, along with others, in his discussion with the man who wanted to know what he must do to inherit eternal life (Mark 10:17–22 = Matt. 19:16–22 = Luke 18:18–25).[14] The Fifth Commandment is quoted in Ephesians 6:2–3, in support of the exhortation

10. For Jewish law specifically related to harvesting on the Sabbath, see Exodus 34:21; *Jubilees* 2:19–30; 50:6–13; *m. Shabbat* 7:2.

11. The critical comment in John 9:16, "He does not keep the Sabbath" (*to sabbaton ou tērei*), is a clear allusion to the Fourth Commandment.

12. The phrase, "according to the commandment," is a clear allusion to the Fourth Commandment.

13. For a reflection on the theological and ethical implications of the Fourth Commandment, see David Novak, "The Sabbath Day," and Marguerite Shuster, "Response," in Van Harn, ed., *The Ten Commandments*, 69–79 and 80–85, respectively.

14. Compare Deuteronomy 5:16 (*tima ton patera sou kai tēn mētera sou*) with Mark 7:10 (*tima ton patera sou kai tēn mētera sou*), and Exodus 20:12 (*tima ton patera sou kai tēn mētera*) with Mark 10:19 (*tima ton patera sou kai tēn mētera*). The quotation in Mark 7 agrees exactly with the form of the commandment in Deuteronomy, while the quotation in Mark 10 agrees exactly with the form of the commandment in Exodus. The quotation in Ephesians 6:2 agrees with the shorter form in Exodus.

that children obey their parents (Eph. 6:1); accordingly, the commandment is probably presupposed in the parallel passage in Colossians 3:20.[15]

Commandment 6 "You shall not commit murder" (Exod. 20:13; Deut. 5:17)

Jesus quotes the Sixth Commandment twice, on the occasion mentioned above, when he conversed with the man who asked about eternal life (cf. Mark 10:19 = Matt. 19:18 = Luke 18:20), and in the Sermon on Mount in the form of the first antithesis: "You have heard that it was said to the men of old, 'You shall not commit murder; and whoever commits murder shall be liable to judgment'" (Matt. 5:21 RSV). Paul quotes this commandment, along with three of the other ten and the command to love one's neighbor (Rom. 13:9). James also quotes this commandment, along with the commandment prohibiting adultery (Jas. 2:11; cf. 4:2).[16]

Commandment 7 "You shall not commit adultery" (Exod. 20:14; Deut. 5:18)

Jesus quotes the Seventh Commandment twice, once in the aforementioned list (cf. Mark 10:19 = Matt 19:18 = Luke 18:20) and as the second antithesis in the Sermon on the Mount (cf. Matt. 5:27). The commandment prohibiting adultery comes into play when Jesus addresses the question of divorce, in what appears to be two occasions (19:9; Mark 10:11–12; Matt. 5:32; Luke 16:18). The Seventh Commandment is also quoted by Paul (explicitly in Rom. 13:9, implicitly in Rom. 2:22) and by James (2:11).[17] John the Baptist's criticism of Herod Antipas, tetrarch of Galilee, was based in part on the Seventh Commandment.[18]

Commandment 8 "You shall not steal" (Exod. 20:15; Deut. 5:19)

Jesus quotes the Eighth Commandment in the list of commandments cited for the benefit of the inquiring man (cf. Mark 10:19 = Matt 19:18 = Luke 18:20). The declaration of Zacchaeus the wealthy tax collector, that he reimburses fourfold anyone defrauded (Luke 19:1–10), probably presupposes the Eighth

15. For a reflection on the theological and ethical implications of the Fifth Commandment, see Byron L. Sherwin, "Honoring Parents," and Anathea E. Portier-Young, "Response," in Van Harn, ed., *The Ten Commandments*, 87–99 and 100–111, respectively.

16. In Greek both Exodus 20:13 and Deuteronomy 5:17 read *ou phoneuseis* (future indicative). It reads this way in Matthew 5:21 (and 19:18) and Romans 13:9, but reads *mē phoneusēs* (aorist subjunctive) in Mark 10:19 (= Luke 18:20) and James 2:11. The grammatical difference is negligible. For a reflection on the theological and ethical implications of the Sixth Commandment, see John K. Roth, "What Have You Done?" Roger Brooks "Response," and Jean Bethke Elshtain, "Response," in Van Harn, ed., *The Ten Commandments*, 113–26, 127–31, and 132–34, respectively.

17. In Greek both Exodus 20:14 and Deuteronomy 5:18 read *ou moicheuseis* (future indicative). It reads this way in Matt. 5:27 (and 19:18) and Rom. 13:9, but reads *mē moicheusēs* (aorist subjunctive) in Mark 10:19 (= Luke 18:20) and James 2:11. Again, there is no significant difference in nuance.

18. For a reflection on the theological and ethical implications of the Seventh Commandment, see Carl E. Braaten, "Sexuality and Marriage," and Elliott N. Dorff, "Response," in Van Harn, ed., *The Ten Commandments*, 135–47 and 148–56, respectively.

Commandment, though the restitution laws of Exodus 22:1–4 (cf. 2 Sam. 12:6) are probably in view.

The Eighth Commandment is presupposed in the parable of the Wicked Vineyard Tenants, in that they rob the owner of the vineyard, refusing to honor the lease agreement (Mark 12:1–9). John's instructions to the soldiers who came to him for baptism (Luke 3:14 RSV: "Rob no one by violence or by false accusation, and be content with your wages") presupposes both the Eighth Commandment and the Ninth Commandment, which forbids bearing false witness. Paul quotes the Eighth Commandment (in Rom. 13:9) and alludes to it (in Rom. 2:22 and in Eph. 4:28).[19]

Commandment 9 "You shall not bear false witness" (Exod. 20:16; Deut. 5:20)

The Ninth Commandment is one of those that Jesus quoted in his exchange with the inquiring man (cf. Mark 10:19 = Matt 19:18 = Luke 18:20).[20] As already mentioned, this commandment is presupposed in John's instructions to the soldiers (Luke 3:14). It is presupposed too in Jesus' third antithesis (Matt. 5:33–37), even though the primary reference is to Leviticus 19:12. The Ninth Commandment is presupposed in Paul's exhortation: "Therefore, putting away falsehood, let everyone speak the truth with his neighbor, for we are members one of another" (Eph. 4:25 RSV).[21]

Commandment 10 "You shall not covet your neighbor's possessions" (Exod. 20:17; Deut. 5:21)

In his discussion of law and knowledge of sin, Paul quotes the Tenth Commandment (Rom. 7:7). He quotes it again, along with several other commandments, in his summation of what constitutes law for Christians (Rom. 13:9, where the law is summed up with Lev. 19:18).[22] James also alludes to the Tenth Commandment, when he admonishes his readers: "And you covet and cannot obtain" (Jas. 4:2 RSV).[23]

19. In Greek both Exodus 20:15 and Deuteronomy 5:19 read *ou klepseis* (future indicative). It reads this way in Matthew 19:18 and Romans 13:9, but reads *mē klepsēs* (aorist subjunctive) in Mark 10:19 (= Luke 18:20). For a reflection on the theological and ethical implications of the Eighth Commandment, see Allen Verhey, "Calvin and the 'Stewardship of Love,'" and Sue Ann Wasserman, "Response," in Van Harn, ed., *The Ten Commandments*, 157–74 and 175–78, respectively.

20. In Greek both Exodus 20:16 and Deuteronomy 5:20 read *ou pseudomartureseis* (future indicative), and it reads this way in Matt. 19:18. But in Mark 10:19 (= Luke 18:20) it reads, *mē pseudomarturēsēs* (aorist subjunctive). Semantically the difference is negligible.

21. For a reflection on the theological and ethical implications of the Ninth Commandment, see Miroslav Volf, with Linn Tonstad, "Bearing True Witness," and David Patterson, "Response," in Van Harn, ed., *The Ten Commandments*, 179–93 and 194–98, respectively.

22. In Greek both Exodus 20:17 and Deuteronomy 5:21 read *ouk epithumēseis tēn gunaika tou plēsion*, etc. (future indicative). It reads this way (*ouk epithumēseis*) in Rom. 7:7 and 13:9. The allusion in James 4:2 reads *epithumeite kai ouk echete* ("You covet and you do not have.")

23. For a reflection on the theological and ethical implications of the Tenth Commandment, see Russell R. Reno, "God or Mammon," and Shalom Carmy, "Response," in Van Harn, ed., *The Ten Commandments*, 199–211 and 212–17, respectively.

The whole of the Law, including the Ten Commandments, is presupposed in various summaries, such as we find in Stephen's speech shortly before his martyrdom: "This is he who was in the congregation in the wilderness with the angel who spoke to him at Mount Sinai, and with our fathers; and he received living oracles to give to us" (Acts 7:38 RSV). As mentioned above, Paul refers to the whole Law by saying that the commandments "are summed up in this sentence, 'You shall love your neighbor as yourself'" (Rom. 13:9 RSV; cf. Lev. 19:18). The apostle has the whole of the Law in mind, perhaps the Ten Commandments specifically, when he declares: "So the law is holy, and the commandment is holy and just and good" (Rom. 7:12 RSV; cf. 7:12; 1 Tim. 1:8).

Jesus' quotation of several of the commandments may have presupposed all ten, though he only cites half of them: "You know the commandments: 'Do not commit murder, Do not commit adultery, Do not steal, Do not bear false witness, Do not defraud, Honor your father and mother'" (Mark 10:19 RSV; Matt. 19:18–19; Luke 18:20). Why he cited these particular ones, and not more of those from the first group of five, will be discussed shortly.

One also observes some variation in the order of the commandments in the few lists we have in the New Testament. Below are the several lists with numbers inserted in parentheses indicating the order of the commandments in the Exodus and Deuteronomy lists. The lists we have in the Synoptic Gospels are interesting:

Mark: (6) Do not commit murder, (7) Do not commit adultery, (8) Do not steal, (9) Do not bear false witness, (?) Do not defraud, (5) Honor your father and mother.

Matthew: (6) You shall not commit murder, (7) You shall not commit adultery, (8) You shall not steal, (9) You shall not bear false witness, (5) Honor your father and mother, (Lev. 19:18) You shall love your neighbor as yourself.

Luke: (7) Do not commit adultery, (6) Do not commit murder, (8) Do not steal, (9) Do not bear false witness, (5) Honor your father and mother.

The first four commandments in Mark's list correspond to what we find in the Hebrew Bible and in some Greek versions of the Old Testament. But the Fifth Commandment that occurs fifth in Mark's list, "Do not defraud" (*mē aposterēsēs*), is curious.[24] The commandment could derive from either Exodus 21:10: "And if he takes another to him, he shall not defraud [*aposterēsei*] her of her necessities and clothing and marital rights"; or Deuteronomy 24:14

---

24. It has been suggested that the commandment not to defraud takes the place of the commandment not to covet, the former hurting one's neighbor, the latter not. Moreover, the wealthy and powerful have greater opportunity to defraud. See Dennis E. Nineham, *The Gospel of St. Mark*, Pelican Gospel Commentaries (New York: Seabury, 1963), 274.

(according to Codex Alexandrinus): "You shall not defraud [*apostereseis*] a poor and needy person of his wages. . . ." One should also consider Sirach 4:1: "Child, do not defraud [*mē apostereses*] the life of the poor"; and Malachi 3:5: "And I will draw near to you in judgment; I will be a swift witness against the sorceresses and against the adulteresses and against those who swear by my name falsely and against those who defraud [*epi tous aposterountas*] the hired worker of his wages and those who oppress the widow and those who buffet orphans. . . ."[25] The commandment against defrauding may have had in mind government officials and tax collectors, who by advantage of office were in a position to cheat people. Mark's list concludes with the commandment to honor one's parents, which in the Decalogue is the Fifth Commandment.

Not surprisingly, both Matthew and Luke elect to omit Mark's curious "Do not defraud," since, after all, it is not one of the Ten Commandments.[26] Perhaps as compensation, Matthew adds the well-known commandment to love one's neighbor as oneself.[27] Luke reverses the order of the first two commandments, placing the prohibition of adultery ahead of the prohibition of murder.[28]

We find a similar reversed order in Paul's list of commandments:

> *Paul*: (7) You shall not commit adultery, (6) You shall not commit murder, (8) You shall not steal, (10) You shall not covet, (Lev. 19:18) You shall love your neighbor as yourself.

Paul's list lacks the Ninth Commandment, which prohibits bearing false witness, but adds the prohibition of coveting (which features prominently in the apostle's discussion in Rom. 7) and the command to love one's neighbor, probably reflecting the influence of the dominical tradition. The order of the commandment against adultery, followed by the commandment against murder, is attested in other sources. In Philo, an older contemporary of Jesus, we find, (7) You shall not commit adultery, (6) You shall not commit murder, (8) You shall not steal (*Decalogue* 36).[29] The adultery–murder order of the

25. For further technical discussion, see Robert H. Gundry, *Mark: A Commentary on His Apology for the Cross* (Grand Rapids: Eerdmans, 1993), 562.

26. For comparison of the commandments in the Synoptic Gospels, see Fuller, "The Decalogue in the New Testament," 245–46.

27. The linkage of Leviticus 19:18 is attested in the *Damascus Document* 6:18–21 ("to keep the Sabbath day . . . to love each his brother as himself").

28. This reverse order is also seen in some Greek manuscripts of Mark. For further discussion of the order of the commandments in the Gospels, see Kenneth J. Thomas, "Liturgical Citations in the Synoptics," *NTS* 22 (1975–76): 205–15, esp. 205–8; Robert H. Gundry, *The Use of the Old Testament in St. Matthew's Gospel with Special Reference to the Messianic Hope*, NovTSup 18 (Leiden: Brill, 1967), 17–19. Gundry thinks the original order was adultery then murder.

29. "'You shall not commit adultery,' 'You shall not murder,' 'You shall not steal,' and the others" (*"ou moicheuseis" legōn, "ou phoneuseis," "ou klepseis" kai ta alla*). See also Philo's later summary: "And the other table of five contains all the prohibitions against [7] adulteries, and [6] murder, and [8] theft, and [9] false witness, and [10] covetousness" (*Decalogue* 51). Josephus, a younger contemporary of Paul, follows the order of Exodus and Deuteronomy in the Hebrew Bible (cf. *Ant.* 3.91–92).

commandments is attested in the Old Greek (e.g., Codex Vaticanus[30]), the Nash Papyrus,[31] Tertullian (*De pudicitia* 5), Clement of Alexandria (*Stromata* 6.146–47), and the second-century apologist Theophilus. According to the latter:

> And concerning piety he says, "You shall have no other gods before me. You shall not make to you any graven image, or any likeness of anything that is in heaven above, or that is in the earth beneath, or that is in the water under the earth: you shall not bow down yourself to them, nor serve them: for I am the Lord your God." And of doing good he said: "Honor your father and your mother [*tima ton patera sou kai tēn mētera sou*]; that it may be well with you, and that your days may be long in the land which I the Lord God give you." Again, concerning righteousness: "You shall not commit adultery. You shall not commit murder. You shall not steal. You shall not bear false witness against your neighbor. You shall not covet your neighbor's wife [*ou moicheuseis, ou phoneuseis, ou klepseis, ou pseudomarturēseis kata tou plēsion sou marturian pseudē. ouk epithumēseis tēn gunaika tou plēsion sou*]. . . ." (Theophilus, *Ad Autolycum* 3.9)

Here we find the order: (7) You shall not commit adultery, (6) You shall not commit murder, (8) You shall not steal, (9) You shall not bear false witness against your neighbor, (10) You shall not covet your neighbor's wife. Elsewhere Theophilus presents the commandments in their standard order:

> Therefore says the holy law: "You shall not commit adultery; you shall not steal; you shall not bear false witness; you shall not covet your neighbor's wife [*ou moicheuseis; ou phoneuseis; ou klepseis; ou pseudomartureseis; ouk epithumēseis tēn gunaika tou plēsion sou*]." (Theophilus, *Ad Autolycum* 2.35)

This time we have: (7) You shall not commit adultery, (8) You shall not steal, (9) You shall not bear false witness, (10) You shall not covet your neighbor's wife.[32]

To bring this part of the discussion to a close, I provide three more partial lists of the Ten Commandments:

---

30. The Decalogue in Deuteronomy in Codex B (Vaticanus) begins two-thirds down in the middle column of p. 199, continues through the column on the right, and concludes half way down the left-hand column on p. 200. Codex A agrees with the Hebrew.

31. For discussion of the Nash Papyrus, see Stanley A. Cook, "A Pre-Massoretic Biblical Papyrus," *Proceedings of the Society of Biblical Archaeology* 25 (1903): 34–56; Francis Crawford Burkitt, "The Hebrew Papyrus of the Ten Commandments," *Jewish Quarterly Review* 15 (1903): 393–408; Innocent Himbaza, "Décalogue de Papyrus Nash, Philon, 4QPhyl G, 8QPhyl 3 et 4QMez A," *Revue de Qumran* 20 (2002): 411–28. The Nash Papyrus, discovered in Egypt in the late nineteenth century, contains the Ten Commandments, followed by Deuteronomy 6:4–5, which apparently was the practice in the early synagogue (cf. *y. Ber.* 1.8; *b. Ber.* 12a). The text of the Nash Papyrus mostly reflects Deuteronomy, but Exodus has exerted some influence. The text, however, is not Masoretic (cf. Burkitt, 398–400). The Nash Papyrus was initially dated to the second century CE (Cook) or first century CE (Burkitt) but is now dated to the first or second century BCE (Himbaza).

32. See also Tertullian, *De pudicitia* 5; Clement of Alexandria, *Stromata* 6.146–47.

James 2:11: (7) Do not commit adultery, (6) Do not commit murder.

Didache 2:1–3: (6) You shall not murder, (7) you shall not commit adultery, (8) You shall not steal, (10) You shall not covet your neighbor's possessions, (9) You shall not give false testimony.

Barnabas 19.4–5: (7) You shall not commit adultery, (3) You shall not take the Lord's name in vain.

The order in James again reflects the reversed order seen in Luke, Paul, the Old Greek, and other writers and sources. The order in *Didache* initially follows the standard order, then curiously reverses the order of the Ninth and Tenth Commandments. What we find in the *Epistle of Barnabas*, a second-century pseudepigraphon, hardly constitutes a list. We have only brief comments on two of the commandments.

The appearance of the Ten Commandments in the New Testament may be tabulated as follows:

Commandment 1: Not quoted, but perhaps alluded to by Jesus and very probably presupposed by Paul and James.

Commandment 2: Not quoted, but perhaps alluded to by the disciples in their question about the man born blind; many other passages probably presuppose this commandment.

Commandment 3: Not quoted, but probably alluded to by Paul.

Commandment 4: Quoted by Jesus' critics; presupposed by the evangelists.

Commandment 5: Quoted by Jesus and Paul.

Commandment 6: Quoted by Jesus, James, and Paul.

Commandment 7: Quoted by Jesus, James, and Paul; perhaps presupposed by John the Baptist.

Commandment 8: Quoted by Jesus and Paul; perhaps presupposed by John the Baptist.

Commandment 9: Quoted by Jesus; presupposed by John the Baptist and Paul.

Commandment 10: Quoted by Paul and alluded to by James.

It is interesting that Jesus and the authors of the New Testament writings do not quote the first three commandments. Nor is the Fourth Commandment quoted by Jesus or a New Testament writer. (Its appearance in the Gospels is on the lips of Jesus' critics.) The implication of this general observation is that the authority, interpretation, and application of the first three commandments were not controversial in the Jewish setting. Jesus and opponents alike readily appealed to Deuteronomy 6:4–5—the Shema—which proclaims God's uniqueness and requirement that worship be directed to God alone. This great commandment presupposes the first two commandments and probably the third as well. Only the Fourth Commandment, the command to observe the Sabbath, was controversial at points. No one disputed its validity; only its application. I shall return to this question below.

MAJOR TEACHERS

At this point I turn to the contributions of major New Testament figures. These include John the Baptist, Jesus, James, Paul, and the author of Hebrews. Although we shall find lines of continuity and overlap, we shall also observe some distinctive features.

John the Baptist

John's location at the Jordan, in a wilderness setting, complete with appeal to Isaiah 40:3 ("Prepare the way of the LORD, make his paths straight"; RSV) and a call to repentance (Mark 1:2–8; Matt. 3:1–12; Luke 3:1–17), strongly suggest that his ministry was one centered on national restoration and spiritual renewal. This point must be kept in mind when we are told later that Herod Antipas arrested John in response to John's criticism of the tetrarch in the matter of dismissing his wife (the daughter of Aretas IV, the Nabatean king) and taking up with the wife of his brother Philip (Mark 6:14–29; Matt. 14:1–12; Luke 3:18–20; 9:7–9). We are told that John said to Antipas: "It is not lawful for you to have your brother's wife" (Mark 6:18). The primary reference is to the proscription against a man having intimacy with his brother's wife, while the brother is still living (Lev. 18:16; 20:21). Levirate marriage, whereby one married the wife of a deceased brother who had not fathered a child, was permitted. But to marry one's sister-in-law, while one's first wife is still living and while one's brother is still living, not only violates the law of Leviticus, it violates the commandment that prohibits adultery and the commandment that prohibits coveting a man's wife.[33]

John's focus on the adultery of Herod Antipas may have had an eschatological dimension as well, for the baptizer evidently was guided by the language and imagery of some of the classical prophets, such as Malachi, who inveighed against divorce and adultery (cf. Mal. 2:16; 3:5) and foretold the day of the Lord (cf. Mal. 3:1), coming fiery judgment (cf. Mal. 3:2–3; 4:1–2), and the return of Elijah the prophet (cf. Mal. 4:5–6). Although Josephus masks the eschatological

---

33. The sensitivity and currency of this moral issue is attested at Qumran (cf. 4Q416 frag. 2, column iv, line 5; 4Q524 frags. 15–22, lines 2b–3a; 11Q19 66:12–13).

dimensions of John's preaching, he too mentions critically the act of Philip's former wife Herodias: "After the birth of Salome, Herodias, thinking to violate the ways of the fathers, abandoned a living husband and married Herod (Antipas)—who was tetrarch of Galilee—her husband's brother by the same father" (*Jewish Antiquities* 18.136).

Jesus and James

Jesus also was very critical of the way some interpreted and applied divorce legislation. His strictures in the matter apparently were consistent with those of John, his associate. It is probably for this reason that Jesus was questioned on this matter:

> And Pharisees came up and in order to test him asked, "Is it lawful for a man to divorce his wife?" He answered them, "What did Moses command you?" They said, "Moses allowed a man to write a certificate of divorce, and to put her away." But Jesus said to them, "For your hardness of heart he wrote you this commandment. But from the beginning of creation, 'God made them male and female.' 'For this reason a man shall leave his father and mother and be joined to his wife, and the two shall become one flesh.' So they are no longer two but one flesh. What therefore God has joined together, let not man put asunder." (Mark 10:2–9 RSV; cf. Matt. 19:3–8)

Pharisees challenge Jesus' strict views of divorce by appealing to Deuteronomy 24:1–4 ("... if then she finds no favor in his eyes ... he writes her a bill of divorce ..." RSV). If Moses makes provision for divorce, then divorce surely is permissible. But Jesus counters this thinking in his appeal to Genesis 1:27 and 2:24, which taken together imply that the marriage union cannot be broken.[34] In private Jesus tells his disciples: "Whoever divorces his wife and marries another, commits adultery against her; and if she divorces her husband and marries another, she commits adultery" (Mark 10:11–12 RSV; cf. Matt. 5:31–32; 19:9; Luke 16:18). Thus, in the view of Jesus, divorce and remarriage result in breaking the Seventh Commandment.[35]

---

34. The men of Qumran apparently held to a very similar view, also appealing to Genesis. According to the *Damascus Document*, Satan has ensnared Israel, including its leader, in the sin of taking two wives in one's lifetime (CD 4.14–5.2, where Gen. 1:27 is cited; cf. 4Q269 frag. 3, lines 2–3, and 6Q15 frag. 1, lines 2–3, where in both passages Gen. 2:24 is cited).

35. Although assembled and edited by the Matthean evangelist, the so-called "antitheses" of the Sermon on the Mount (i.e., Matt. 5:21–48) exemplify Jesus' strict understanding of the ethical dimension of the commandments found in the Second Table. See Fuller, "The Decalogue in the New Testament," 246–48; Christian Dietzfelbinger, *Die Antithesen der Bergpredigt* (Munich: Kaiser, 1975); Robert A. Guelich, "The Antitheses of Matthew V 21–48: Traditional and/or Redactional?" *NTS* 22 (1976): 444–57; John P. Meier, *Law and History in Matthew's Gospel: A Redactional Study of Mt. 5:17–48*, Analecta biblica 71 (Rome: Pontifical Biblical Institute Press, 1976); Hans Dieter Betz, *The Sermon on the Mount*, Hermeneia (Philadelphia: Fortress, 1995), 198–328. For important background, see Hermann von Lipps, "Jüdische Weisheit und griechische Tugendlehre. Beobachtungen zur Aufnahme der Kardinaltugenden in hellenistisch-jüdischen Texten (Aristeasbrief, Sapientia Salomonis, 4. Makkabäerbuch)," in Henning Graf Reventlow, ed., *Weisheit, Ethos und Gebot.*

Jesus' understanding of what is permitted on the Sabbath differed sharply from Pharisaic understanding. Jesus and his disciples are criticized for plucking grain on the Sabbath (Mark 2:23–28). They are asked: "Why are they doing what is not lawful on the Sabbath?" (v. 24 RSV). Jesus justifies the actions of his disciples by appealing to the example of David and his men, who technically broke the law when they ate consecrated bread, and by making the extraordinary claim that because the "Sabbath was made for man, not man for the Sabbath," as "Son of man" he is "lord even of the Sabbath" (vv. 27–28 RSV).[36] So far as the Pharisees were concerned, Jesus and his disciples had broken the Fourth Commandment.

Sabbath controversy was also occasioned by acts of healing. When on the Sabbath Jesus heals the woman with the curved spine (Luke 13:10–17), he is rebuked by the ruler of the synagogue, who says to the congregation: "There are six days on which work ought to be done; come on those days and be healed, and not on the Sabbath day" (v. 14 RSV). Such a rebuke may strike us moderns as curious, but in Jesus' day there was a fine line between the ministrations of a physician and the charismatic actions of a holy man with the power to heal. However one heals, one should not heal on the Sabbath.[37]

Jesus justifies his healing of the woman by pointing out that even Pharisees allowed some work to be performed on the Sabbath, in order to care for animals. Jesus reasons that because the life of a human being is more valuable than that of an animal, a compassionate healing act for a human should be allowed on the Sabbath (v. 15).[38] Jesus makes similar arguments elsewhere (Mark 3:1–6; Luke 14:1–6; John 5:9–16; 9:14–16).[39] In the case of the woman with the curved spine, Jesus adds an eschatological argument, when he asks rhetorically, "And ought not this woman, a daughter of Abraham whom Satan bound for eighteen years, be loosed from this bond on the Sabbath day?" (v. 16 RSV). This argument is consistent with Jesus' claim that his power over Satan is evidence of the reality of the in-breaking rule of God (cf. Luke 11:20).

These examples should not lead us to conclude that Jesus had no respect for the Sabbath. On the contrary, his view was that the Sabbath was a gift of God,

---

Weisheits- und Dekalogtraditionen in der Bibel und im frühen Judentum, Biblisch-theologische Studien 43 (Neukirchen-Vluyn: Neukirchener Verlag, 2001), 29–60. The purpose of the antitheses is summed up well in Charles H. Talbert, *Reading the Sermon on the Mount: Character Formation and Decision Making in Matthew 5–7* (Columbia: University of South Carolina Press, 2004), 68: "The religious leaders, scribes and Pharisees, use their interpretive tradition to evade the true intent and meaning of the Scriptures. Jesus recognizes the evasion and his reading focuses on God's intent in the Scriptures."

36. For a learned discussion of this passage, see John P. Meier, "The Historical Jesus and the Plucking of the Grain on the Sabbath," *CBQ* 66 (2004): 561–81.

37. This is also the view of the men of Qumran: "No one should carry medicine on his person, either going out or coming in, on the Sabbath" (CD 11.9–10).

38. This is *not* the view of the men of Qumran: "No one should help an animal give birth on the Sabbath; and if it falls into a well or a pit, he may not lift it out on the Sabbath" (CD 11.13–14).

39. For further discussion of Sabbath in the Gospel of John, see Martin Asiedu-Peprah, *Johannine Sabbath Conflicts as Juridical Controversy*, WUNT 2, no. 132 (Tübingen: Mohr Siebeck, 2001).

whose purpose was to benefit, not burden, humanity. As a day of rest it was only appropriate to liberate the woman in bondage to an affliction linked in some way to Satan. So also in other cases of healing on the Sabbath. Far from violating the Sabbath, it could be said that Jesus' actions sanctified the Sabbath.[40]

The Fifth Commandment, the command to honor one's father and mother, was invoked by Jesus in his debate with Pharisees and scribes who were critical of the disciples for eating with hands not properly washed according to their understanding of purity (Mark 7:1–13; Matt. 15:1–9). Jesus regarded this criticism as highly hypocritical, for how one washes one's hands was part of an oral tradition (a "tradition of the elders") and not a written commandment; but honoring one's parents was a very important commandment, one of the Ten Commandments. Yet, this commandment was in effect nullified by another oral tradition, which elaborated on the laws of oaths. The qorban tradition (by which property or money could be dedicated to God's use and for no other use) could have the effect of making it impossible for a son to care for his parents, because his means to do so have been set aside for divine use only. Failure to care for one's parents not only violated the Fifth Commandment, the invoking of an oath that brings about this deplorable situation is tantamount to speaking "evil of father or mother," something prohibited elsewhere in Mosaic law (cf. Exod. 21:17; Lev. 20:9). Failure to keep the Fifth Commandment hints at a shorter life span; speaking evil of one's parents could result in death.

We find that Jesus appears to have quoted or alluded to Commandments 4–7, though other commandments were uttered in his presence and with his approval. The non-appearance of the first three commandments is probably due to their noncontroversial nature. Faith in only one God, the God of Israel, avoidance of idolatry, and respecting the divine name were givens. How to apply

40. That Jesus' following respected the Sabbath is seen in the Easter narrative, where we are told that the women did not visit the tomb of Jesus until "the Sabbath was past" (Mark 16:1). The Sabbath day was controversial in the Christian church. Indeed, the Sabbath remains sacred among many Jewish Christians and, of course, among Sabbatarian groups, such as Seventh Day Adventists. On this topic, see Samuele Bacchiocchi, *From Sabbath to Sunday: A Historical Investigation of the Rise of Sunday Observance in Early Christianity* (Rome: The Pontifical Gregorian University Press, 1977). An issue of the journal *Interpretation* is devoted to the question of the Sabbath: see, among others, Sharon H. Ringe, "'Holy, as the Lord your God commanded you': Sabbath in the New Testament," *Int* 59 (2005): 17–24; Dorothy C. Bass, "Christian Formation in and for Sabbath Rest," *Int* 59 (2005): 25–37; and Robert Sherman, "Reclaimed by Sabbath Rest," *Int* 59 (2005): 38–50. On the thorny question of how early and what evidence there is for the Christian practice of assembly and worship on Sunday instead of on the Sabbath, see the debate between Stephen R. Llewelyn, "The Use of Sunday for Meetings of Believers in the New Testament," *NovT* 43 (2001): 205–23, and Norman H. Young, "'The Use of Sunday for Meetings of Believers in the New Testament': A Response," *NovT* 45 (2003): 111–22. It has been argued that Christians met evenings following Sabbath services (and by Jewish reckoning, this meant that Christians met on Sundays). See Harald Riesenfeld, "The Sabbath and the Lord's Day in Judaism, the Preaching of Jesus and Early Christianity," *The Gospel Tradition* (Oxford: Blackwell, 1970), 111–37. On the expression "Lord's Day" (cf. Rev 1:10 *en tē kuriakē hēmera* ["on the Lord's day"]), see Clifford William Dugmore, "Lord's Day and Easter," in *Neotestamentica et Patristica: Festschrift for Oscar Cullmann*, NovTSup 6 (Leiden: Brill, 1962), 272–81; Kenneth A. Strand, "Another Look at 'Lord's Day' in the Early Church and in Rev. I.10," *NTS* 13 (1967): 174–81.

Commandments 4–7 was far more controversial, and it was here that Jesus engaged his fellow teachers of faith and practice.

The Tenth Commandment, the prohibition of coveting, appears in the teaching of James, the brother of Jesus. The leader of the Jerusalem church chastises believers for their feuds and infighting (4:1–10), at one point declaring: "You desire and do not have; so you kill. And you covet and cannot obtain; so you fight and wage war. You do not have, because you do not ask.[3] You ask and do not receive, because you ask wrongly, to spend it on your passions" (4:2–3 RSV). What is interesting here is that James has linked coveting to the failure to petition God rightly. The words "you ask and do not receive" are unmistakable allusions to the teaching of Jesus: "Ask, and it will be given to you . . . for every one who asks receives . . ." (Matt. 7:7–8 RSV).

Commentators have long recognized the many echoes of the teaching of Jesus in the letter of James. In this particular case I wonder if James' application of Jesus' teaching on asking has not in fact teased out an element implicit in this teaching. That is, lying behind Jesus' teaching on prayer, on asking and receiving, in Matthew 7:7–11, is the solution to the temptation to covet.[41] After all, it is difficult for the poor not to covet the comfort and security of their wealthier neighbors. Jesus implies and James teaches explicitly that instead of coveting, one must petition God and petition God rightly and with a pure heart (Jas. 4:3, 8).[42]

Paul

Paul quotes or alludes to Commandments 1–3 and 6–10. He may also allude to the Fourth Commandment.[43] Beyond what was said above I have nothing to add, except with regard to the Tenth Commandment.

Paul cites the Tenth Commandment, along with several others from the Second Table, in Romans 13:9. But it is in Romans 7 that this commandment receives special attention. Part of Paul's argument in this chapter is that the purpose of the Law is to expose sin:

> What then shall we say? That the law is sin? By no means! Yet, if it had not been for the law, I should not have known sin. I should not have known what it is to covet if the law had not said, "You shall not covet

41. Rightly Ben Witherington III, *Letters and Homilies for Jewish Christians: A Socio-Rhetorical Commentary on Hebrews, James and Jude* (Downers Grove, IL: InterVarsity, 2007), 512.

42. The coveting and killing to which James alludes may have referred to anti-Roman zealotry among some Jewish Christians, which included resentment toward the wealthy and the temple establishment who collaborated with Roman authority. On this point, see Ralph P. Martin, *James*, WBC 48 (Dallas: Word, 1988), 146–47. On praying wrongly, see Luke Timothy Johnson, *The Letter of James*, AB 37A (Garden City, NY: Doubleday, 1995), 278.

43. Paul may be alluding to the Fourth Commandment, the commandment to honor the Sabbath, when he enjoins the Christians of Colossae "not to permit anyone to pass judgment on them with respect to food or drink or with regard to a festival or a new moon or a Sabbath" (Col. 2:16). Even if "Sabbath" here means any holy day, the seventh day itself is surely included.

[*ouk epithumēseis*]." But sin, finding opportunity in the commandment, wrought in me all kinds of covetousness. Apart from the law sin lies dead. I was once alive apart from the law, but when the commandment came, sin revived and I died; the very commandment which promised life proved to be death to me. (Rom. 7:7–10 RSV)

Paul defends the Law,[44] arguing that one of its benefits is its revelation of God's righteous standards and, when applied, human shortcomings. Why Paul chose to focus on the Tenth Commandment has intrigued interpreters. The most likely explanation is that covetousness, that is, the desire for the illicit (which the Tenth Commandment in its full form makes clear),[45] is what lies behind all sin, beginning with Adam and Eve who desired to acquire knowledge though commanded not to do so (Gen. 2:16–17; 3:6; Rom. 5:12–21). The idea that violation of the Tenth Commandment is the root of human sin is not unique to Paul. It is attested in James: "Then desire [*epithumia*] when it has conceived gives birth to sin; and sin when it is full-grown brings forth death" (1:15); and in several Jewish writings from late antiquity. Philo, Paul's older contemporary, explains:

> Last of all, the divine legislator prohibits covetousness [*epithumein*], knowing that desire is a thing fond of revolution and of plotting against others; for all the passions of the soul are formidable, exciting and agitating it contrary to nature, and not permitting it to remain in a healthy state, but of all such passions the worst is desire. On which account each of the other passions, coming in from without and attacking the soul from external points, appears to be involuntary; but this desire alone derives its origin from ourselves, and is wholly voluntary. (*Decalogue* 142)[46]

In the pseudepigraphical work, the *Life of Adam and Eve* (according to the Greek version misnamed the *Apocalypse of Moses*), the repentant Eve admits: "And when he (the serpent) had received the oath from me, he went and poured upon the fruit the poison of his wickedness, which is lust [*epithumia*], the root and head of every sin, and he bent the branch on the earth and I took of the fruit and I ate" (19:3).[47]

Paul's focus on the commandment not to covet, seen as a summing up of the whole Law, provides the apostle with the opportunity to explain and defend the righteous function of the Law. The Law is good, holy, and just (Rom. 7:12, 16; cf. 1 Tim. 1:8). Apart from the Law, humanity would not be in a position to recognize its sinfulness and its failure to measure up to the holy standard of

---

44. For a list of major Pauline interpreters who argue this point, see James D. G. Dunn, *Romans* 2 vols., (WBC 38A, 38B; Dallas: Word, 1988), 1:377.

45. It is not lust, per se, but "coveting what belongs to others"; cf. Robert Jewett, *Romans*, Hermeneia (Minneapolis: Fortress, 2007), 449.

46. See also Philo, *Opif.* 152; *Decal.* 150, 153, 173; *Spec.* 4.84–85.

47. See also *Apocalypse of Abraham* 24:9: "And I saw there desire [Slavonic *zelanie* = Greek *epithumia*], and in her hand was the head of every kind of lawlessness . . ."; and 4 Macc 2:5–6.

God. But the Law does not serve merely to expose human sinfulness; it serves as a tutor (Gal. 4:2), leading human beings to Christ (Gal. 3:24–25), the true goal of the Law (Rom. 10:4), through whom forgiveness of sin can be obtained (Rom. 4:7; Col. 1:14).[48]

CONCLUDING REMARKS

In the writings that make up the New Testament there is a surprising degree of consistency in the understanding of the Ten Commandments. The validity of these commandments is not in doubt; they are understood to reflect God's righteous standards. How they are to be applied may vary, but their goodness and truth are not questioned.

Some interpreters may wonder if there is a contradiction between Jesus and Paul. Whereas the latter recognizes the Law, summed up in the Tenth Commandment, as incapable of saving, the former assures an expert in the Law that if he does the commandments, "he will live." Perhaps I should conclude this chapter with a few brief comments on this problem.

In Mark 10:17–22 a man asks Jesus what he must do "to inherit eternal life?" As already noted, Jesus reviews the commandments from the Second Table, and the man declares that he has observed all of them since childhood. But when Jesus tells him that he lacks one thing and that he should give his wealth to the poor, the man walks away saddened, unable to comply. I suspect that what Jesus laid bare was the man's covetousness. He had wealth and wanted more of it; parting with it was not an option. This may well be why the Tenth Commandment did not appear in the list that Jesus recited to him. It appears implicitly at the conclusion of the story.

In Luke 10:25–29 we find a similar story, in which an expert in the Law asks Jesus what he must do to inherit eternal life. Although some interpreters think this story is no more than a variation of the story in Mark 10, the many differences suggest that it probably is a distinct story. In this story Jesus asks the inquirer to cite what is written in the Law. He does not cite the Ten Commandments, but the Shema (Deut. 6:4–5) and the command to love one's neighbor as one's self (Lev. 19:18). Jesus approves his reply and assured him, "Do this and you will live" (Luke 10:28 RSV). However, the legal expert is not assured and asks Jesus for clarification of who his neighbor is. The famous parable of the Good Samaritan follows (Luke 10:30–37).

In both of these encounters the Ten Commandments, or the summary of them in the form of the two "Great Commandments," prove difficult. This is clear in the story in Mark 10, where the wealthy man walks away downcast,

---

48. The Sabbath commandment is cited in Heb. 4:4, but the subsequent application is metaphorical, as seen in 4:9–10. It is likely that the believers to whom Hebrews was addressed honored the Sabbath.

unable to comply. The outcome of the story in Luke 10 is probably the same, where most readers would assume that the legal expert would find it very difficult to follow the example of the good Samaritan, who had mercy on the injured Jewish man lying on the side of the road.[49]

I believe Paul would interpret both of these stories as proving his point. In human strength, or in the strength of the flesh, as he would put it, men and women cannot fulfill the Law. They agree with the Law, as to what is morally right and wrong, but in their own power they cannot fulfill it and therefore cannot escape God's wrath. It is only in the power of the Holy Spirit that people can please God and so satisfy the righteous requirements of God.

49. This mercy included the sharing of wealth.

Chapter 3

Early Syriac, Greek, and Latin Views of the Decalogue

ALISON G. SALVESEN

The picture we are given by the Synoptic Gospels is that Jesus Christ, without having abandoned ritual observance or temple worship, taught the observance of the ethical aspects of Judaism but also emphasized inner intentionality. Not much more than a generation after his earthly ministry, the movement of his followers had been impacted by two major developments: namely, the entry of Gentile believers into the movement and the destruction of the Jerusalem temple. The effects of these two events and the accommodations to them are of course already seen in the documents that make up the New Testament. Discussed in Craig Evans's chapter, the writings of the New Testament are of course foundational to approaches in the following three centuries. The downplaying of ritual and ceremonial aspects to Jewish practice continues within most churches, though apparently not without opposition from certain groups. In practice, maintaining a claim to the heritage of the Jews as God's chosen people, and therefore not appearing to the Roman authorities as a new sect, while discarding practices commonly associated with Judaism and regarded by many as central to that religion, proved to be something of a tightrope walk. The linkage between divine covenant and Law is clear in many parts of Scripture:

how to claim the former without taking on observance of the latter required some justification even in the second century. The type of debate recounted in the Acts and Epistles continued to be played out in one way or another.

Central to much of the thinking in the early church communities is the Sermon on the Mount, in which Christ says he has come to fulfill the Law, not abolish it, while he also raises the bar for ethical conduct: intent and attitude also count.[1] He reiterates several commandments of the Decalogue, while elsewhere he provides a summary of the whole Law as consisting of the First Commandment on loving God, plus Leviticus 19:18b on loving one's neighbor as oneself, or a similar "ethic of reciprocity" (in this case, the positive form of the "Golden Rule").[2]

It is unlikely that such an emphasis was at all foreign to the Judaism(s) of the period. The *Didache*,[3] an early though composite work very influential in the first centuries of Christianity, is widely agreed to have Jewish roots, principally in its first two sections, which may have been used for the instruction of Jewish proselytes.[4] These outline the "Two Ways, one of Life and one of Death," and

---

1. Matthew 5:17–48.

2. Luke 10:26–28 (NRSV): "Just then a lawyer stood up to test Jesus. 'Teacher,' he said, 'what must I do to inherit eternal life?' He said to him, 'What is written in the law? What do you read there?' He answered, 'You shall love the Lord your God with all your heart, and with all your soul, and with all your strength, and with all your mind; and your neighbor as yourself.' And he said to him, 'You have given the right answer; do this, and you will live.'" (cf. Matt. 22:36–40; Mark 12:28–34); also Matthew 7:12 "In everything do to others as you would have them do to you; for this is the law and the prophets"; cf. Luke 6:31 "Do to others as you would have them do to you" and Romans 13:8–10 "Owe no one anything, except to love one another; for the one who loves another has fulfilled the law" [followed by the four commands on adultery, murder, theft, covetousness]. . . . Love does no wrong to a neighbor; therefore, love is the fulfilling of the law"; Galatians 5:14 "For the whole law is summed up in a single commandment, 'You shall love your neighbor as yourself.'" James 2:8 "You do well if you really fulfill the royal law according to the scripture, 'You shall love your neighbor as yourself.'" See Philip S. Alexander, "Jesus and the Golden Rule," *Hillel and Jesus: Comparative Studies of Two Major Religious Leaders*, ed. James H. Charlesworth and L. L. Johns (Minneapolis: Fortress, 1997), 363–88. Note that as Alexander points out (p. 371), the Golden Rule was an "ethical commonplace" in the ancient world, and offered by both Hillel and Jesus as "a summation of age-old teaching." Greek philosophy knew the principle in various forms, usually in the negative form of the Golden Rule, "do not do to other what you would not wish them to do to you," found also in the Western text of Acts 15:29. The Babylonian Talmud also gives the negative form: "That which is hateful to you, do not do to your fellow. That is the whole Torah; the rest is the explanation; go and learn" (*b.Shabb.* 31a).

3. Current consensus dates the *Didache* around the end of the first century CE or beginning of the second. It has been variously placed in Syria or Egypt. See Huub van de Sandt and David Flusser, *The Didache: Its Jewish Sources and Its Place in Early Judaism and Christianity* (Assen: Van Gorcum; Minneapolis: Fortress, 2002), 48–52.

4. For instance, there are some points of contact with the *Rule of the Community* found at Qumran (1QS 3.13–4.26). See also Jonathan A. Draper, "Torah and Troublesome Apostles in the Didache Community," *Novum Testamentum* 33 (1991): 347–72, esp. 357–59, on the way in which the *Didache* inserts the commands to love God and neighbor into the "Two Ways" to become the first principle of the Way of Life, while the expansion of the moral parts of Torah especially the Decalogue, become the second principle (2:1), and material from 'Q' is added to form 1:3–6. Draper argues that the section on apostles indicates that some in the community were advocating abolition of Torah, a position rejected by the *Didache*.

cite the First Commandment and the Golden Rule[5] before fleshing them out in a number of ethical instructions that incorporate other commands of the Decalogue and teachings of Jesus, along with prohibitions of pederasty, abortion, and witchcraft.[6] Although there is no specific reference to their original context in the Sinaitic Decalogue, it is clear that the *Didache* argues *from* the Law, not *to* it, as being self-evidently authoritative. Thus the Decalogue is regarded as fundamentally valid for Christians.[7]

EPISTLE OF BARNABAS

Another authoritative document in Greek of a slightly later period[8] is the so-called *Epistle of Barnabas*.[9] This work differentiates clearly between ethical instructions and ritual commandments. The author states that, given the evil times, "we should apply ourselves to searching out the ordinances of the Lord."[10] The writer argues from Scripture that the Lord never needed sacrifices and has abolished them, in favor of the new law of Jesus Christ, which has "no yoke of necessity."[11] Other passages in the Old Testament are brought forward in support of an ethical service of God, and in rejection of ceremonial and sacrificial laws. The crux of the author's argument appears in IV.7–8, where he says that Moses received the covenant from the Lord (represented by the tablets of stone) but the Israelites' idolatry with the Golden Calf destroyed "their" covenant, a destruction dramatically portrayed by Moses' breaking of the stone tablets. This was in order for the covenant of Jesus to be sealed upon believers' hearts through the hope of faith in him.[12] Aspects of the ritual law, argues *Pseudo-Barnabas*, were intended to act as types of the coming of Christ,[13] as was circumcision.[14] The dietary rules had a spiritual significance, which Jews failed to understand but Christians do.[15] The Letter implies, however, that

---

5. "Now the Way of Life is this: first, you shall love God who made you; secondly, your neighbor as yourself; and all things that you wish should not be done to you, you shall not do to another." J. P. Audet, *La Didachè. Instructions des Apôtres*, Études bibliques (Paris: Gabalda, 1958), I.2.

6. See Audet, *La Didachè*, 226–42 and Willy Rordorf, "An aspect of the Judeo-Christian Ethic: The Two Ways," in *The Didache in Modern Research*, ed. Jonathan A. Draper (New York: Brill, 1996), 148–64 [156].

7. J. S. Kloppenborg, "The Transformation of Moral Exhortation in Didache 1–5," in *The Didache in Context, Essays on Its Text, History and Transmission*, ed. C. N. Jefford, NTS 77 (New York: Brill, 1995), 88–109 [102].

8. A date preceding the Bar-Kokhba Revolt of 132 CE is agreed on because the reference to an imminent rebuilding of the temple in 16.3–4 is incompatible with a later period.

9. R. A. Kraft, ed., *Épître de Barnabe*, SC 172 (Paris: Cerf, 1971).

10. *Ps-Barn.* II.1. Translations of this text are my own.

11. *Ps-Barn.* II.6.

12. *Ps-Barn.* IV.8c. The author of *Ps-Barn.* returns to this theme in XIV.

13. *Ps-Barn.* VII, VIII.

14. *Ps-Barn.* IX.

15. *Ps-Barn.* X.12.

the Decalogue is still to be observed, with the exception of the Sabbath. This can only be truly kept by those with pure hands and heart, thus hinting that it is impossible to do so in this age. Instead, the "eighth" day, when Christ arose, is the day that Christians are to observe, and this same day will mark the beginning of a new world.[16]

Pseudo-Barnabas eventually provides some more specific instructions on how Christians are to conduct themselves, mentioning the "Two Ways" familiar from the *Didache*.[17] The first injunction corresponds to the First Commandment and to *Didache* 1.2: "you shall love the One who made you," but expands this into "you shall fear the One who formed you, you shall glorify the One who redeemed you from death."[18] The rest of chapter XIX is generally composed of prohibitions, and like the *Didache* includes and expands on some of the commands of the Decalogue, while the author enjoins his readers not to forsake the commands of the Lord.[19] These presumably include both the traditional Ten Words and their outworkings, with the result that the prohibition of adultery naturally implies a prohibition of fornication, and the prohibition of killing applies to abortion and infanticide. The order in which these injunctions are listed seems rather arbitrary: the ban on taking the Lord's name in vain follows a prohibition on being double-minded and precedes a command to love one's neighbor more than oneself.[20] Next come the prohibitions of abortion and infanticide, of failing to discipline one's children, and then of covetousness.[21] The rest of the chapter gives various further injunctions for following the Way of Life.

Thus the *Epistle of Barnabas* has an oddly ambivalent attitude to the Decalogue. The author mentions it in relation to Sabbath observance and the law-giving at Sinai,[22] but since he argues that true Sabbath observance is impossible and the Sinaitic covenant had been immediately destroyed by the Israelites' idolatry (represented by the breaking of the stone tablets), with the Law having only typological function as far as believers are concerned, it is difficult to see how the Decalogue as such can be recovered from the wreckage. Instead its precepts appear scattered through chapter 19, with no clear relationship to the Pentateuch or even to any New Testament works that could have been in existence at that date.

---

16. *Ps-Barn.* XV.9.

17. *Ps-Barn.* XVIII. For the relationship between the *Didache* and *Ps.-Barn.* regarding the Two Ways, see van de Sandt and Flusser, *The Didache*, 49, and 70–80.

18. *Ps-Barn* XIX. See van de Sandt and Flusser, *The Didache*, 76.

19. *Ps-Barn.* XIX.2.

20. However, Kloppenborg has pointed to the influence of Hellenistic Jewish elaborations of Torah on the *Didache* and *Ps-Barn.* ("The Transformation of Moral Exhortation in Didache 1–5," 101). He notes similar treatments in Philo's *Hypothetica*, Josephus's *Contra Apionem*, and *Pseudo-Phocylides*.

21. *Ps-Barn.* XIX.5–6.

22. *Ps-Barn.* XV.

JUSTIN MARTYR

Moving on a few decades, Justin Martyr (d. 165) in his *Dialogue with Trypho*[23] argues that the Jewish law is obsolete and has been replaced by a new, universal and eternal code, identified with the person of Christ himself. Circumcision was given merely as a mark to separate out the Israelites from other nations and make them identifiable,[24] and Christians do not need to observe the law of physical circumcision, Sabbath, and feasts since it was given only by God for their hardness of heart:[25] the righteous up to the time of Abram were pleasing to God without being circumcised.[26] God imposed dietary laws and Sabbaths and sacrifices for their sin.[27] As for the commandments of the Decalogue (a term that Justin does not use), they are natural and universal precepts to which Christ appealed when he summed up "all righteousness and piety" in two commands. All righteousness is thus divided in two.[28]

Given that Justin is engaged directly in anti-Jewish argument, it is not surprising that he focuses on the rejection of ceremonial laws, circumcision and Sabbath. Necessary Christian conduct is summed up by the two great precepts of Christ, and the rest of Torah is rather summarily dismissed as natural and universal laws, which people should observe.

In his *First Apology*,[29] Justin is presenting Christian faith to a non-Jewish audience with philosophical leanings, and perhaps this is why he stresses that religious practice for Christians consists of *imitatio Dei*[30] with thanksgiving and no sacrificial cult.[31] However, though Justin does present Christ's teachings, starting with those on adultery,[32] he does not link the prohibition to the Decalogue or to the Mosaic Law more generally. This is no doubt because although adultery would have been frowned on in philosophically inclined pagan circles, the concept of Jewish law would have been either unfamiliar or rejected.

IRENAEUS

Justin's younger contemporary Irenaeus originated from Asia Minor but became bishop of Lyons in Gaul. In his work written against Gnostic heresies, the *Adversus*

---

23. E. J. Goodspeed, ed., *Die ältesten Apologeten* (Göttingen: Vandenhoeck & Ruprecht, 1915), 90–265. *Dial.* XI.2.
24. *Dial.* XVI.
25. *Dial.* XVIII.
26. *Dial.* XIX; XCII.
27. *Dial.* XXI–XXII; XXVII.
28. Goodspeed, ed., *Dial.* 93.1–3.
29. Goodspeed, ed., *Die ältesten Apologeten*, 26–77.
30. *1 Apol.* X.
31. *1 Apol.* XIII.
32. *1 Apol.* XV.

haereses,[33] written circa 180, he employs similar arguments to Justin (whose work he may have known), but in a much more developed form. Following Paul, he says that the Law was both instruction for Israel and a prophecy of things to come. Yet immediately after, Irenaeus argues that God was merely reminding people of natural law by means of the Decalogue, without which no one can be saved. God demanded no other observance from them.[34] Irenaeus rejects circumcision and the Sabbath as being unnecessary for righteousness since the patriarchs were pleasing to God even before the observance of either was revealed. He applies similar argumentation to the Law as a whole, including the Decalogue. The Law was not necessary for the righteous (cf. 1 Tim. 1.9) but was written on their hearts: "that is, they loved the God who made them, and held back from acting unjustly towards their neighbor".[35] When this natural righteousness came to an end during Israel's residence in Egypt, God instituted the Law. However, Irenaeus sees the Sinaitic Law in a more positive light than some other writers of the period:

> And it taught love towards God, and recommended just conduct towards one's neighbor, so that no one should behave unjustly, nor unworthily towards God, *who prepares man for His friendship through the Decalogue*, and also for harmonious relations with his neighbor. These [commandments] were for the benefit of man himself, since God needs nothing from man.[36]

Irenaeus also sees the Ten Commandments as universal and permanent:

> to prepare man for this [eternal] life, the words of the Decalogue were spoken to all alike by the Lord Himself in His own person, and similarly therefore, they remain with us. When he came in the flesh they were extended and increased but not abrogated.[37]

Other laws, however, were given as a bondage, a theme that we will find in other writers of the subsequent period,[38] though Irenaeus does not present these laws as a punishment for the Israelites out of God's anger. This is likely to be because his argument in this book is aimed in part against the Marcionites, who rejected the Old Testament as being the work of the old and jealous god rather than the loving God of the New Testament.[39] Irenaeus, like Barnabas, points to the many passages in Scripture where God apparently rejects the sacrificial cult, in preference for ethical conduct.[40]

---

33. A. Rousseau et al., *Irénée de Lyon, Contre les Hérésies, Livre IV/1*, SC 100 (Paris: Cerf, 1965). Irenaeus wrote in Greek, but his works survive mainly in Latin and Armenian translation.

34. *Haer.* IV.15.1.

35. *Haer.* IV. 16.3.

36. *Haer.* IV. 16.3 end; emphasis added.

37. *Haer.* IV. 16.4.

38. *Haer.* IV.16.5.

39. Note that Irenaeus says that God gave the "natural precepts" of the Decalogue to all people generously and without jealousy in order to allow people to know God as Father by adoption (*Haer.* IV.16.5).

40. *Haer.* IV.17.

TERTULLIAN

Tertullian was a Latin writer active in Carthage at the turn of the second century. He evidently knew of the work of his predecessors, Pseudo-Barnabas, Justin, and Irenaeus.[41] In one section of his work *Adversus Judaeos,* he tackles the question of Israelite/Jewish particularism: why would the one God, Creator of the whole universe, give a law to one people only?[42] Therefore the Law must have been given to all, starting with Adam and Eve. The very first divine command was given to Adam, and it stated that he was not to eat of the tree in the middle of paradise. This Law would have been sufficient for Adam and Eve, if they had kept it, since, according to Tertullian, it summarized all other commands:[43] love for God, love for neighbor, the prohibitions on killing, adultery, theft, false witness, covetousness, and the command to honor one's parents (since God was effectively the primordial couple's father). Tertullian argues that there was a pre-Mosaic, unwritten, natural law kept by the righteous forefathers such as Abraham and Noah,[44] and that this remains and continues to have priority for Gentiles also.[45]

Tertullian wrote the rather different treatise *De pudicitia* in his later, Montanist period, when his moral views had become even more stringent. It appears to have been composed as a reaction to an episcopal edict in Carthage granting pardon to adulterers and fornicators who had performed due penitence. Tertullian disapproved very strongly of this lenient attitude, as he believed (following 1 John 5:16) that adultery and other grave offences such as murder, idolatry, and apostasy, should lead to the permanent exclusion of offenders from the church (though this would not necessarily mean that they were destined for hellfire).[46]

Tertullian says that the seriousness of adultery (and by extension, fornication) can be gauged by the "first law of God," in other words the Decalogue.[47] The treatise has a section on the prohibition of adultery there,[48] which Tertullian says follows the ban on worship of other gods, the making of idols, the commendation of the Sabbath, and the command to honor one's parents. (In fact,

---

41. O. Skarsaune, "The Development of Scriptural Interpretation in the Second and Third Centuries—Except for Clement and Origen," in *Hebrew Bible/Old Testament: The History of Its Interpretation, I/1, From the Beginnings to the Middle Ages,* ed. M. Saebø (Göttingen: Vandenhoeck & Ruprecht, 1996), 373–442 [430].

42. H. Tränkle, ed., *Q.S.F. Tertulliani Adversus Iudaeos, mit Einleitung und kritischen Kommentar* (Wiesbaden: Steiner, 1964), *Adv. Jud.* II.1–9.

43. *Primordialis enim lex est data Adae et Evae in paradiso quasi matrix omnium praeceptorum dei* (*Adv. Jud.* II.4).

44. *Adv. Jud.* IV.7.

45. *Adv. Jud.* IV.9.

46. See R. P. C. Hanson, "Notes on Tertullian's Interpretation of Scripture," *Journal of Theological Studies,* New Series 22 (1961): 273–79: "It is clear that Tertullian held that what was permanent or unchanged in the old law was its moral commandments" (277). With regard to ritual laws as well, Hanson also notes that Tertullian would only eat meat from which the blood had been drained, and that he is aware of Christians who observe the Sabbath.

47. C. Micaelli and C. Munier, ed., *Tertullien, La Pudicité* I., SC 394 (Paris: Cerf, 1993).

48. *Pud.* V.

the commandment against murder comes before it in Exodus, Deuteronomy, and Matthew.) He sees in this order a deliberate grouping of spiritual sanctity followed by physical chastity and equates adultery with idolatry (as did, of course, many prophets in the Old Testament). He claims that adultery precedes murder in the code because it is more serious (presumably because of this spiritual aspect), while it often goes hand in hand with both idolatry and murder.[49]

He argues against the view that the precepts of the Law are no longer operative, since only the "yokes of works" has been rejected, not the "yokes of [moral] discipline."[50] Freedom in Christ does no wrong to innocence.[51] The entire law of piety, sanctity, humanity, truth, chastity, justice, mercy, benevolence, modesty remains.[52]

Tertullian seems to be doing the tightrope walk between Law and Grace mentioned at the beginning of this essay.[53] He is arguing that while there is liberty in Christ, who has fulfilled the law (but not abolished it), adultery remains a very serious offense for which there is no easy route out through penitence. Biblical precedents in which God pardoned adulterers and murderers should not be used to imply that divine mercy is somehow automatic and expected, since there are other examples (such as Num. 25:7–8) where fornicators were executed immediately. In the parables concerning the restoration of the lost sheep, lost coin, and prodigal son, which Tertullian's opponents were using as a precedent for restoring penitent adulterers, Tertullian says that they overlook the fact that these parables do not apply to baptized Christians, but to lost heathens who are found by God. For Christians who break the commandments after baptism, restoration in this life is not an option.[54] The Scriptures that Tertullian cites in De pudicitia VI, from both Old and New Testaments, are used to support his view that the Decalogue remains in force, and that the prohibition of adultery has been made even more stringent by Christ's censure of lustful thoughts.

CLEMENT OF ALEXANDRIA

Clement of Alexandria (d. c. 215) shows a good deal of interest in the Decalogue. In his work the *Paedagogus*, or "Instructor," a kind of manual of instruction on practical Christian living, he underlines the fundamental importance of the Decalogue. He starts with the Great Commands, but then speaks of the role of the other commandments.

49. *Pud.* V.1–5.
50. See Draper, "Torah and Troublesome Apostles in the Didache Community," 347 on the concept of "yoke" in the Church Fathers, and Pseudo-Barnabas's "yoke of necessity" above.
51. *Pud.* VI.3.
52. *Pud.* VI.4.
53. Although in fact this is what he accuses his opponents of doing: "Go on, you who walk the tightrope of modesty, chastity and every sort of sexual purity, treading the finest thread of a discipline of this sort, you progress with careful step away from the true path . . . " (*Pud.* X.9).
54. *Pud.* VII.

> Remarkable is the love of the Instructor towards mankind set forth in various life-giving commandments, in order that we might discover salvation more readily through the generous provision and arrangement of the Scriptures. We have the Decalogue through Moses, which . . . defines sins in a way conducive to salvation: 'Do not commit adultery. Do not worship idols. Do not corrupt boys. Do not steal. Do not bear false witness. Honor your father and your mother,' and so on. These things must be observed by us, and whatever else is commanded according to Scripture.[55]

However, in Clement's work the *Stromata*, written for a more intellectual Christian readership (he terms these Gnostics, in a positive, non-heretical sense) he expounds what he considers to be the true spiritual meaning of the Decalogue.[56] For this he reflects on the cosmic significance of the numbers one to ten, but especially ten, which he regards as a sacred number. God's writing of the Decalogue on the stone tablets with God's own hand is understood as symbolizing the creation of the universe by God's power. The tablets of stone are a prophecy of the two covenants. Ten also represents the physical world, and also the senses and principles in each human being, which should be governed by the ruling principle of reason, the Logos, which is the point of resemblance between man and God referred to at the creation of humanity in Genesis 1:26–27.

Clement introduces the idea that the Decalogue is represented by the letter iota (the "jot" Jesus said would not pass away), which signifies the name of Jesus. However, Clement mentions this motif almost in passing, at the end of a long explanation of the true meaning of various other numbers included in his comments on the Fourth Commandment (on the Sabbath).[57]

The Fifth Commandment, on honoring one's parents, Clement relates to honoring God the Father and divine wisdom as mother. The prohibition on murder is related to denial of true Christian doctrine, and similarly the prohibition of adultery is compared to idolatry and heresy, because it is the abandonment of God and espousal of false teachings. Theft is robbing God of credit as creator by claiming to be a creator oneself (e.g., an artist) or that it is the stars that are responsible for ordering the cosmos. The command against coveting is extended to false desires or supposing that inanimate objects are able to do good or harm of themselves.

Clement's exposition is a kind of meditation on the philosophical meaning of the practical commandments of the Decalogue, and it is at times very convoluted, though the general approach is not so different from that of Philo in the *De decalogo*. However, as also with Philo, Clement was hardly advocating that the "higher" meaning replaced the actual observance of the commands.

---

55. M. Harl et al., ed., *Clément d'Alexandrie: Le pédagogue*, SC 158 (Paris: Cerf,1970): *Paed.* III.12.88–89.

56. L. Früchtel, O. Stählin, and U. Treu, *Clemens Alexandrinus*, vol. 3, 2nd ed., GCS 52 (Berlin: Akademie Verlag, 1970), 15, 17: "Let us set out the Decalogue cursorily as an example for a gnostic explanation" (*Strom.* VI.16.133). However, there is nothing cursory about the explanation!

57. Früchtel et al., *Strom.* VI.16.145.7.

He merely presented a way of approaching them that would prove satisfying to those of a more intellectual bent.

Annewies van der Hoek has commented on the complete lack of negativity in Clement towards the Law, which may be due to Clement's stance against the Marcionites, and also less directly to the influence of Philo's thought. For Clement, *nomos* leads to *logos* and has an educational role, but it is also both given and accomplished by Christ.[58]

ORIGEN OF ALEXANDRIA

As one would expect, Origen of Alexandria, Clement's pupil, takes a similarly allegorical line with the Decalogue in his Exodus homilies, which were originally given for the moral instruction of the congregation in Caesarea and taken down by stenographers. For Origen, Moses is not merely the lawgiver, but the law of God himself, displayed in his chastisement of the Egyptians with the Ten Plagues and his wonder working. This "law," Moses, is given to correct and reform the world by means of the Ten Commandments. Thus Origen equates the Mosaic Law with the Decalogue, and sees it as a necessary measure for human discipline, paralleled by the Ten Plagues, which were needed to enforce God's will in Egypt. This is of course not a wholly positive depiction of the role of the Decalogue, but perhaps ties in with Paul's view that the Law is a tutor to lead us to Christ (Gal. 3:24).[59]

Origen's eighth homily on Exodus is centered on the Decalogue, which he sees as addressed as much to those hearing his sermon as to those Israelites who left Egypt to worship God at Sinai: for Christian believers have also, in a spiritual sense, left Egypt, which represents servitude to the present age.[60] Thus the First Commandment of the Decalogue reminds the people of their new liberty: "I am the LORD your God who brought you out from Egypt, from the house of slavery".[61] However, Origen's exposition of the Decalogue is largely limited to defining the implications of the command of monolatry and the prohibition of idol making and idol worship. He says that not all of the commandments concern the "exterior man," several being addressed to the "interior man," and

---

58. A. van der Hoek, *Clement of Alexandria and His Use of Philo in the* Stromateis: *An Early Christian Reshaping of a Jewish Model*, Supplements to Vigiliae Christianae 3 (New York: Brill, 1988), 227–29.

59. M. Borret, ed., *Homélies sur l'Exode*, SC 321 (Paris: Cerf, 1985), *Hom. Exod.* IV.6.

60. Compare Philo's view of Egypt as the land of the Body: Sarah J. Pearce, *The Land of the Body: Studies in Philo's Representation of Egypt*, WUNT 208 (Tübingen: Mohr Siebeck, 2007). Note that Philo in his treatise *De decalogo* I–IV has an extended explanation of why the people had to leave the city and enter the wilderness in order to hear the Law. Origen by contrast states that the people could not hear the Law while they were in a condition of servitude in Egypt, up to the moment when they reached Sinai.

61. Borret, *Hom. Exod.* VIII.1.

he then talks about the role of the devil in temptations to sin, the call of God to the soul to repent, and so on. Thus he provides no discussion of the other eight commandments.

In the next homily, IX, on the Tabernacle, he exhorts each person to erect within themselves a tabernacle to God, and expand their hearts to the ten curtains of the Tabernacle (Exodus 26:1–3 etc.), which represent the perfect number ten and symbolize the Decalogue.[62] These ten curtains can be stretched out within a person when he is able to enlarge the breadth of the spiritual understanding of the Law to the whole of the Decalogue, or produces the nine fruits of the Spirit.[63] How useful Origen's congregation found all this in their daily lives is debatable.

DIDASCALIA APOSTOLORUM

Treatments such as those of the Alexandrians Clement and Origen belong more to the realms of ideas and abstruse theology. More practical expositions of the nature of the Decalogue and its place in Christian life are found in works from the Syrian region of the third and fourth centuries.

An influential document is the early third-century pseudepigraphical and composite work, the *Didascalia Apostolorum*, which claims to represent the traditions of the twelve apostles. It originated in a Syrian environment and was translated from the lost Greek original into Syriac at some point in the fourth century[64] and also into Latin. It formed the basis for the work known as the *Apostolic Constitutions*, which unlike the *Didascalia*, does survive in Greek and possibly dates from 400 CE. The *Didascalia* claims to be speaking from a "catholic," or orthodox Christian, standpoint. For the most part it explicitly addresses those brethren who have converted from Judaism and clearly warns them away from adherence to Jewish ritual practices.

The *Didascalia* commences almost immediately with an exhortation to shun evil, and launches into a defense of the Decalogue and its reiteration by Jesus:

> And you shall not desire that which is anyone's, for it is written in the Law (Syriac *namosa*): You shall not desire what is of your neighbor: neither his field, nor his wife, nor his servant, nor his maidservant, nor his ox, nor his ass, nor anything of his property. For all these desires are from the Evil One.

---

62. *Hom. Exod.* IX.3.
63. *Hom. Exod.* IX.4. Cf. Galatians 5:22.
64. Vööbus's edition relies on eighteen manuscripts dating from the eighth to the twentieth century for the *Didascalia* itself. The number of surviving manuscripts attests to the enduring influence of the work in the Syriac church. See Robert Murray, *Symbols of Church and Kingdom* (Cambridge: Cambridge University Press, 1975; repr. Gorgias Press, Piscataway, NJ, 2004), 26; Walter Bauer, *Orthodoxy and Heresy in Earliest Christianity* (original German edition Tübingen, 1935; English translation Minneapolis: Fortress Press, 1971), 244–57.

For he that desires the wife of his friend, or his servant, or his maidservant, is already an adulterer and a thief, and condemned of uncleanness, like those who lie with males, by our Lord and Teacher Jesus Christ . . . As also in the Gospel He renews and confirms and fulfills the Ten Words of the Law, because it is written in the Law: You shall not commit adultery: yet I say unto you this, *I who in the Law spoke through Moses, but now I myself say to you*: Whoever looks upon the wife of his neighbor to desire her, has already committed adultery with her in his heart. And thus was he who desired condemned like an adulterer. He also that desires the ox or the ass of his neighbor, he wishes to steal it and to take it away. And he again who desires the field of his companion, does he not wish to force it within his own boundary, and trick him that he may sell it to him for nothing?[65]

This understanding draws the closest possible link between the authorship of the Decalogue at Sinai and the authority of Jesus in the Gospel, drawing out the concept of fulfillment and completion by the One who originally spoke it.[66]

The *Didascalia* goes on to indicate that there is one single, simple law for Christians: this turns out to be the negatively framed Golden Rule, which summarizes precepts found in the Decalogue and Gospel.[67]

While championing the "simple Law," the *Didascalia* distinguishes it from the "Second Law," Greek *deuterosis*[68] or Syriac *tinyan namosa*.[69] (This Syriac term is the same as that used for the title of the book of Deuteronomy, which effectively moves the thrust of the argument away from possibly Tannaitic oral interpretations of Torah to the biblical Mosaic Law.) Though mentioned in passing elsewhere in the *Didascalia*, the work dedicates its entire last chapter to what it calls "the Bonds of the Second Legislation of God."[70] It is addressed to "you who have been converted from the People," i.e., Christian converts from Judaism, to dissuade them from keeping "purifications, sprinklings, baptisms, and distinctions of foods."[71] Instead, they are reminded that God gave a simple, pure, and holy law of life, on which the Savior set his name. "For (when) he spoke the Ten Words, he therefore indicated Jesus, for 10 signifies Yod, and Yod is the first letter of the name of Jesus." The writer cites several Old Testament passages in support of the excellence of this simple Law, finishing with Jesus' command to the leper to show himself to the priests and make the due offering, "in order to show that he was not abolishing the Law but teaching what is the Law and in the Second Law."[72] The (simple) Law cannot be abolished, but the Second Law is temporary and can be abolished. So the Law consists of the Ten Words and the judgments, about which Jesus testified, saying,

65. A. Vööbus, ed., *The Didascalia Apostolorum in Syriac*, I, CSCO 401, SS 175 (Louvain: Secrétariat du CorpusSCO, 1979), ch. 1, p. 2, line 4, p. 13, line 2 (AT and emphasis added).
66. A point hinted at by Irenaeus, *Haer*. IV.16.4.
67. Vööbus, I. ch.1, p. 13, lines 5–7.
68. Note Jerome's negative attitude towards this term, e.g., in *Comm. Habac*, 1.2, line 420.
69. In the *Constitutiones Apostolorum*, Book 1, chapter 6, line 22.
70. Vööbus, *Didascalia* I. ch. 26, 241–65.
71. Ibid., 241, lines 12–13.
72. Ibid., 242, lines 19–21.

A single letter Yod shall not pass from the Law. The Yod that does not pass from the Law is known from the Law itself through the Ten Words: it is the Name of Jesus.[73]

The writer then proceeds to identify the Law and judgments (he does not specify what these are!) with what God told Moses before the making of the Golden Calf. It belongs to the dispensation of the Church and the Gentiles, whereas the Second Law was used by God to bind the Israelites after their worship of the Calf, out of anger and yet also in mercy.

The theme is developed at some length, but it is interesting that the *Didascalia* insists on the validity of the true Law and its identity with the Decalogue, rather than arguing that Christians are free of Law altogether. The "simple" Law is intimately linked to the very name of Jesus, and he commands believers to be under it: as the author says, "indeed everyone who is not under the Law is a transgressor."[74] The argument is ostensibly aimed at Jewish Christians (perhaps in fact at the actual date of writing also at Judaizers), and secondarily at heretics who do not cleave to the (simple) Law and the Prophets.[75]

APHRAHAT

It has been argued that Aphrahat, a Syriac writer of the mid-fourth century based around what is now the Mosul area, knew the *Didascalia* in Syriac.[76] Concerning the Decalogue, Aphrahat uses very similar arguments. A number of his twenty-three Demonstrations are aimed at combating Jewish arguments for the sanctity of the Sabbath, circumcision and dietary laws, at a time when a number of Christians in the Persian Empire appear to have been either Judaizing or converting to Judaism, in the hope of escaping the state persecution of the Church. Like the *Didascalia* he vehemently opposed ceremonial observances, while advocating observance of the Decalogue. This of course produces a contradiction when it comes to the commandment concerning the Sabbath, which other writers had already tried to remedy, usually by spiritualizing or allegorizing the concept of sacred rest. Aphrahat is more ingenious, in that he starts from the problem of having animals required to keep the Sabbath, during which leisure time, he says, they are able to commit major infractions of the Law, for instance killing each other, committing adultery and incest, licking their own blood, and eating unclean flesh.[77] If the Sabbath is meant to be of (spiritual) benefit

73. Ibid., 242, line 24–243, line 6.

74. Ibid., 248, lines 19–20.

75. Ibid., 254 end–255, line 7.

76. R.H. Connolly, *Didascalia Apostolorum: The Syriac Version Translated and Accompanied by the Verona Latin Fragments with an Introduction and Notes* (Oxford: Clarendon, 1929; repr. 1969), xvii, 265–70; Murray, *Symbols* (1975), 26, 155 n.3, 164 n.12, 193, 202 nn.5, 6; 337.

77. J. Parisot, ed., *Aphraatis sapientis persae demonstrations*, Patrologia Syriaca (Paris: Firmin-Didot et socii, 1894), *Dem.* XIII.2, pp. 543–46.

to domestic animals, the Law should surely first restrain them from these defiling acts and then confer righteousness on them for Sabbath observance. This *reductio ad absurdum* means that Aphrahat can undermine the idea that keeping the Sabbath is a matter of vital spiritual importance on the level of the other commands, when in fact, he argues, it was given only for physical rest.

In his first Demonstration, on Faith,[78] he presents an anti-Jewish caricature, in which the woman with the lost coin from the Gospel parable represents the "synagogue of the house of Israel" who was given the Decalogue but lost the First Commandment through worshiping other gods. Without it, Israel cannot keep the other nine commandments, which depend on it.

Further on in the same Demonstration, Aphrahat summarizes the faith and provides a kind of creed. He adds that it is necessary to break free of observing the Sabbaths and festivals, witchcraft and auguries, and one must avoid fornication, singing, the teaching of false doctrines, flattering words, blasphemy, adultery, bearing false witness, and duplicity. Thus as in earlier sources such as the *Didache*, key commands of the Decalogue have been integrated into a moral code including precepts from the Gospels and Epistles.

In his second Demonstration, on Love, Aphrahat discusses in what way Jesus needed to fulfill the Law and Prophets: what was lacking in them that needed to be fulfilled?[79] The answer is that the testament, the word of promise, was hidden within them. The Mosaic covenant was not ratified until the last covenant arrived, which was in fact the prior covenant, promised in advance. Christ's death confirmed both covenants, made the two one, and (following the Syriac Peshitta reading of Eph. 2:15) "abolished the law of commandments *by his own commandments*" (AT and emphasis added): Christ's sacrifice of himself nullified the purpose of the Law and the sacrificial system, which had never been pleasing to God, according to numerous passages of the Old Testament. Instead, the word (*meltha*) on which the Savior said the Law and Prophets hung is right and good.[80] For he said, "The single letter Yod shall not pass away from the Law and the Prophets until all shall come to pass" (Matt. 5:18, AT). Our Lord took the Law and Prophets and hung them upon just two commands, abrogating nothing from them. The dual commands to love God above all else and one's neighbor in the flesh as one's self are "above" the whole Law: here Aphrahat seems to be playing on the concept of having a "higher" law from which the other commands hang suspended. Aphrahat argues that the Law was not intended for the righteous (*ki'ne*) since whoever maintains righteousness is above[81] commandment, the Law and the Prophets. This confirms the word our Lord spoke, that the letter Yod would not pass away from the Law and Prophets, because it sealed and hung them on the two commands.

---

78. Parisot, *Dem.* I.19, col. 44.
79. Parisot, *Dem.* II.6, cols. 57–60.
80. Ibid., *Dem.* II.7, cols. 61–64.
81. Ibid.

Aphrahat's reasoning seems obscure until we look back at more explicit state-ments in earlier writers connecting the name Jesus with the initial letter of his name, Yod or iota: what Aphrahat is saying is that everything is confirmed by Jesus himself, the Yod that will not pass away, and the only one able to "main-tain righteousness." By his authority Jesus made all commands hang (depend) on the two Great Commandments of Love.

In his Demonstration XV on the dietary laws[82] Aphrahat picks up on the notion that God gave the Israelites two different types of law, based on Ezekiel 20: one set by which they would live by observing them (Ezek. 20:11) and one set as punishment for disobedience. The first, life-giving set Aphrahat identifies with the holy Decalogue that God wrote with his own hand, while the ceremo-nial and purity laws were given after the making of the Golden Calf. The Law can justify no one, and because the Law was burdensome, Jesus said, "Come to me who labor and are heavy laden . . . take my yoke on you, because my yoke is light and pleasant": Aphrahat implies that this light yoke is the Decalogue, the "simple" Law of the *Didascalia*.[83]

In his last Demonstration,[84] he says that if someone confesses that God is one, and yet breaks God's commandments and fails to do them, he is contradict-ing his own confession of God's unity. Aphrahat details these commandments as "You shall not kill, you shall not commit adultery, you shall not give false witness, honor your father and mother, what is hateful to you, do not do to your fellow." Anyone who believes that God will truly act as judge will not do such things. The next section of the Demonstration discusses the meaning of "You shall not take the Lord's name in vain" and the problem of swearing oaths: if someone commits perjury, how can he or she expect help from the God whom he or she has made out to be a liar? There is no wisdom like the fear of the Lord, and the person who keeps God's commands is to be praised.[85] Thus observance of the Decalogue is proof of faith in one God.

EPHREM

Ephrem, the most famous Syriac writer of all, was Aphrahat's younger contemporary and was active just over the border from him, in Roman territory. He lived most of his life in Nisibis, and then moved west to Edessa for the last ten years after Nisibis was ceded to the Persians in 363 CE. Though Ephrem is known principally for his wonderful poetry, we also have commentaries on

---

82. Parisot, *Dem.* XV.7–8, cols. 753–58.
83. Note the use of Matthew 11:28–30 in *Didascalia* IX (Vööbus, I. pp.112–113) in relation to the ceremonial laws and ch. XXIV (Vööbus, II, p.235) in the context of Peter's speech in Acts 15:10.
84. Parisot, *Dem.* XXIII.62, pp.128–29.
85. Ibid., *Dem.* XXIII.67, col. 148.

Genesis and Exodus by him,[86] and one on the *Diatessaron,* or Gospel harmony.[87]
In his commentary on Exodus[88] Ephrem discusses the commandments in
relation to the two Great Commands in the Gospel, with the Golden Rule
framed in the negative, as in Aphrahat:

> Do not do what is hateful to you to your fellow: do not kill, so that no
> one will kill you either; do not commit adultery with your neighbor's
> wife so that you will not have to repay through your own wife what you
> exacted from the wife of your fellow. Do not steal what is not yours, so
> that others do not steal what is yours. Do not bear false witness against
> your neighbor, so that another does not make a lying testimony against
> you. Do not covet what your neighbor has, so that another does not covet
> what you have in your house. See how fittingly our Lord said that "on
> these two commandments hangs the Law." It is natural law[89] that is in
> the Law[90] and the Prophets, apart from the precepts created for contin-
> gent circumstances.[91]

Ephrem's *Diatessaron* commentary presents a much more detailed (and complex) view of the Decalogue and Christ's claim to have fulfilled the Law.

> In order that the disciples should not suppose that by the Perfect Com-
> mands that our Lord introduced he did away with those of the Law, he
> warned them, "If you hear that I am bringing in Perfection, do not suppose
> that I am abolishing the Law: rather, I am actually fulfilling it. For I did
> not come to abolish but to fulfill."[92] For a scribe who perfects a child does
> not clash at all with the tutor, nor does a father wish his son to be always
> a child, nor a nurse wish that an infant should always be asking for milk.
> For milk is appropriate in its time, but when a child is robust, he does not
> need milk.

86. R.M. Tonneau, ed. *Sancti Ephraem Syri in Genesim et in Exodum commentarii*, CSCO 152,
SS 71 (Louvain 1955); English translation E. G. Mathews, J. P. Amar and K. McVey, *St. Ephrem
the Syrian, Selected Prose Works (Commentary on Genesis, Commentary on Exodus, Homily on our Lord,
Letter to Publius)*, Fathers of the Church 91 (Washington, 1994).
87. L. Leloir, ed., *S. Ephrem. Commentaire de l'évangile concordant. Texte syriaque (Manuscrit
Chester Beatty 709)* Chester Beatty Monographs 8 (Dublin: Hodges Figgis, 1963); L. Leloir, ed., *S.
Ephrem. Commentaire de l'évangile concordant. Texte syriaque (Manuscrit Chester Beatty 709) Folios
Additionels*, Chester Beatty Monographs 8 (Leuven, Paris: Peeters, 1990); C. McCarthy, *Saint
Ephrem's Commentary on Tatian's Diatessaron: An English translation of Chester Beatty Syriac MS
709*, Journal of Semitic Studies Supplement Series 2 (Oxford: Oxford University Press, 1993). I use
my own translation of this section in order to highlight some of the wordplay.
88. R.M. Tonneau, *Comm. Gen.* XX.1–3.
89. Literally, "precepts/laws of nature."
90. Here Ephrem uses the native Aramaic term *'orayta* instead of the Greek loan *namosa* nor-
mally used in Syriac.
91. Ephrem follows this defense of the Decalogue with a slightly curious reference to the command about building an altar of earth (Exod. 20:24). It is possible that the positioning of this citation this is influenced by the argument in the *Didascalia* II. XXVI, p.243 where the author states that
the text says '*If* you make an altar . . .', arguing that this implies that God did not at first instruct the
Israelites to make sacrifices to him. If so, Ephrem does not have the odd conditional "if" in his text.
92. Ephrem uses the verb *šra'* from Matthew 5:17 for the idea of abrogating the Law, rather than
baṭṭel from Ephesians 2:15, which Aphrahat prefers.

To the scribes and Pharisees who were present and seeking a pretext, he said, "I have not come to abolish the Law and the Prophets but to fulfill them," and he is the fulfillment of what is lacking. He makes known what this fulfillment consists of: "We are going up to Jerusalem, and the end of what is written about me." About these "deficiencies" he says, "The former things have passed away." But of those things that have entered into fulfillment and were absorbed into growth, and renewed into excellence he says, "It is easier for heaven and earth to pass away than for one of these letters of the Law to fall," and "Whoever abolishes one of the commands"—of the *New* Testament.[93]

Thus the Law is presented as a necessary but preliminary stage, to be fulfilled by Christ's death and replaced by the "solid food"[94] of the New Testament commands, which lead to "Perfection." Perfection is an important concept in early Syriac thought, related to the idea of becoming "perfect" or "complete," Greek *teleios* (Matt. 5:48).

Ephrem continues,

Whoever strikes you on your cheek, prepare for him the other: to maintain the [principle] of blow for blow is something inferior, because it is to maintain Justice in the period of Grace. "However, if your righteousness does not exceed [that of] the scribes, you shall not enter the kingdom of heaven." For it was said to [Israel], "Do not kill," but to you, "Do not become angry"; to them, "Do not commit adultery," and to you, "Do not desire." To them, "Blow for blow," but here, "Whoever strikes you, make ready for him the other." . . .Therefore he wished to bring the mature into the place of the mature, that is, the Perfect to the place of the angels.[95]

In this way Ephrem can demonstrate the spiritual superiority of the new moral code of the Gospel without undermining the authority or effectiveness of the Decalogue. Ephrem develops this line of thought at some length in the following sections, including the idea that the implied command of Jesus, "Do not desire" (§11a: cf. Matt. 5:28), sums up both the prohibition of adultery and fornication, and is therefore the "Perfection" or Completion of the Law. For Ephrem, the period of the "first covenant" of Justice had to reach perfection or fullness, and then Grace could produce its own perfection. The "water" of the old covenant, made to keep people from error and estrangement from God, is transformed by baptism into the "wine" of the new order, which is an aid to prevent us from turning aside to do what is merely transient.[96] The notion of progression in ethical revelation emerges, since Moses is said to have brought the

93. Leloir, ed., *Comm. Diat.* VI.3a–3b.
94. See §11b: "when the times set for the period of education were completed, then the solid food was proclaimed."
95. Leloir, ed., *Comm. Diat.* VI.4–5.
96. *Comm. Diat.* VI.12.

people up from the stage of iniquity and established them at the stage of Justice, while Jesus raised people to the level of Grace.[97]

LIBER GRADUUM

The final Syriac source to be surveyed is the *Liber Graduum*, or Book of Steps, an intriguing collection of thirty *memre*, or homilies on the spiritual life.[98] A single author appears to be behind them, who worked in the late fourth or early fifth century CE. The *memre* are remarkable in that they present a two-tier Christian community, consisting of the Upright (*ki'ne*) and the Perfect (*gmire*), who have different roles and responsibilities. Among other things, the Upright are meant to follow the basic commandments while the Perfect are called to observe a higher moral code. Thus the author argues in Memra XI that there are two types of commandments, major and minor, humble and harsh, "vegetable and milk" versus "solid food," commands that save those who keep them and others which do not. (These concepts are not dissimilar to what we have seen in Aphrahat and Ephrem, but the two older writers do not suggest anywhere that they are intended for different categories of believer but that all should aspire to the higher level of the two Great Commands of Christ.) Exegetically, the approach of the *Liber Graduum* is a useful one as it effectively resolves the apparent contradiction between certain precepts, as such "Do not judge" and "shame a person before the whole church": the first is a major command for the Perfect, the second a minor one for the Upright. The minor commands are not to be ignored, and must be kept if one is unable yet to aspire to the higher level.[99]

This is very relevant to the *Liber Graduum*'s teaching on the Decalogue. In Memra VII on the commandments of the Upright,[100] the author insists that since not everyone aspires to Perfection, they should observe the commandments not to kill, commit adultery, or steal; they should honor their parents, have mercy on the oppressed, refrain from fornication, bearing false witness, plundering or defrauding, coveting a fellow's property or wife, or removing his boundary. They should not do to others what is hateful to them but what they wish others would do to them. Later on the writer also states that various types of witchcraft and magic are forbidden.[101] He concludes the Memra by stating that if the Upright are not able to attain the major Law and be perfected, then they can still live by the minor one (i.e., the "extended" Decalogue and the ethic of reciprocity). In contrast, the Perfect should live by the two Great Commands

---

97. *Comm. Diat.* VI.14.
98. M. Kmosko, *Liber Graduum*, Patrologia Syriaca Pars Prima 3 (Firmin-Didot et socii: Paris, 1926). There is an English translation by R. A. Kitchen and M. Parmentier, *The Book of Steps: The Syriac Liber Graduum* (Kalamazoo, MI: Cistercian Publications, 2004).
99. See also Kmosko, Memra XIX.5, cols. 456–57, and XXX.3, col. 868.
100. Kmosko, Memra VII.1, col. 145.
101. Note the strong influence of the *Didache*.

(Matt. 22:37, 39), on which the Law and Prophets hang and by which a person can fulfill both of these.

The *Liber Graduum* takes a tougher line to Ephrem on the *lex talionis*:[102] Ephrem in the *Diatessaron* commentary had seen it as a reasonable command in the Covenant of Justice/Uprightness (provided one did not hit another unjustly), but it was superseded by the Covenant of Grace. However, the *Liber Graduum* regards this judgment of an eye for an eye as giving "evil for evil," having no virtue and unable to save. The author also appears to know of Aphrahat's second Demonstration,[103] as he uses the same texts, including Ephesians 2:15 on Christ making the two covenants or testaments one and abolishing the commandments of the Law by his own commandments. Like Aphrahat, the author speaks of "the Yod that shall not pass away." However, whereas Aphrahat hinted that this symbolized the name of Jesus, the *Liber Graduum* connects it with the number ten, and thus the Decalogue, which is the thing that will never pass away. The Decalogue will therefore endure even though since the coming of John the Baptist the rest of the Law and the Prophets served their purpose and passed away because they were old and obsolete.[104] These must refer to the Jewish ceremonial laws, and are presumably what the writer has in mind when he says that certain commandments should not be observed since they do not bring life and have been annulled. However, in contrast to the situation in the *Didascalia*, purity and dietary laws do not seem to be a live issue for the community of the *Liber Graduum*.

The *Liber Graduum*'s view of the history of the Decalogue resembles that of Irenaeus in some respects. According to the short Memra XXVI, "On the Second Law that the Lord gave Adam," Adam was given a first Law in Eden, which he broke. So God gave him another Law, that of Uprightness (*ki'nutha*). This corresponds to the content if not the wording of the Decalogue:

> See the possession that you loved, without understanding your own glory. Possess whatever you wish, only walk in uprightness. See, the earth that you have loved is given to you: only do not take what is your neighbor's. See, the labor that you have sought is given to you: only do not covet [the fruit of] your neighbor's labor. See, the marriage that you sought on the advice of the Evil One is given to you: only do not desire the wife of your neighbor, do not take two wives, do not let your sons commit fornication nor your daughters become prostitutes. Pass on the commands to your descendants, until I come and become for you all the example of Perfection . . . Adam and Eve, it is enough that you have fallen from Virginity and Perfection: do not fall from Uprightness and Justice.[105]

Thus the essence of the Decalogue is seen as primordial and pre-Mosaic, and both necessary and sufficient for salvation, yet a far cry from God's original plan

---

102. Kmosko, Memra XXII.1, cols. 633–36.
103. Parisot, Aphrahat, *Dem.* II, §6 and 7.
104. Kmosko, Memra XXII.21 cols. 683–84.
105. Kmosko, Memra XXVI.2, cols. 760–61.

of Perfection for humankind.[106] The whole "vexation" (or "bother") of the Law and Prophets was intended so that people should arrive (back) at the "Yod," the Ten Commandments,[107] which represent the beauty of the best commands in the Law and Prophets.[108] Anything outside the "Yod" in Scripture is called the "Covenant of Debts," because of the sins (debts) of the Israelites.

However, in Memra XXX, the last in the work, the author of the *Liber Graduum* stresses that though salvation is possible through obedience to the "Ten," there is a higher commandment than those of the Decalogue, including the two Great Commands. It is the "great and perfect portion," in fact the imitation of Christ, which involves leaving everything and taking up one's cross to follow him.[109]

CONCLUSION

This survey of sources from a wide geographical area up to the end of the fourth century amply demonstrates that the Decalogue formed a central part of Christian ethical teaching. A more systematic approach was about to be brought forward by Augustine of Hippo, in part as a response to his own Manichaean past. At this earlier stage, the difficulty was in proving that Christians still needed to observe a key part of the Mosaic Law. The words of Christ in the Gospel affirming the Decalogue, summarizing it, and extending its scope, do not seem to have been sufficient justification for several writers. Further arguments were necessary, in particular to show that Jesus was not referring to the whole Mosaic Law when he said that nothing of the Law would pass away. The reference to the "jot," the Greek letter iota or Syriac Yod is particularly ingenious in that it can signify either the Ten Commandments or the Name of Jesus who reauthorizes them, or both.

Less obvious is the process by which other precepts outside the Decalogue were tacked on as if self-evident, such as the ban on magical practices, and ironically these were as Jewish, even Mosaic, in origin as the traditions and ritual laws that Christians rejected. No doubt the real reason for these distinctions was the early established and soon dominant branch of the Church that saw Christian religious practice as primarily an ethical rather than ritual stance.

---

106. Kmosko, Memra XXII.22, col. 683–85.
107. It conceivably may also refer to Jesus himself as indicated by "Yod," since the *Liber Graduum* then speaks about the Lord's teaching that the whole force of the Law and Prophets hangs on the two Great Commands.
108. Kmosko, Memra XXII.23, col. 685.
109. Kmosko, Memra XXX.26, cols. 921–24.

Chapter 4

Thomas Aquinas

MATTHEW LEVERING

Addressing the question of whether the Old Law (Torah) was suitably given at the time of Moses rather than after Adam and Eve's sin, Thomas Aquinas explains that among the reasons why God did not immediately give the Torah was to make manifest the futility of pride: "man was left to the guidance of his reason without the help of a written law: and man was able to learn from experience that his reason was deficient, since about the time of Abraham man had fallen headlong into idolatry and the most shameful vices."[1] For our purposes, the important point is not the accuracy of Aquinas's history of religion,

An earlier version of this chapter was published as chapter 4 in Matthew Levering, *Jewish-Christian Dialogue and the Life of Wisdom: Engagements with the Theology of David Novak* (New York: Continuum, 2011). Used by permission of Continuum.

1. Thomas Aquinas, *Summa theologiae* 1–2, q.98, a.6, trans. Fathers of the English Dominican Province (Westminster, MD: Christian Classics, 1981). For the Jewish and Christian medieval background to Aquinas's theology of law, see the excellent article by Juan-Fernando Chamorro, O.P., "Ley Nueva y Ley Antigua en Santo Tomás," *Studium* 7 (1967): 317–80; Sean Eisen Murphy, "'The Law Was Given for the Sake of Life:' Peter Abelard on the Law of Moses," *American Catholic Philosophical Quarterly* 81 (2007): 271–306. For discussion of Aquinas on Christ's fulfillment of the Torah, see my *Christ's Fulfillment of Torah and Temple: Salvation according to Thomas Aquinas* (Notre Dame, IN: University of Notre Dame Press, 2002). See also Jean-Pierre Torrell, O.P., "*Ecclesia Iudaeorum*—Quelques jugements positifs de saint Thomas d'Aquin à l'égard des

but rather his emphasis, in Russell Hittinger's words, on the fact that "God left men in such a condition . . . in order to chastise them."[2] Once human pride was deflated, God promised covenantal intimacy to Abraham, Isaac, and Jacob and through Moses gave the people of Israel the Torah. Since the restoration of human relationship with God requires human holiness, Aquinas observes, "just as the principal intention of human law is to create friendship between man and man; so the chief intention of the divine law is to establish man in friendship with God."[3] Within the Torah, the Decalogue reveals the foundational moral precepts. The ceremonial and judicial laws of the Torah then apply the Decalogue's precepts to the liturgical practices and economic-political structures of the people of Israel.[4]

Given that Aquinas envisions the Decalogue as contributing to "friendship with God," I examine Aquinas's theology of the Decalogue in his *Summa theologiae* by focusing on four overlapping topics.[5] First, I inquire into the Decalogue's status, according to Aquinas, as revealed natural law. Second, I explore the relationship in the Decalogue between revelation and the created order by taking as a test case the commandment to observe the Sabbath. Third, I ask whether obedience to the Decalogue is meritorious, that is, how it pertains to friendship with God. Last, I comment briefly on how Aquinas interprets certain biblical passages that suggest that God violates the Decalogue.

---

juifs et du judaïsme," in *Les philosophies morales et politiques au Moyen Âge*, ed. B. Carlos Bazán, Eduardo Andújar and Léonard G. Sbrocchi (Ottawa: LEGAS, 1995), 1732–41.

2. Russell Hittinger, *The First Grace: Rediscovering the Natural Law in a Post-Christian World* (Wilmington, DE: ISI Books, 2003), 11. This does not mean that humans had no knowledge of the natural law between Adam and Eve's sin and the time of Moses. On the contrary, Aquinas notes, "human reason could not go astray in the abstract, as to the universal principles of the natural law; but through being habituated to sin, it became obscured in the point of things to be done in detail" (1–2, q.99, a.2, ad 2). For further discussion see Pamela Hall, *Narrative and the Natural Law: An Interpretation of Thomistic Ethics* (Notre Dame, IN: University of Notre Dame Press, 1994); David McIlroy, "A Trinitarian Reading of Aquinas's Treatise on Law," *Angelicum* 84 (2007): 277–92.

3. 1–2, q.99, a.2. Although friendship with God comes through the Paschal mystery, nonetheless the Torah is not extrinsic to this friendship, since the Torah prepares for and points to the Messiah. Aquinas states that "it was possible at the time of the Law, for the minds of the faithful, to be united by faith to Christ incarnate and crucified; so that they were justified by faith in Christ: of which faith the observance of these ceremonies was a sort of profession, inasmuch as they foreshadowed Christ. Hence in the Old Law certain sacrifices were offered up for sins, not as though the sacrifices themselves washed sins away, but because they were professions of faith, which cleansed from sin. In fact, the Law itself implies this in the terms employed: for it is written (Leviticus iv.26, v.16) that in offering the sacrifice for sin *the priest shall pray for him . . . and it shall be forgiven him*, as though the sin were forgiven, not in virtue of the sacrifices, but through the faith and devotion of those who offered them" (1–2, q.103, a.2).

4. For further discussion see my *Christ's Fulfillment of Torah and Temple: Salvation according to Thomas Aquinas* (Notre Dame, IN: University of Notre Dame Press, 2002), chapter 1.

5. Aquinas treats the Decalogue in many other places as well, most notably his *De decem praeceptis*: for an English translation see Aquinas, *God's Greatest Gifts: The Commandments and the Sacraments*, trans. Joseph B. Collins (Manchester, NH: Sophia Institute Press, 1992). His *De decem praeceptis* briefly interprets the commandments and exhorts obedience to them.

THE DECALOGUE AS NATURAL LAW

Among the laws given to Israel, the Decalogue has a special place, as indicated by the two tablets of stone that Moses received from God. Aquinas suggests that God directly gives the Decalogue so as to underscore that humans know the precepts of the Decalogue without needing instruction from human lawgivers.[6] For Aquinas, "the precepts of the Decalogue are such as the mind of man is ready to grasp at once."[7]

If the Decalogue consists in precepts "such as the mind of man is ready to grasp at once," then why is violation of the Decalogue, for instance by idolatry and irreverence, so common? Aquinas holds that sin obscures, without effacing, human apprehension of the natural obligation to worship God. Describing the consequences of sin, he says that "when man turned his back on God, he fell under the influence of his sensual impulses: in fact this happens to each one individually, the more he deviates from the path of reason, so that, after a fashion, he is likened to the beasts that are led by the impulse of sensuality" rather than by rational reflection.[8] Sin cannot efface from the human mind the natural law in its first principles, including love of God and love of neighbor. But the natural law "is blotted out in the case of a particular action, in so far as reason is hindered from applying the general principle to a particular point of practice, on account of concupiscence or some other passion."[9] In idolatry, irreverence, and so forth, we lose touch with what is reasonable.[10]

Despite the fact that the natural law precepts are in accord with reason, then, God reveals such precepts in the Decalogue because human beings, weighed down by sin, have difficulty making right judgments in moral reasoning. It follows that the Decalogue can be expected to be the central source of natural law, not despite of the Decalogue's covenantal character, but because of it. God makes covenant with Israel so that Israel might become holy. The Decalogue holds a central covenantal place because it communicates the natural law as elevated into the covenantal context of God's call to Israel to be God's people and to be holy.

This covenantal context becomes further evident in light of Aquinas's three-fold ordering of the moral precepts of the Torah. He begins with the moral

6. Aquinas states, "The precepts of the Decalogue differ from the other precepts of the Law, in the fact that God himself is said to have given the precepts of the Decalogue; whereas he gave the other precepts to the people through Moses. Wherefore the Decalogue includes those precepts the knowledge of which man has immediately from God" (1–2, q.100, a.3).

7. 1–2, q.100, a.6.

8. 1–2, q.91, a.6. Aquinas here quotes Psalm 48:21 from the Vulgate: "*Homo in honore cum esset non intellexit; conparatus est iumentis insipientibus, et similes factus est illis.*" Cf. Psalm 49:20 (RSV): "Man cannot abide in his pomp, he is like the beasts that perish."

9. 1–2, q.94, a.6; see also 1–2, q.100, a.11.

10. Frank Mobbs argues that since "[i]t is *the mode of knowing* that distinguishes natural from revealed," no precept of the natural law can be "natural" if one knows it from God's revelation: see Mobbs, "Is Natural Law Contained in Revelation?" *New Blackfriars* 85 (2004): 453–58, at 456. Mobbs overlooks the way in which the light of faith heals reason.

principles that are "so evident as to need no promulgation; such as the command-ments of the love of God and our neighbor."[11] Rather than solely being mere commandments, these principles provide "the ends of the commandments."[12] Thus the Torah commands the act of charity toward God and neighbor: "you shall love the LORD your God with all your heart, and with all your soul, and with all your might" (Deut. 6:5) and "[y]ou shall not take vengeance or bear a grudge against any of your people, but you shall love your neighbor as yourself" (Lev. 19:18).[13] Following upon these commandments, about which "no man can have an erroneous judgment," are commandments that are first conclusions from basic natural law principles. The Decalogue reveals these first conclusions, whose truth most people recognize.[14] Lastly, following upon the command-ments of the Decalogue stand the moral precepts of the Torah that require fur-ther reasoning to deduce.

The foremost place given to the commandments regarding charity under-scores the relationship of covenant and creation in Aquinas's theology of the Decalogue. As he does with respect to all the precepts of the Torah, he argues that the Decalogue requires, for its fulfillment, the New Law: "Man cannot ful-fill all the precepts of the law, unless he fulfill the precept of charity [Deut. 6:5; Lev.19:18], which is impossible without charity."[15] Aquinas specifically means the supernatural virtue of charity, as becomes clear from his conclusion: "Con-sequently it is not possible, as Pelagius maintained, for man to fulfill the law without grace."[16] In this covenantal context the commandments of the Deca-logue, including those commandments that are knowable solely from within the created order, do not form an autonomous morality. Thus, inquiring whether "peace is the proper effect of charity," Aquinas quotes Psalm 119:165, "Great peace have those who love thy law."[17] To love the Mosaic law, Aquinas explains, requires both loving God with one's "whole heart, by referring all things to

11. 1–2, q.100, a.11.

12. Ibid.

13. 1–2, q.100, a.10. Christ Jesus teaches that these two commandments provide the key to the whole Mosaic Law: "On these two commandments hang all the law and the prophets" (Matt. 22:40).

14. 1–2, q.100, a.11.

15. 1–2, q.100, a.10, ad 3. This point is one of the similarities that David VanDrunen identifies between Aquinas and Calvin on natural law. VanDrunen also observes that "Thomas and Calvin agree that the Mosaic law is properly distinguished into moral, ceremonial, and judicial laws" and that "Thomas and Calvin both see a basic identity of the natural law, moral law, and Decalogue": see VanDrunen, "Medieval Natural Law and the Reformation: A Comparison of Aquinas and Cal-vin," *American Catholic Philosophical Quarterly* 80 (2006): 77–98, at 89. Comparing Aquinas with Calvin, VanDrunen also finds a "relative absence of the topic of sin in Thomas's discussions" (95), but this seems to me not accurate. VanDrunen similarly notes that "[f]or Calvin, all people know the requirement of charity through the law of nature" and so "in some ways Calvin, rather than Thomas, has the richer substantive view of natural law" (97). In this regard compare the reflections on natural and supernatural love in Thomas M. Osborne Jr., *Love of Self and Love of God in Thirteenth-Century Ethics* (Notre Dame, IN: University of Notre Dame Press, 2005).

16. 1–2, q.100, a.10, ad 3.

17. 2–2, q.29, a.3, *sed contra*.

Him," and loving "our neighbor as ourselves."[18] Such love comes about not through our natural powers, which are insufficient to make us friends with God, but through "the infusion of the Holy Spirit, who is the love of the Father and the Son, and the participation of whom in us is created charity."[19]

It follows that the precepts of the Torah, including the Decalogue, are far from a mere list of rules. Rather, Aquinas treats them under the rubric of Psalm 19:8, "the precepts of the Lord are right, rejoicing the heart; the commandment of the Lord is pure, enlightening the eyes."[20] As Psalm 19 goes on to say of the precepts of the Mosaic Law, "More to be desired are they than gold, even much fine gold; sweeter also than honey and drippings of the honeycomb. Moreover by them is your servant warned; in keeping them there is great reward" (19:10–11). They belong to the covenantal drama of the law and the prophets. Aquinas remarks in this respect, "As anyone can see, who reads carefully the story of the Old Testament, the common weal of the people prospered under the Law as long as they obeyed it; and as soon as they departed from the precepts of the Law they were overtaken by many calamities."[21]

THE SABBATH COMMANDMENT

Aquinas holds that the precepts of the Decalogue do not all belong to the law of nature "in the same way": the Decalogue includes both precepts of natural law and precepts inaccessible to human reason alone.[22] With respect to the former, he notes that "there are certain things which the natural reason of every man, of its own accord and at once, judges to be done or not to be done: e.g., *Honor thy father and thy mother*, and, *Thou shalt not kill, Thou shalt not steal*: and these belong to the law of nature absolutely."[23] While these precepts of the Decalogue

---

18. 2–2, q.29, a.3. The moral virtue of justice, by itself, cannot achieve peace. Responding to an objection that proposes that peace can be achieved without sanctifying grace, Aquinas observes, "Peace is the *work of justice* indirectly, in so far as justice removes the obstacles to peace: but it is the work of charity directly, since charity, according to its very nature, causes peace. For love is *a unitive force* as Dionysius says (*Div. Nom.* iv): and peace is the union of the appetite's inclinations" (2–2, q.29, a.3, ad 3). Peace requires the interior harmony of one's rational and sense appetites, whose disorder is the root cause of conflicts. I have Gregory Reichberg to thank for drawing my attention to this text.

19. 2–2, q.24, a.2.

20. 1–2, q.100, a.11, *sed contra*.

21. 1–2, q.99, a.6, ad 3. Qualifying this point (which reflects the witness of such books as Deuteronomy, Judges, 1 and 2 Kings, Ezra, and Nehemiah), he adds, "But certain individuals, although they observed the justice of the Law, met with misfortunes,—either because they had already become spiritual (so that misfortune might withdraw them all the more from attachment to temporal things, and that their virtue might be tried);—or because, while outwardly fulfilling the works of the Law, their heart was altogether fixed on temporal goods, and far removed from God, according to Isaiah xxix.13 (Matthew xv.8): *This people honoreth Me with their lips; but their heart is far from Me*" (1–2, q.99, a.6, ad 3).

22. Ibid.

23. Ibid.

play a role within the covenantal particularity of Israel,[24] nonetheless they flow from the created order. Other precepts of the Decalogue, however, are not accessible to natural human reason. As an example, Aquinas gives, "Thou shalt not take the name of the Lord thy God in vain."[25] Only by Revelation can we know "the name of the Lord."

In Aquinas's view, the covenantal particularity of the Decalogue explains the Decalogue's combination of natural law with precepts not accessible to reason alone. Uniquely among the laws given to Israel, the Decalogue is God's direct instruction: "God Himself is said to have given the precepts of the Decalogue; whereas He gave the other precepts to the people through Moses."[26] The Decalogue does not include either the first principles of practical reason (which need not be promulgated anew) or those precepts that must be more laboriously deduced from natural law principles, which God teaches through the mediation of "wise men" such as Moses.[27] Instead, the purpose of the Decalogue is to renew creation by recalling the basic precepts of the natural law, and to elevate creation by placing it within the context of covenantal Revelation, of knowing the very "name" of the Lord. Recall Jacob's plea: "Tell me, I pray, your name" (Gen. 32:29, RSV)—and his exultation that same night, "For I have seen God face to face, and yet my life is preserved" (Gen. 32:30).

For Aquinas, then, the Decalogue calls into question efforts to isolate natural law doctrine, rooted in our natural knowledge of the created order, from the covenantal particularity in which it comes fully to light. Consider Aquinas's treatment of the commandment of Sabbath observance. Against Hesychius's exclusion of the commandment regarding the Sabbath from the Decalogue, Aquinas notes, "it seems unbecoming for the precept of the Sabbath-day observance to be put among the precepts of the Decalogue, if it nowise belonged to the Decalogue."[28] Following Origen's and Augustine's commentaries on Exodus, Aquinas therefore argues for the inclusion of the Sabbath in the Decalogue.[29] One might ask, however, why observing the Sabbath should have a special place among the ten words (Deut. 4:13) that Moses singles out as the heart of the Law. Would it not fit better among the ceremonial precepts, which are "determinations of the precepts of the Decalogue"[30]—laws that apply the principles articulated by the Decalogue to Israel's particular time and place? If,

24. For the illustration of the Decalogue in the covenantal history of Israel, see David Noel Freedman with Jeffrey C. Geoghegan and Michael M. Homan, *The Nine Commandments: Uncovering the Hidden Pattern of Crime and Punishment in the Hebrew Bible*, ed. Astrid B. Beck (New York: Doubleday, 2000).

25. 1-2, q.100, a.1.

26. 1-2, q.100, a.3.

27. Ibid. Aquinas adds, "Nevertheless both kinds of precepts are contained in the precepts of the Decalogue; yet in different ways. For the first general principles are contained in them, as principles in their proximate conclusions; while those which are known through wise men are contained, conversely, as conclusions in their principles" (ibid.). See also 1-2, q.100, a.11.

28. 1-2, q.100, a.4.

29. Ibid.

30. 1-2, q.100, a.11, ad 2.

as Aquinas states, "the precepts of the Decalogue need to be such as the people can understand at once,"[31] is Sabbath observance such a precept?

In reply, Aquinas suggests that the Sabbath commandment can at the same time be universal (linked to the order of creation) and covenantal.[32] The Sabbath commandment is a universal moral precept, knowable by natural law, "in so far as it commands man to give some time to the things of God, according to Psalm xlv.11: *Be still and see that I am God.*"[33] As Aquinas points out, the Sabbath commandment, understood as a moral precept, is the foundation of all the ceremonial precepts.[34] Worship is not an irrational impulse: "It belongs to a dictate of natural reason that man should do something through reverence for God."[35] In principle, therefore, human beings can understand the Sabbath commandment "at once," although in practice many reject the commandment. In addition to being a moral precept, however, the Sabbath commandment is also a ceremonial precept regarding God's choice of the seventh day for the people of Israel to worship God.[36] The seventh day need not be set apart for human beings to "give some time to the things of God"; God could have chosen another day, and in the New Covenant God does so.

The determination of the seventh day as a day of rest and worship for the Israelites is not the only way in which the Sabbath commandment is covenantal as well as universal. Aquinas argues that the Sabbath commandment both points back to creation and points forward to the elevation of creation in eschatological new creation. Understanding the Decalogue as law for the human community under God, Aquinas notes that "man owes three things to the head of the community: first, fidelity; secondly, reverence; thirdly, service."[37] The Sabbath pertains to the service of the "head," God. Such service arises in response to the

31. 1–2, q.100, a.5.

32. David Novak suggests otherwise, although he recognizes that the Sabbath has a "semi-universal status" (Novak, *Natural Law in Judaism* [Cambridge: Cambridge University Press, 1998], 72). He comments, "The semi-universal status of the Sabbath might be due to the fact that two reasons are given for it. The first is the reason from creation given in the Exodus version of the Ten Commandments. The second reason, though, is the one in the Deuteronomic version of the Ten Commandments, namely, 'in order (*le-ma'an*) that your male slave and your female slave rest like you. And you shall remember that you were a slave in the land of Egypt and the Lord your God brought you out from there' (Deuteronomy 5:14–15). This latter reason is clearly covenantal, hence historical not natural" (72). Aquinas proposes that a commandment can be both covenantal/historical and natural.

33. 1–2, q.100, a.3, ad 2. J. P. M. van der Ploeg, O.P., argues that Aquinas "does not take account of the fact that the law does not command *vacare rebus divinis*, but rather not to do work on this day" (van der Ploeg, "Le traité de saint Thomas de la loi ancienne," in *Lex et Libertas*, ed. Leo Elders, S. V. D. and K. Hedwig [Vatican City: Libreria Editrice Vaticana, 1987], 185–99, at 192). By not doing work on the Sabbath, the Israelites participate in the Lord's hallowing of the Sabbath, as Exodus 20:11 shows. Such participation is what is meant by *vacare rebus divinis*.

34. See 1–2, q.100, a.11.

35. 2–2, q.81, a.1, ad 3. Aquinas goes on to say, "it is a dictate of natural reason in accordance with man's natural inclination that he should tender submission and honor, according to his mode, to that which is above man" (2–2, q.85, a.1).

36. 1–2, q.100, a.3, ad 2.

37. 1–2, q.100, a.5.

divine gifting that constitutes the community: "Service is due to his master in return for the benefits which his subjects receive from him: and to this belongs the Third Commandment of the sanctification of the Sabbath in memory of the creation of all things."[38] The Sabbath hearkens back to the seven days of creation, as the commandment makes clear: "for in six days the LORD made heaven and earth, the sea, and all that is in them, and rested the seventh day; therefore the LORD blessed the sabbath day and hallowed it" (Exod. 20:11, repeating Gen. 2:3, RSV).

Human community under God, which begins at creation, is ordered by God's grace to the perfect Sabbath, beatific union with God. Aquinas notes, "it is right that the seventh day should have been sanctified, since the special sanctification of every creature consists in resting in God."[39] This special sanctification is envisioned by God in creating from eternity. Here Aquinas differentiates between the "first perfection" of a creature, in which it fully receives its substantial form, and the creature's "second perfection," which is the final attainment of the creature's end or goal. This "end" can be "either an operation, as the end of the harpist is to play the harp; or something that is attained by the operation, as the end of the builder is the house that he makes by building."[40] In this sense the "end" is caused by the form as the principle of operation. What then are the "first perfection" and "second perfection" of the entire created universe? Aquinas answers that "the final perfection, which is the end of the whole universe, is the perfect beatitude of the Saints at the consummation of the world; and the first perfection is the completeness of the universe at its first founding, and this is what is ascribed to the seventh day."[41]

The "completeness of the universe at its first founding" does not require that new creatures or new species not come into existence later. As Aquinas notes, individual things now being generated can be said to have existed "in their causes" (including their material cause), and new species "existed beforehand in various active powers."[42] Even spiritual souls, fashioned by God at the instant of the conception of each new human person, "existed beforehand by way of similitude," as did the incarnate Son who was made "in the likeness of men" (Phil. 2:7, RSV).[43] While insisting upon the completeness of the universe in its natural integrity (inclusive of its natural teleology), Aquinas never envisions this "first perfection" as cut off from the supernatural grace of the Holy Spirit. Against the view of a number of his contemporaries, Aquinas argues that human beings were created in grace.[44] Without grace, Adam and Eve's original justice could not have been sustained: as Aquinas says, "it is clear that such a subjection

---

38. Ibid.
39. 1, q.73, a.3.
40. 1, q.73, a.1.
41. Ibid.
42. 1, q.73, a.1, ad 3.
43. Ibid.
44. For discussion see Jean-Pierre Torrell, O.P., "Nature et grâce chez Thomas d'Aquin," *Revue Thomiste* 101 (2001): 167–202, at 168–79.

of the body to the soul and of the lower powers to reason, was not from nature; otherwise it would have remained after sin; since even in the demons the natural gifts remained after sin."[45] Already, then, Adam and Eve received the gift of intimate friendship with God in charity, whose perfection is found in the new creation, the state of glory.[46]

Discussing the Decalogue, Aquinas quotes Augustine to the effect that "by the First Commandment we reverence the unity of the First Principle; by the second, the Divine truth; by the third, His goodness whereby we are sanctified, and wherein we rest as in our last end."[47] By calling to mind both the beginning and the end, creation and new creation, the Sabbath commandment illustrates how the Decalogue weaves together creation and covenantal particularity. As Aquinas explains, this union of creation and (covenantal) new creation is why the Decalogue includes the Sabbath but not the other festivals or sacrifices.[48] He adds that the first three commandments can also be viewed as teaching the right ordering of deeds, words, and thoughts, the last of which applies to the Sabbath commandment, since "the sanctification of the Sabbath, as the subject of a moral precept, requires repose of the heart in God."[49]

THE DECALOGUE AND JUSTIFICATION

Aquinas raises the question of human obedience to the Torah in light of Jesus' teaching to a young man of Israel, "If you would enter life, keep the commandments" (Matt. 19:17, RSV).[50] Aquinas notes that full obedience can only be achieved in the context of covenantal union with God. Deepening God's promise that Israel would be his own people, Jesus makes us his friends by giving us a share in his Spirit. But if obedience to the Decalogue requires charity, how does one address the striving of human beings who lack charity? Can such persons follow the Decalogue?

Outside charity, Aquinas suggests, human beings can certainly understand, and often follow, the Decalogue. The commandment "Honor your father and your mother" (Exod. 20:12), for example, "does not mean that a man must honor his father from charity, but merely that he must honor him. Wherefore

---

45. 1, q.95, a.1.

46. Cf. 1, q.95, a.3. That the natural and supernatural gifts might not be blurred, Aquinas comments on Genesis 2:15 ("The LORD God took the man and put him in the garden of Eden to till it and keep it"): "Paradise was a fitting abode for man as regards the incorruptibility of the primitive state. Now this incorruptibility was man's, not by nature, but by a supernatural gift of God. Therefore that this might be attributed to God, and not to human nature, God made man outside of paradise, and afterwards placed him there to live there during the whole of his animal life; and, having attained to the spiritual life, to be transferred thence to heaven" (1, q.102, a.4).

47. 1–2, q.100, a.5.

48. See 1–2, q.100, a.5, ad 2.

49. 1–2, q.100, a.5.

50. See 1–2, q.100, a.10, obj.1 and ad 1.

he that honors his father, yet has not charity, does not break this precept."[51] No human beings, even those who have no share in covenantal relationship with God, stand outside the reach of the Decalogue. Yet full obedience to the natural law requires charity. Interpreting Romans 2:14–15, Aquinas holds that the Gentiles who are able to fulfill the natural law, rather than merely to obey one or another commandment, do so by a certain graced participation in "the Israel of God" (Gal. 6:16).[52] He explains that implicit faith allows for this participation in the covenant: "If, however, some [gentiles] were saved without receiving any revelation, they were not saved without faith in a Mediator, for, though they did not believe in Him explicitly, they did, nevertheless, have implicit faith through believing in Divine providence, since they believed that God would deliver mankind in whatever way was pleasing to him" (cf. Heb.11:6).[53]

Aquinas's position here also has to do with his understanding of what law is. He holds that God draws human beings toward himself by means of law: "the extrinsic principle moving to good is God, Who both instructs us by means of His Law, and assists us by His Grace."[54] Since natural law belongs to the teleological constitution of the rational creature, the goal of natural law in the concrete historical order cannot be fulfilled without covenantal charity. This is so not only because of the consequences of original sin, but also because only charity unites us to the ultimate end for which we were created, namely God himself. Lacking charity, human actions—even those which accord with the Decalogue, such as "Honor your father and your mother"—miss the good toward which God has ordained human beings.[55] It is better to honor one's father and mother than not to do so; and yet if one does so for self-serving reasons, one has failed to fulfill the commandments "you shall love the LORD your God" (Deut. 6:5) and "you shall love your neighbor as yourself" (Lev. 19:18). These commandments are certainly in accord with natural reason, but they require charity to be fulfilled. Lacking charity, one can neither "keep the commandments" nor "enter into life" (Matt. 19:17).

Although the Decalogue commands certain human actions, such precepts themselves, on their own, cannot bring about the divine action needed for the restoration of "that justice which is before God."[56] In this regard Aquinas quotes 2 Corinthians 3:6, where Paul writes that God "has qualified us to be ministers

51. 1–2, q.100, a.10.

52. In his commentary on Romans, Aquinas interprets Romans 2:14–15—"When Gentiles who have not the law do by nature what the law requires, they are a law to themselves. . . . They show that what the law requires is written on their hearts"—to be speaking of Gentiles who share in the grace of the Holy Spirit and have faith, hope, and charity. For further discussion, see my "Knowing What Is 'Natural': Thomas Aquinas and Luke Timothy Johnson on Romans 1–2," *Logos* 12 (2009): 117–142.

53. 2–2, q.2, a.7, ad 3. Cf. 2–2, q.2, a.8, obj.1 and ad 1.

54. 1–2, q.90, preface.

55. 1–2, q.100, a.10.

56. 1–2, q.100, a.12, ad 3.

of a new covenant, not in a written code but in the Spirit; for the written code kills, but the Spirit gives life."[57] Here Paul is emphasizing the insufficiency of fallen human resources to attain covenantal life with God: "Such is the confidence that we have through Christ toward God. Not that we are sufficient of ourselves to claim anything as coming from us; our sufficiency is from God" (2 Cor. 3:4–5, RSV). In the same vein Aquinas recalls Genesis 15:6, "And he [Abraham] believed the Lord; and he reckoned it to him as righteousness," which Paul interprets in Romans 4:2, "For if Abraham was justified by works, he has something to boast about, but not before God."[58]

On the other hand, Aquinas takes equal notice of Romans 2:13, "For it is not the hearers of the law who are righteous before God, but the doers of the law who will be justified," as well as of such Old Testament texts as Leviticus 18:5, "You shall therefore keep my statutes and my ordinances, by doing which a man shall live."[59] If those who do the law "will be justified" and "shall live," then why should not the fulfillment of the Decalogue make human beings just in the presence of God? Aquinas distinguishes between possessing justice as a virtuous "habit"—in which case the infused virtue of justice justifies the human person—and doing "works of justice."[60] In this latter sense, Aquinas observes that doing "works of justice," as commanded by the Decalogue, does indeed pertain to the justified person. Indeed, in this sense obeying all the precepts of the Mosaic Law pertains to justification, although the mode of obedience differs before and after Christ, because Christ fulfills the Mosaic Law by his cross and thereby establishes the New Law.[61] Doing good actions pertains to justification, even though human beings cannot justify themselves by their actions alone without the grace of the Holy Spirit.

According to Aquinas, "the Old Law ordained men to Christ in two ways. First, by bearing witness to Christ. . . . Secondly, as a kind of disposition, since by withdrawing men from idolatrous worship, it enclosed (*concludebat*) them in the worship of one God, by whom the human race was to be saved through Christ."[62] Both the Torah and the "law of Christ" (Gal. 6:2) "have the same end, namely, man's subjection to God."[63] In this sense, divine law is one. Thus Aquinas can affirm that both the Torah (inclusive of the Decalogue) and Christ connect one to the grace of God, so long as one allows for the key distinction regarding causality: the Messiah of Israel accomplishes the Torah's covenantal promises of full intimacy between Israel and God. As Aquinas observes, "the

57. 1–2, q.100, a.12.

58. Ibid.

59. 1–2, q.100, a.12, obj.1 and 2 (and ad 1 and 2).

60. 1–2, q.100, a.12.

61. See 3I, q.47, a.2, ad 1; for discussion see my *Christ's Fulfillment of Torah and Temple*, chapter 3.

62. 1–2, q.98, a.2.

63. 1–2, q.107, a.1. For discussion see *Christ's Fulfillment of Torah and Temple*, chapter 5.

proper effect of law is to lead its subjects to their proper virtue."[64] Christ leads us to this end by uniting us to him. "Do we then overthrow the law by this faith? By no means! On the contrary, we uphold the law" (Rom. 3:31).

DISPENSATIONS FROM THE DECALOGUE?

The pre-Sinai narratives, however, seem to make God complicit in violations of the Decalogue. Among the examples cited by Aquinas, consider the Lord's command to the people of Israel through Moses after the ninth plague: "Speak now in the hearing of the people, that they ask, every man of his neighbor and every woman of her neighbor, jewelry of silver and gold" (Exod. 11:2, RSV). Since the Lord intends for the people to leave Egypt with this jewelry, never to return, does not the Lord here command theft—contrary to "You shall not steal" (Exod. 20:15)? Similarly, God commands Abraham to offer Isaac as a human sacrifice: "Take your son, your only son Isaac, whom you love, and go to the land of Moriah, and offer him there as a burnt offering upon one of the mountains of which I shall tell you" (Gen. 22:2, RSV). This appears to violate the commandment "You shall not kill" (Exod. 20:13, RSV).[65] Is God's involvement so arbitrary that he can change his mind about what to command Israel? Is God a reliable covenant partner, or does God violate the moral norms that God has given to God's own creation?

Aquinas answers by appealing to the covenantal context of the Decalogue. He quotes Isaiah 24:5: "The earth lies polluted under its inhabitants; for they have transgressed the laws, violated the statutes, broken the everlasting covenant."[66] If God has transgressed God's laws, then God has broken God's covenant. But just as God's covenant is "everlasting," so are God's laws. Sinai confirms that the God who is personally involved in Israel is also the God who created the world and established the universal norms for human nature. Quoting 2 Timothy 2:13's commendation of this God, "if we are faithless, he remains faithful—for he cannot deny himself," Aquinas affirms that God "would deny himself if he were to do away with the very order of his own justice, since he is justice itself."[67]

He argues, therefore, that the apparent dispensations of the Decalogue in the pre-Sinai narratives, such as God's command to Abraham to slay Isaac, do not in fact violate the natural law but rather involve the divine Lawgiver acting directly to achieve the just end, known by God, that the law entails. Thus with regard to the near-slaying of Isaac, Aquinas comments that God "is the Lord of life and death: for He it is who inflicts the punishment of death on all men, both

---

64. 1–2, q.92, a.1.
65. 1–2, q.100, a.8, ad 3.
66. 1–2, q.100, a.8, *sed contra*.
67. 1–2, q.100, a.8, ad 2.

godly and ungodly, on account of the sin of our first parent."[68] For Aquinas, God's commands never contradict the Decalogue, because God can directly will the end toward which its precepts aim. Speaking philosophically, Aquinas notes, "the intention of every lawgiver is directed first and chiefly to the common good; secondly, to the order of justice and virtue, whereby the common good is preserved and attained. If therefore there be any precepts which contain the very preservation of the common good . . . such precepts contain the intention of the lawgiver, and therefore are indispensable."[69] The Decalogue consists of just such precepts. The first three laws, concerning human-to-God relations, "contain the very order to the common and final good, which is God."[70] The last seven laws, concerning human-to-human relations, contain the "very order of justice and virtue." Insofar as all the moral laws included in the Mosaic Law are good moral laws, and thus are in accord with reason (divine and human), "all the moral precepts belong to the law of nature,"[71] and cannot be dispensed.

CONCLUSION

At first sight, Aquinas's theology of the Decalogue as natural law might seem to correspond to a rationalist view of the revelation of the Torah. On such a view, the Torah has significance as a philosophical achievement; the glow that suffuses Moses' face after speaking with the Lord "face to face" (Exod. 33:11) would mark Moses not so much as a prophet, even the greatest prophet of Israel, but rather as a great philosopher, whose teachings could and should be separated from their covenantal context.[72] Against a rationalist interpretation

68. 1–2, q.100, a.8, ad 3. For further discussion, contrasting Aquinas's position with that of John Duns Scotus, see my "God and Natural Law: Reflections on Genesis 22," *Modern Theology* 24 (2008): 151–77. Scotus argues that only the first two (or perhaps the first three) precepts of the Decalogue cannot be dispensed. In Scotus's view, God sometimes dispenses the Decalogue's precepts regarding the relationship of humans to each other. Scotus thereby severs the law of love toward neighbor from its intrinsic bond to the law of love toward God. The law regulating human relationships takes on a certain autonomy, rather than participating intrinsically in the law of love toward God. For this reason, although David VanDrunen suggests that "Duns Scotus's view of natural law moved away from that of Thomas on the mutability of the second table of the Decalogue, but on the whole their views were very close" (VanDrunen, "Medieval Natural Law and the Reformation," 82 n. 18), I argue that their views significantly diverge.

69. 1–2, q.100, a.8.

70. Ibid.

71. 1–2, q.100, a.1.

72. David Novak describes this separation of a universal ethics from covenantal/historical particularity in the work of Hermann Cohen, Martin Buber, and Emmanuel Levinas. As he notes, "Even though the thought of Buber and that of Levinas are usually seen in contrast to Cohen's Kantian rationalism, all three of them, nonetheless, are very much beholden to Enlightenment notions of universality. One could argue that for all of them, God's only function is to provide some sort of undergirding for ethics, and that is their view of God's function in Judaism as well. And for all of them, both the singularity of revelation and the singularity of the Jewish people as the community elected to receive that revelation in the covenant, sooner or later become subsumed into universal

of Aquinas on the Decalogue, I have emphasized the theological character of Aquinas's understanding of the Decalogue as natural law. For Aquinas, the Decalogue refers both to creation and to the new creation, and the Decalogue can be fulfilled only by supernatural charity. Jesus Christ fulfills the Decalogue on the Cross, and in Christ and his Spirit we too fulfill the Decalogue through the "works of justice" proper to the justified person. The Decalogue can never be dispensed, even by God—although God can directly accomplish the goals of its precepts.

Yet while Aquinas offers a resolutely theological portrait of the Decalogue, he does not hesitate to describe it philosophically as natural law. In this regard we can appreciate the role of Aquinas's doctrine of creation in his theology. David Burrell observes that creation, despite its status in the creeds of the church, has in recent years been "virtually suppressed in Christian theology."[73] Aquinas's theology of the Decalogue thus offers a way to reclaim the doctrine of creation in relation to the doctrine of redemption, so as to understand properly the covenantal pattern of the redemption of fallen creation.

---

nature" (Novak, *Natural Law in Judaism*, 84). On the grounds that Maimonides does not envision God as truly in an active relationship with Israel, Novak argues that Maimonides's treatment of the moral laws of the Torah, "what for us is the locus of the natural law," is likewise insufficiently covenantal/historical: "That is the theological problem with Maimonides' natural law theory. Minimally, it is non-covenantal; maximally, it is counter-covenantal" (135–36). See also Novak, "Maimonides and Aquinas on Natural Law," in *Talking with Christians: Musings of a Jewish Theologian* (Grand Rapids, MI: Eerdmans, 2005), 67–88, at 87. For an excellent discussion of the "theological character of Aquinas's natural law theory," see Russell Hittinger, "Theology and Natural Law Theory," *Communio* 17 (1990): 402–8. Hittinger concludes, "A careful reading of Aquinas will show that positive laws, both divine and human, are crucial to the way we come to learn about the natural law" (408). For this argument see also my *Biblical Natural Law: A Theocentric and Teleological Approach* (Oxford: Oxford University Press, 2008).

73. David B. Burrell, C.S.C., "Incarnation and Creation: The Hidden Dimension," in Burrell, *Faith and Freedom: An Interfaith Perspective* (Oxford: Blackwell, 2004), 234–44, at 234–35.

Chapter 5

Moses Maimonides

DAVID NOVAK

MAIMONIDES AND CHRISTIANS

Moses Maimonides was born in 1135 in Cordova in Muslim Spain, in the region called Andaluz. He died in the year 1204 in Fustat, the old city of Cairo in Egypt. I think that in virtually everyone's opinion he was the most structured, comprehensive Jewish thinker who ever lived. Therefore, it is extremely important to understand his importance in the Jewish tradition and indeed his influence on non-Jewish thinkers as well.

Since I am addressing a theological issue in a Christian context, I am reminded of a *responsum* that Maimonides wrote. It is very interesting because there he seems to be saying something very different from some of his other views about Christianity. He was asked the question, "Are Jews allowed to teach the Torah to gentiles?" Now this question was already asked in the Talmud. The Talmud answered that Jews should only teach those aspects of the Torah which are universal, which apply to all humankind. These are the only aspects of Torah that should be discussed with gentiles. The implication here is that this is a somewhat limited area, because most of the Torah is Moses speaking to the Children of Israel, either as a direct divine command or on his own initiative for

81

the sake of God. Maimonides' answer, interestingly enough, is that the Torah may not be taught to Muslims, but that it may be taught to Christians. This is quite interesting and rather unusual, since at least at a metaphysical level, when it came to the question of monotheism, Maimonides' criticism of the Christian doctrine of the Trinity as being problematic for monotheists was very similar to Islamic criticisms of the doctrine of the Trinity. Yet that metaphysical criticism notwithstanding, still on biblical grounds he said that Muslims do not accept the Torah as the word of God, for they say only some of it is the word of God, but much of it is human fabrication. Whereas he said about Christians that they accept word for word what we Jews consider to be God's perfect Torah. Now, if that is the situation, if Christians and Jews agree word for word what is the text of the Torah and that it all has the stamp of divine revelation, then the question is, What is the difference between Jews and Christians? To this underlying question Maimonides answered that the Christians have interpreted at least some of the Torah very differently from the way Jews have interpreted it. That is an essential difference. But, of course, even though the Christians have interpreted some of the Torah differently from the way Jews have interpreted it, nevertheless they do not interpret all of it differently.

To examine Maimonides in the context of the history of the interpretation of the Decalogue is to speak of Maimonides talking about something about which Jews and Christians share in common as a revealed text. And at least on some of the commandments of the Decalogue, and I would say on all of them, with the exception of the Sabbath commandment (for most Christians, with the exception of seventh-day Christian Sabbatarians), the interpretations might differ on some secondary points, yet they are not at loggerheads. That is, there might be certain very specific differences, let us say on the prohibition of idolatry, but for the most part that prohibition of idolatry is going to be interpreted similarly; so also with the prohibitions of murder, adultery, and stealing.

With that background in mind, I think it is important to mention that before I begin my treatment of Maimonides' understanding of the First Commandment, there is nothing that I am saying about Maimonides' position that one could not say about very similar positions in certain Christian theologians; I am especially thinking of Thomas Aquinas. Aquinas was very influenced by Maimonides, not only in metaphysics, but especially in his interpretation of biblical law.[1]

THE DECALOGUE

In Hebrew, the Decalogue is called *Aseret ha-Dibbrot*, which doesn't mean "the Ten Commandments" but, rather, "the Ten Statements." *Dibbur* (plural: *dibbrot*) in Hebrew is like the Greek *logos*, hence there are "ten statements" or *deka logoi*. And,

---

1. My references to Maimonides are *Book of Commandments*: positive commandment, no. 1; *Mishneh Torah: Fundamentals of the Torah*, 1.1, 5; *Commentary on the Mishnah: Sanhedrin*, chap. 10.

actually for the Jewish tradition, in the *Aseret ha-Dibbrot*, there are more than *ten* commandments (*mitsvot*). In traditional Jewish teaching, it has been determined that there are 613 norms that are considered to be perpetual commandments, that is, commandments that are not ad hoc commands given only for a certain time and place. So, for example, in Egypt the Jews were commanded to paint blood on their doorposts on the eve of the first Passover (what the Talmud calls "Egyptian Passover" as distinct from "Passover of the generations"). It is a one-time commandment, never to be observed again. But the tradition asserts that there are 613 perpetual commandments, and the beginning of the giving of these commandments is considered to be at Mount Sinai with the giving of the *Aseret ha-Dibbrot*, "the Ten Statements." So the question becomes, therefore, What is the First Commandment, which would be the First Commandment in the Decalogue? And whatever the First Commandment is, it will not just be first in a sequence from one to 613; it will be first in order of importance. It will be the foundational commandment of the entire Torah (what a famous philosopher of law, Hans Kelsen, called a *Grundnorm*). This is the theological question Maimonides is addressing. Moreover, he is dealing with a question as he has inherited it from Talmudic and post-Talmudic tradition.

What is the First Commandment in the Decalogue? Clearly, most Christian interpreters have said it is *You shall have no other gods but Me*. That seems to be the first imperative (*mitsvah*) one finds in Exodus 20. Nevertheless, that is not the first statement (*dibbur*) one finds there; for *You shall have no other gods but Me* is preceded by the statement, *I am the LORD your God, who has taken you out of the land of Egypt, from out of the house of slavery* (that is, from the institution of Egyptian slaveholding). So there you have what seems to be a declarative statement rather than an actual commandment. But, if so, why is an "is" statement put in a sequence of "ought" statements? (Indeed, some philosophers have argued that one of the biggest philosophical mistakes one can make is to confuse a declarative sentence with an imperative sentence; this has been called "the modal fallacy.") So we can at least wonder whether *I am the LORD your God* might perhaps be a prescriptive statement after all. Might it not be a statement by which one is commanded to do something? Could it not be a *mitsvah*, a commandment? Or is it a prelude, a preamble, a preparation for the giving of the commandments?

An ancient rabbinic text called *The Mekhilta*, which is a midrash, or a collection of rabbinic comments and discussions about most of the book of Exodus, asks the following question: "Why was the Decalogue not uttered at the beginning of the Torah?" In other words, the Torah begins with the words: *In the beginning God created the heavens and the earth*; then in Exodus it goes on to talk about the enslavement of the people of Israel and their being freed from slavery. So the Rabbis ask the question, If after all, the Torah is *the Law* (what in the New Testament is called *ho nomos*), if it is the book of Commandments in effect, then why wasn't the First Commandment uttered on page 1 rather than in the middle of the book of Exodus? The Rabbis answered that with the following parable.

> It is like a king who entered into a province and he said to the people: "I want to rule over you. I want to be your king." And the people said to him, "Well, what have you done for us? Why should we accept your kingship?" So the king reminds them that before he even made any claims upon them he built walls, he repaired the city, and thus saved them from disaster. After the people heard that, they said to the king, "Yes, yes, do rule over us!" So the Rabbis said that is exactly what God did with the people of Israel. God tells the people of Israel: "I want to rule over you. And you should accept my kingship because of what I have done for you."[2]

Thus the analogue of the king saving the city from danger and building up its fortresses is God's redemption of the people of Israel from Egypt and allowing them to survive in the wilderness.

Now you have to understand the logic of this passage. It is frequently misinterpreted. The logic of the passage is not that this is what God has done for the people and therefore the people owe something to God. In other words, this is not a kind of quid pro quo; namely, that is what I have done for you, now this is what I want you to do for me. But, rather, this is an expression of the fact that God's act is an act of pure grace: God has acted graciously for the people of Israel. They have experienced God's grace in terms of God's having redeemed them from Egypt. So, what God seems to be saying is, *I want to give you more of My grace by giving you a body of perpetual commandments by which you are to live and flourish.* In other words, this reflects the very important rabbinic notion that the Torah as Law, as a body of commandments, is not something that is different from or opposed to divine grace. It is divine grace; indeed, it is the epitome of divine grace.

That God commands the people and gives them this way to live, and will hold them responsible for it, is not considered to be an imposition of power but, rather, it is a gracious expression of God's goodness and God's love. So this is how the passage interprets: *I am the LORD your God who has taken you out of the land of Egypt.* There are two clauses: (1) *I am the LORD your God;* (2) *who has taken you out of the land of Egypt, out of the house of slavery.* The logic of this passage seems to be this: Because I have taken you out of the land of Egypt, I am to be your God. In other words, because of what I have done for you, I have a claim on you, not to take *from* you what you owe me, but I have a claim because of what I have already done *for* you; I want you to accept My kingship so I can continue to benefit you, so I can continue to be gracious to you. In other words, I took you out of Egypt, out of slavery, to another culture, *in order that I be your God thereafter.*

Being "God" (*Elohim*) means to be able to command you with both just and beneficent authority. So, one could say that "I took you out of the land of Egypt" is the major clause, which then leads to the normative conclusion: "I am the LORD your God." That is, being *your God* means God's being the source

---

2. Mekhilta attributed to R. Ishmael 51 (AT). See Jacob Neusner, *Classics of Judaism: A Textbook and Reader* (Louisville, KY: Westminster John Knox Press, 1995), 107.

of all commandments. It is the general commandment presupposed by all the specific commandments. It is what the Rabbis called the "acceptance of the yoke of the kingship of God." One could say it is the first normative principle; then the first specific commandment is, *You shall have no other gods before Me.* Accordingly, what you have here is a normative introduction, a justification for why the people should accept the various commandments of God, not out of fear but out of love. As such, the commandments are one more expression of God's love, they can be accepted in love and not as the imposition of an all-powerful ruler who expects something in return. Surely that is *sola gratia.* And I think when you understand that logic, you can then see this is the rabbinic tradition that Maimonides has inherited, but with which he is going to do something very different.

MAIMONIDES ON THE FIRST COMMANDMENT

One of Maimonides' major works is called *Sefer ha-Mitsvot,* "Book of the Commandments." Here he enumerates and briefly explicates each of the six hundred thirteen commandments of the Written Torah (that is, the Pentateuch). Now, in the Jewish tradition, there were those who did not innumerate the commandments of the Torah, since their number is potentially infinite; perhaps new commandments will be discovered by new interpretations of the scriptural text. But Maimonides, following an earlier post-Talmudic source, is quite clear that he wants the finite number 613, and for each of those 613 commandments to be distinguished. I think he is adamant on this point because he wants normative revelation to be a finite datum. Perpetually authoritative normative revelation has *already* been given. It is now complete. No one may add to it. There is and will never be any supplement to the Mosaic Torah. Everything thereafter is only justified normatively when it can be shown to be a valid interpretation of the Mosaic Torah, either of its specific norms or of its more general principles. The commandments of God have been given and it is now the task of human reason to interpret what the commandments presuppose, what the commandments imply, how they are to be applied, and so on. To allow any addition to or subtraction from the perpetually binding Mosaic Torah and its commandments is to imply that it needs to be changed. However, the perfect Torah comes from the will of the perfect God. Hence one cannot, one may not, improve on perfection itself.

In the *Book of Commandments,* one sees how much Maimonides diverges from the rabbinic interpretation of *I am the LORD your God,* which it will be recalled, was taken by an earlier rabbinic source to be a preamble to the specific commandments themselves. Nevertheless, there he writes, "The First Commandment He commanded us is to believe the existence of the divine [*ha'elohut*], namely, that we are to believe that there is a first cause who effects everything that exists, as it says: *I am the Lord your God*" (AT). We are thus commanded to affirm God as the Creator of the entire universe. In other words, God Himself commands us to affirm God's creative existence. Following another rabbinic tradition, Maimonides asserts here and elsewhere that God gave this commandment directly to the people. As such, this commandment and the prohibitions of polytheism and idolatry that follow after it are unlike the other 611 commandments of the Torah, since all these other commandments were given by God to the people through Moses. Most of them are presented with the preamble "the LORD spoke to Moses saying: 'speak to the children of Israel, etc. . . .'"

Now the question is what happened to the second clause in that first statement of the Decalogue, that is, *who has taken you out of the land of Egypt, out of the house of slavery*? Well, it would seem that for Maimonides, this second clause is a subordinate clause. In other words, it is just the most recent example of God's general rule, God's general control, of the universe as its Creator and King. That is, God builds into the natural order that at this particular point in history the people of Israel would leave Egypt, that they would be freed from slavery. So the statement, *I am the LORD your God*, is an eternal truth to be always affirmed; not because of any particular historical event, but because God's existence cannot be denied without denying existence itself. But how could anyone who himself or herself exists still deny God's existence—which for Maimonides is *Being per se*—when that very denial of God's existence could not be made unless that denier himself or herself exists? (This is a point made by such Christian thinkers as Anselm of Canterbury and T. S. Eliot, among others.)

The Exodus from Egypt, which culminated in the theophany at Sinai, was a unique occasion when an entire people experienced this truth of all truths collectively. In this sense, then, *I am the LORD your God* is to be affirmed, not because of anything God has done in history, but *I am the LORD your God* is a commandment whose revelation is *occasioned by* an extraordinary historical event. It is not a commandment that is a *response to* or an *inference from* that historical event. Accordingly, *I am the LORD your God* is God's self announcement of God's own being, something that is eternally true, even though humans can only apprehend that truth intermittently; and human communities can only collectively apprehend that truth shining through mighty historical events, which they have experienced and which they subsequently commemorate. Along these lines of *I am the LORD your God* being a commandment, one of the German-Jewish translations of the Bible translates the Hebrew *anokhi adonai eloheykha* as *Ich sei der Herr euer Gott*, namely, "I am to be the Lord your God."

MAIMONIDES' LOGICAL PROBLEM

All this notwithstanding, Maimonides seems to have gotten himself into a logical bind by asserting that God directly commands us to believe that God exists. After all, if I think God has commanded me to believe that God exists, isn't the conclusion already contained in the premise? Don't I have to believe that God exists before I can be commanded to believe God exists? That is what medieval philosophers called *petitio principii;* and it is what we would call "begging the question." Surely, it is question begging to assert that I should be commanded to affirm what I have already affirmed by accepting this commandment in the first place. This is the logical problem that was raised by a number of critics of Maimonides, most prominently by the late fourteenth-century Spanish Jewish philosopher-theologian, Don Hasdai Crescas, and then by his most notable disciple, the early fifteenth-century Spanish philosopher-theologian, Joseph Albo. And, interestingly enough, those of you who are students of modern Christian theology will recognize that this same problem was dealt with by the great Protestant theologian Karl Barth in his 1931 book, *Fides Quaerens Intellectum,* or *Faith Seeking Understanding.* In this book, Barth was dealing with the so-called Ontological Argument of Anselm, himself arguing that unlike the philosophers Descartes and Leibniz (and Kant who argued against the Ontological Argument), Anselm is not really trying to prove the existence of God, since he begins the so called proof for the existence of God with a prayer to the very God whose existence he is supposed to be proving. Just as Barth shows that Anselm cannot be trying to prove the existence of the very God to whom he is already praying, Crescas and Albo question Maimonides for trying to see God commanding belief in God's existence to the people who couldn't be so commanded unless they believed that the God so commanding them does exist.

How, then, can one get Maimonides out of this logical critique of his assertion that God commands us to believe God exists? Can we get Maimonides out of this vicious circle, this logical conundrum?

One way out of this seeming circularity is to change the commandment to believe God's existence into a creedal statement. Thus in some Jewish prayer books (written long after Maimonides' time), thirteen articles of faith are presented (although, unlike Christian creeds like the Apostles' Creed, this creed is not an integral part of the liturgy, but added as a supplemental devotion after the morning service). The first article of this creed is, in the words of a popular British prayer book: "I believe [*ani ma'amin*] with perfect fact that the Creator, blessed be his name, is the Author and Guide of everything that has been created, and that he has made, does make, and will make all things."[3] This creed is based on a work of Maimonides, written before the *Book of Commandments,* in which he enunciated what he took to be the thirteen fundamental, indispensable principles of Judaism (*yesodot*), principles that if denied would quickly render Judaism unintelligible. So, a first person commandment, in which God as "I" commands you as "thou" to affirm the existence of God, is changed into a first person statement of a creature, who is speaking of God in the third person. As such, this is not what *I* have been commanded but, rather, what *I* believe about God. The subject of this sentence is no longer God, but *I.* God, then, becomes the object of my belief rather than the object of God's commandment being *me.*

3. *The Standard Prayer Book,* trans. Simeon Singer (New York: Bloch, 1949), 107.

As you can see, once we have turned believing God's existence into a creedal statement, the logical problem is solved. Thus it is not that God has literally commanded me to affirm God's existence, it is I—and the *I* here is not just I as an individual, but I as part of the *keneset yisrael*, the faithful community of Israel—who does freely choose to affirm that there is the Creator, who is the absolute, who is the source of all existence, and not only the source of all existence, but the continual foundation of all existence, the continual governor of the entire universe. And in that way, it is not that I am affirming something that has already been affirmed by my acceptance of a commandment, but it is the community of Israel deciding what it is that requires affirmation on the part of all the members of that faithful community.

By changing a prescriptive statement *from* God *to* man into a declarative statement *from* man *about* God, later theologians and liturgists got Maimonides out of the logical conundrum we have just examined. As Joseph Albo pointed out in his *Sefer Ha-Iqqarim*, his *Book of First Principles* (which is still the most comprehensive systematic Jewish theology ever written), in order for the commandments themselves to function as the normative components of an intelligible system, one must understand the principles all these commandments presuppose. Thus one could well say that they are necessary for Judaism as a system of ideas that explains the specific and general meaning of each of the commandments. They are what medieval philosophers called *conditio sine qua non*. They are what faithful Jews must necessarily affirm if their observance of the commandments is to be intelligent action. And, of course, the first of these principles is the existence of God, a point with which Maimonides begins the first book of his *Mishneh Torah*, his great compendium of both Jewish law and Jewish theology.

In that way, one can look at these foundational principles as functioning much the same way dogmas function in Christian theology. That is, these dogmas are the presuppositions of Christian practice, both in speech and deed. This point, by the way, has been brought out by George Lindbeck, a Lutheran theologian who taught for many years at Yale (and who has influenced some of the best and the brightest younger Christian theologians today). In his most influential work, his 1984 book *The Nature of Doctrine*, Lindbeck emphasized that Christian dogma functions as the explanation of Christian praxis. In other words, if Christians were just simply uttering these principles without them being the explanation of what they are saying and doing in worship and in practice, this would then be some kind of abstract exercise that would have little meaning and connection to the reality of the God-human relationship Christians enjoy. So this is how reading Barth, reading Lindbeck, and then dealing with this question in my own tradition of Maimonides' problem of declaring belief in God's existence to be a commandment, one can understand how this functions and see this as something that is quite coherent. Accordingly, this is not what we are directly commanded to affirm, but what we have ourselves decided must be affirmed about God in order to give meaning to our practice of God's commandments.

MAIMONIDES' PSYCHOLOGICAL PROBLEM

We might have solved the logical problem of God commanding us to believe God exists by not interpreting *I am the LORD your God* literally as a commandment to be received directly from God but, rather, as a theological-dogmatic statement of the most important truth Judaism teaches and which is thus presupposed by all the commandments of the Torah. However, we have not solved the psychological problem of how belief (*emunah*) can be commanded by anyone. For a modern person, being especially attuned to psychology and its questions, that is the more important question, even though it was also raised in the fourteenth century by Crescas, the same philosopher-theologian who raised the logical question we have just examined.

Interestingly enough, a number of scholars have pointed out that the word that Maimonides uses in terms of the First Commandment is *emunah*—a word that is used for both belief and faith. So, perhaps he is not talking about a state of inner certainty, where I am commanded (by whomever) to be inwardly certain that God exists. The question is, How I can be commanded to believe what I have to discover for myself before I can be certain about it? How can certainty or inner conviction be commanded anymore than love can be commanded? (Kant asked a similar question about how one can be commanded to love one's neighbor.) How can anyone—even God—command what seem to be feelings or attitudes rather than overt actions? How can attitudes and feelings, which seem to be involuntary, be chosen? Indeed, Maimonides himself argued elsewhere for the reality of freedom of choice by noting that it makes no sense to command beings who could not choose to either obey or disobey what they have been commanded. Since the purpose of the Torah is to give a body of commandments from God to human subjects, therefore one must assume by the very fact that God commands, that this presupposes God has already endowed the human recipients of God's commandments with freedom of choice.

Maimonides wrote the *Book of the Commandments* in Arabic. Now a number of scholars have pointed out that in the Arabic text Maimonides is talking about knowledge: that is, we are not being commanded to *believe* God exists, we are being commanded to *know* it (*it'aqad*). Moreover, even in his *Mishneh Torah* (written in Hebrew), for which his Arabic *Book of Commandments* is written as a prolegomenon, Maimonides states, "The foundation of all foundations, the fundament of all fundamentals is to know [*le-yd'a*] that there is Prime Existence." And he goes on to say a few sentences thereafter, "this knowing [*yedi'at davar zeh*] is a positive commandment as Scripture says: *I am the Lord your God.*"

Now what is the difference between saying you are commanded to *believe that* and that you are *commanded to know*? The difference would be as follows: To be commanded to *believe* something is simply a requirement that you verbally affirm (especially in worship) a truth, but which you do not really know by your own process of inquiry. In other words, you assume it is true, even though you may not be convinced inwardly of this truth or be able to demonstrate it to be true. Making such a creedal statement works better when it is not put forth as a direct commandment of God but, rather, that this is what the tradition has told you to affirm, basing itself of what God declared to the people Israel at Mount Sinai. But with knowledge, on the other hand, one is not commanded to affirm what one has not experienced or learned. Instead, one is commanded to inquire and learn a truth one can only affirm at the present point of one's intellectual and spiritual development. One is being commanded, then, to engage in a process of constant inquiry, the results of which cannot be ascertained at present. Thus, if this is a process of inquiry that one is being commanded to begin as soon as one understands what he or she is being commanded *to do*, then one could even say that this commandment could be experienced as a direct divine prescription. What God seems to be commanding us to do is to seek some objective certainty of God's creative existence, without which our apprehension of God's existence might well be nothing but a subjective experience without any real external referent.

One is not being commanded in a way that involves logical and psychological paradoxes, which the Rabbis said would make the Torah (of which this is the First Commandment, the archetype of all the other commandments) look ridiculous. Instead, God commands you to inquire into God's relationship with the whole universe—and not just into God's relationship with you—by your own powers of reasoning. And that commandment is mediated by the tradition. So, even though there is a rabbinic legend that all Israel stood at Mount Sinai and heard God's commandments, nonetheless Maimonides would have to admit that for almost all of us, that First Commandment, like all the others, has been given to us, at least initially, by tradition. Thus the divine commandment, mediated by tradition, tells us to affirm God's existence. Usually that affirmation is given to us when we first use the name "God," namely, when we were taught to pray, usually by our parents when we were little children. And then as we grow older, the Torah itself commands us, even understanding this to be the direct commandment of God, to inquire, to be able to ascertain by rational means that which we have been taught and accepted on faith, is actually true and intelligible, that is, objectively knowable.

This commandment to engage in a process of inquiry is very similar to what the prophet Isaiah commanded us: *Seek God where and when God may be found* (Isa. 55:6). But the commandment to actually seek God is obviously addressed to people who are already in some kind of relationship with God. But it is a relationship that is based on faith, that is, trust in those who told it to me and what they told me, which is distinct from my knowing God's existence myself. In fact, in the *Summa theologiae* of Thomas Aquinas, in part 1, question 2, where Aquinas questions whether one should prove or can prove the existence of God, the first objection is *No, we should not try to prove the existence of God because the existence of God is something we accept on faith.* Therefore, there is this seeming dichotomy between faith and reason. And if the fact of God's existence is accepted by faith, then, in effect, by attempting to prove it one doubts what one should not doubt, since all knowledge begins in doubt seeking certainty. But, if you already have certainty, why do you need to engage in a process of inquiry that raises all kinds of doubts? Couldn't one be tempted into heresy thereby?

Aquinas's answer to that first objection—if I understand his answer correctly—is that most people need to be told that they ought to affirm and thereby accept the existence of God as the truth of all truths. And it follows that if some of those people can also thereafter prove or rationally demonstrate that which they have been told, then all the better. This is an example of *credo ut intelligam*—"I believe in order to understand": or *fides quaerens intellectum*—"faith seeking understanding." But, with the possible exception of Abraham, who in rabbinic tradition discovers God at a time when the very name "God" had been forgotten, everyone else can only discover a God whose name they have already heard. And, for most of us, we have not only heard the name "God," we have already been taught to use this name, and intending by that use the One who exists outside of ourselves and who is then affirmed by our mouths in the prayers we were taught in childhood. But the true process of internalization happens when we begin the effort by our minds, by our intelligence, to understand the deeper meaning of what we have been speaking in the language of worship. Surely, this point about Aquinas concerning faith and reason could be said about Maimonides on faith and reason. Neither Maimonides nor Aquinas is an advocate of what has come to be called "blind faith." Both would reject the famous statement attributed to the early Christian thinker Tertullian: "I believe because it is absurd" (*credo quia absurdum*).

In his great work of philosophical theology, the *Guide of the Perplexed*, Maimonides picks up on this point again. There he says that the first two commandments, which now in his counting are *I am the LORD your God* (to be understood as *I am to be the Lord your God*), and *You shall have no other gods but Me*, these two commandments are in a class by themselves. (The Talmud had taught the same thing, but the reason there is probably different from Maimonides' reason for this special classification.) And, just as the First Commandment pertains to the affirmation of God's existence (followed by the imperative to inquire into the rationality of that affirmation), the Second Commandment is taken by Maimonides to be an affirmation of the uniqueness of God. This is what the great German-Jewish philosopher, Hermann Cohen called *Einzigkeit Gottes*, which means not that God is one in the numerical sense (*Einheit* in German), but that God is totally unique. Well if God is totally unique and is our God, then obviously there can be no other gods who can share divinity with this one and only God. And that is because these "other gods" do not really exist as *gods* at all, since only one God can exist. At most, what are mistakenly taken by idolaters to be "gods" are only exalted creatures like the heavenly bodies. Thus what is not divine is unworthy of worship, and if what is divine is only the One God, then this God alone can be truly worshiped.

As Maimonides pointed out in an earlier discussion of the essence of idolatry, worshiping any other "god" is a violation of what for him might well be the most basic epistemological norm: "From falsehood [*dvar sheqer*] you shall keep yourself afar" (Exod. 23:7, AT), whose positive inverse is: *seek truth*. After all, how can one know what is false unless one has some idea of what is true, since we only know what is false when we at least know *that* it denies something that is true, even if we don't know what that truth really is? Accordingly, these two foundations, these two fundaments, namely the existence of God and God's uniqueness, are not things that simply come to us through some kind of intuition; rather, we come to them by means of rational enquiry, by mean of the perpetual human search for truth. Thus these are the things that can be known by rational demonstration. Any rational human being can know them; one need not have any special prophetic inspiration. The prophets might well have special experience of God; but even prophets have to first engage in the type of philosophical inquiry that makes them reasonably certain that their experience of God is not a figment of their imagination, not a human project, not mere wish fulfillment.

Now this, I think, solves the logical problem that it is not that we are commanded by God to affirm God's existence, but that we are commanded by God to inquire on our own, so we can actually have a rational understanding of what it means to say that God exists. This inquiry is supposed to show God's relations to the world. Therefore, proofs of the existence of God are attempts to show how the world and its immanent order imply a transcendent divine creator, who is thereby the first intelligent cause of everything in the universe and of the universe itself.

MAIMONIDES' PHILOSOPHICAL AND THEOLOGICAL PROBLEMS

It now seems we have found some good answers to those who question the logical and psychological cogency of Maimonides' location of an imperative to prove—or at least to show the strong probability of—the existence of God. Nevertheless, there are still two other questions raised against Maimonides' whole approach in ascertaining God's existence. These two objections, of course, are not only raised as criticisms of Maimonides: they are raised against Aquinas and certain Muslim thinkers as well, especially Ibn Sina (Avicenna).

First, there is the philosophical problem. So what if you think that you can infer that there is a creator of the world? This is the so-called argument from design: you look at the world; it looks like it's been put together intelligently; it doesn't look haphazard; therefore someone put it together; someone thought out its plan (its nature) and seems to be continually directing it; and that is *who* we call God. The problem is that this argument (or inference) tells you nothing about God, and it tells you nothing about the world. In other words, it doesn't tell you *how*, let alone *why*, God created the world. As such, it gives us no special way of knowing (*scientia*) either God or the world or any interrelation between God and the world. What difference does it make to say that God created the world or that the world is just there? Therefore, it makes no difference to say either that God created the world or that the world created itself (*causa sui*). Are we not simply adding an unneeded assumption in our approach to the world, and in our approach to God? Maybe, we should be looking elsewhere for both God and the intelligibility of the universe. This is done by the philosophical device of Occam's razor, which eliminates assumptions that add nothing to any proposition; that is, the proposition itself tells us just as much as its subject without any such additional (hence superfluous) assumptions. So, all that the argument from design tells us is *that* it is not unreasonable to assume the world is a creature (*ens creatum*). Nevertheless, it does not tell us *what* God is; it does not tell us *how* God created the world by realizing one possibility among many; and it does not tell us *why* God created the world instead of remaining in God's own self-sufficient perfection. This overall philosophical objection was most famously and most effectively raised against this whole approach to God's existence (though not against Maimonides particularly) by Immanuel Kant in his *Critique of Pure Reason*. There Kant attacks what he thinks he can show are the pretensions of metaphysics, especially metaphysical theology.

Second, there is the theological problem. This was something that was best understood by the great Protestant Reformers, but also by the great twentieth-century Jewish philosopher-theologians, Martin Buber, Franz Rosenzweig, and my late revered teacher Abraham Joshua Heschel. In one way or another, they all argued that the biblical doctrine of humans being created in the image of God (*tselem elohim*) clearly teaches that human beings are capable of a direct relationship with God; that they do not have to go *through* the world to reach God. Instead, God reaches humankind directly by revealing God's self to people and calling for our *immediate* response. To be sure, the world or the rest of creation does not disappear when this relationship is operating between God and humankind. (Asserting the disappearance or nonreality of the world for the sake of God constitutes the temptation of Gnosticism, a temptation that periodically crops up in both Jewish and Christian traditions.) Nevertheless, the world is only the context or the background *for* this relationship (called *ha-berit* or "the covenant"); the world is not in the foreground of this relationship, and the world does not function as the *medium of* this covenantal relationship. However, if the relationship with God is mediated by the world, then why can't there be some kind of semi-divine status for the world, thus taking God to be the chief God but not the only God? Yet, surely, God's uniqueness in relation to us means that there are no other gods; there are no other semi-gods; there is only a direct relationship between God and human beings. Therefore, we cannot, we should not try, to reach God except when God approaches us *in* the world (but not *through* the world) *by* revelation.

There seem to have been two possible ways out of this philosophical and this theological problem.

First, there is the approach of what has been called "pietism," like Quakerism among Christians and Hasidism among Jews. This approach looks to inner experience of God's presence, what is called in German *Erlebnis* (which is distinct from *Erfahrung*, meaning experience of the external world). Here we are urged to look inward into our hearts for the true experience of the divine presence (what in Hebrew is called *penimiyut*). Now that is certainly to be commended. After all, what is prayer if it is not looking for God in your heart and speaking to God from your heart? (Indeed, the Talmud calls prayer *avodah she-be-lev*, meaning "worship which is in the heart.") However, this is not a process of sustained and systematic intellectual inquiry; hence while it is commendable, it should not be presented as a substitute for rational inquiry into God's relation to the world in concert with God's relationship to God's unique human creatures who are created in God's image. Indeed, those of us who are sympathetic to Maimonides' whole philosophical approach to God, however much we might now differ with some of his specific philosophical assumptions and conclusions, are suspicious of pietism as the primary way to do theology. That is because history has shown us how often pietism becomes anti-intellectual, excessively emotional, and totally closed to any other religious approach to God other than its own.

The second approach is closer to Maimonides' use of what has been called the *via negativa*. Here Maimonides (and others both before him and after him) have emphasized that we can only say *what God is not*, but not *what God is*. Thus this approach does not attempt to even prove *that* God exists; it only rules out saying anything about God that would make God a member of a category God shares with any creature (even if God is *primus inter pares* or "first among equals"). In other words, this approach or method prevents us from making any assertion about God that would in any way compromise God's transcendence. Therefore, our similar method today, when engaging any philosophical atheism or denial or assertion of the impossibility of God's existence (like that of Richard Dawkins or Daniel Dennett, for example), should be to show that the "god" they are rejecting is not the God Jews, Christians, and Muslims, affirm and worship, especially those Jews, Christians, and Muslims who have not rejected the significance of the external world for their obedient and rational relationship with their God. Accordingly, we are not going to simply dismiss atheists, especially the atheists who bring scientific findings to their arguments against God, as "the knave [*naval*] who says in his heart there is no God" (Ps. 53:2). These atheists are not fools. Instead, rather than trying to prove God's existence to them (or to anyone else, like "agnostics" who lack the certainty of atheists and the faith of the faithful), we should *negate* their atheistic conclusions as being no more convincing than the very metaphysical theology (what some Continental philosophers call "onto-theology") they think that by rejecting they have eliminated even the possibility of God's existence from the minds of intelligent, critical-thinking persons. Here Maimonides' theological approach to the deniers of the Creator-God of his day is still helpful to us, that is, when we properly understand its methods.

USING MAIMONIDES TO ARGUE
AGAINST CONTEMPORARY ATHEISTS

There are basically two kinds of such atheism, and each one of them calls for a different defense from Jews, Christians, and Muslims, in the face of their aggressive denial of the ground of our faith.

The first kind of atheism regards the unique human qualities associated with the image of God as being an island of apparent rationality and freedom in an otherwise absurd cosmos, that is, a universe lacking intelligence, freedom, and purpose. However, we must ask, How can human rationality and freedom realistically survive if our human existence is nothing but "dust you are and to dust you shall return" (Gen. 3:19, AT)? In such a universe, will not our rationality and freedom cave in on themselves simply because they will be reclaimed by this absurd universe as if they had never been there at all? How could it be otherwise if our brief existence in the universe makes no difference to the universe? Does not the universe simply cave in on us, making us something like the "black holes," the cosmic negativity physicists speculate about? Is not our very assumption of this ultimate negativity a cause for intellectual and moral paralysis?

The very fact, however, that most of us are not paralyzed either intellectually or morally means that most of us do not really believe this kind of atheism, even those of us who have no recognizable relationship with God. In other words, this kind of atheism underestimates the human condition. Indeed, if we have neither origin nor destiny in the world outside of ourselves, then it would seem that our only succor in this initially and ultimately absurd journey through the world would be the kind of instant bodily gratification advocated by hedonists, for whom assuming human rationality and moral freedom is considered to be a nuisance. Yet atheists of this kind do value their rationality; and when they are scientists, they obviously think their rationality somehow or other does mirror or intend a rational order "out there," to which they are beholden for revealing some of its secrets to them. (No one understood this better than Albert Einstein.) And they value their moral freedom, often invoking moral arguments that seem to assume that some moral norms are more than human whims but, somehow or other, fit into a purposeful universe. Therefore, without claiming to be able to prove God's existence, we can show that the underestimation of the human condition implied by this kind of atheism is belied by the very rationality and moral responsibility exercised by these atheists. In other words, we can engage in a negation of their very negativity, only emphasizing the greater plausibility of our position, yet not claiming any final victory in this battle of ideas.

The second kind of atheism overestimates the human condition by looking at the world as nothing but raw material for human technology. In this view, the world belongs to us; it is there for the taking; it is there for our control. But, after all, isn't this the attitude that has brought about the ecological crisis that most of us recognize as one of our biggest threats to our very survival, both physically and civilizationally, in the world? Now, whereas in the first kind of atheism, humanity is not the reflection of anything greater than itself, this second atheism puts humanity in place of God. Therefore, what we need to argue is that when humans place themselves in place of God, they quickly discover that they are most godlike, not when they are engaged in their rather puny creative efforts but, rather, when they destroy themselves and as much of the world as they can take along with themselves into oblivion. Here we have the nihilism that is the flipside of the mania of exalting *homo faber*, "man the maker." Here we have a collective manic-depressive or "bipolar" condition, a condition rightly to be feared and thus a temptation we must try to avoid at all costs. Accordingly, we need to deflate this kind of human overestimation, and do so, not by agreeing that despair or hedonism is the only realistic alternative, but that our very spiritual survival, that our ability to live hopefully and purposefully is not an impossibility or even an anomaly in the world. Here again, we have by no means proven the existence of God. We have only more humbly tried to show that humanity is not God, and that it is not good for humans, whether individually or collectively, to try to replace God—nor is it good, let alone even possible, for humans to suppress the human desire to seek what is above and beyond themselves in every way.

In dealing with both kinds of atheism, we have tried to show their inner paradoxes, just like Maimonides showed the inner paradoxes of those who denied the Creator-God in his day. As such, we can try to think like Maimonides, who affirmed the existence of God as a divine imperative, and who suggested how we could ascertain that affirmation by rational means. Nevertheless, despite paradigm shifts that make the way we can do metaphysics and ethics quite different from the way Maimonides did them, we can still emulate his overall methods of inquiry. Accordingly, the God whom we have heard of from our ancestors is a God whose existence we should and therefore we can discover by our own means of reasoning, or we can at least refute those who say that what we have accepted on faith is not true, but only our delusion.

Chapter 6

Martin Luther

TIMOTHY J. WENGERT

THE BEGINNINGS: 1516–1520

Decem praecepta Wittenbergensi praedicata populo (1518)

Sebastian Münster, later Hebrew professor at the University of Basel, thought a person could not find anything like it anywhere in the world. Johann Oeco-lampadius, later a Reformer in the same city, wrote, "Luther has taken the veil from Moses' face."[1] They were both referring to the first publishing sensation to roll off the presses of the small university town of Wittenberg—not the paltry Ninety-five Theses but a Latin version of Martin Luther's sermons on the Ten Commandments, published on 20 July 1518 and based on sermons given in Wittenberg's city church from late 1516 to early 1517.

From the introductory questions that Luther posed, one can indeed see why these two Reformers-to-be reacted the way they did. With one stroke Luther simply rewrote the way in which the Ten Commandments would be viewed—at

---

1. *Luthers Werke: Kritische Gesamtausgabe [Schriften]*, 73 vols. (Weimar: H. Böhlau, 1883–2009), 1:384 (henceforth cited as WA [Weimarer Ausgabe]).

least among Lutherans but perhaps even within the larger Protestant movement as well.

> First it is asked, "Why does [God] not command something affirmatively, as 'Have the proper or one God' or 'Adore me, the one God'?" Second, "Why does he not speak in the imperative voice rather than the indicative: 'May you not have other gods'?" To both questions I respond at the same time that every commandment of God is established so that it now shows past and present sin rather than that it prohibits future sin, since (according to the Apostle [Romans 3:20]), "Through the law comes only the knowledge of sin," and again [Romans 11:32], "God shut up all people under sin, so that he might have mercy on all." Therefore, when the commandment of God comes, it finds sinners and increases [sin], so that sin may abound more fully (Romans 5[:20]). But human laws are established on account of future sins. Therefore the Spirit, since he is the most blessed Teacher, speaks instead in the indicative, as if to say, "O miserable human, behold I show your depravity to you. You ought to be such a person who has no gods, who does not take the name of God in vain, who sanctifies the Sabbath, who does not kill, does not covet, etc. Now, however, you are totally opposite [alius] and perverse." Thus, finally, he commands negatively because a negative is more vehement than an affirmative, since the Samaritans, too, always worshiped one God but at the same time their (other) gods. And now [the same is true of] Jews and Gentiles, heretics and evil people. Indeed, every human being in the world worships one God, whom all know, as the Apostle says in Romans 1[:19]. But there they sin, because they worship this [God] so that at the same time they may worship their idols.[2]

If anything shapes Martin Luther's interpretation of the Ten Commandments throughout his career, it is simply this one verse of Paul: "Through the law comes only knowledge of sin"—another example, by the way, of Luther adding a *sola* where lesser exegetes have missed Paul's point. To be sure, God had also other uses for the law. However, the chief use of the law (what later Lutherans called its "theological use") revealed sin and went hand in hand with the gospel, which far from revealing sin revealed the savior.

This "use" of the law was by no means Luther's invention. We can clearly see this hinted at in Augustine's *On Christian Doctrine*, III.xxxiii.46, with which Luther was doubtless familiar and also in Luther's favorite Augustinian tract, *On the Spirit and the Letter*.[3] Nevertheless, Luther brought what was probably for Augustine and certainly for the Western theological tradition that followed him a secondary insight to the fore and shaped his interpretation of the law around it. No wonder that Sebastian Münster and Johann Oecolampadius were so excited when they first read these sermons! Here finally was an exegetical way out from under the ceaseless legislation of medieval theology and practice. God gave the

---

2. WA 1:398, 6–399, 5.

3. Indeed, the notion of "uses" of the law comes from Nicholas of Lyra's comments on Galatians 3 (applied only to the Jews), which Luther brought into his Christmas postil of 1522 on the epistle for New Year's Day (Gal. 3:23–29) by applying it to *God's* uses on *all* people. See WA 10/1/1:449–503.

law not for humankind to fulfill in the future but to show right now that human beings did not and could not fulfill it.

More important, already at this very early stage Luther demonstrated his conviction that God's Word *does* something to its hearers. Here again, Augustine's *On the Spirit and the Letter* played an influential role, as the nascent Reformer interpreted the Psalms and, especially, Romans from 1513–1516.[4] To be sure, simply to quote Romans 3:20 in defining what task the law performs would result in a rather mild and intellectualized form of Luther's insight. It is not just that the law informs us of a problem (as if Paul were saying, "By the law we learn something about sin"), which we must then fix. Instead, the law (to use Luther's other metaphors) thunders, breaks, threatens, and (in agreement with 2 Cor. 3:6) "puts to death." Or, rather, God uses the law to do these things. God's work with the gospel, then, matches this use of the law exactly. The letter kills; the spirit (gospel) gives life. The law thunders and threatens; the gospel consoles, heals, and comforts.

Die zehen gepot gottes mit einer kurtzen außlegung jrer erfullung und vbertretung von Doctor Martin Luther Augustiner gemacht (1518)

Luther's second published explication of the Decalogue also saw the light of day in 1518, this time in a short German tract (a single sheet in quarto with eight pages of text) titled *The Ten Commands of God with a Short Explanation Done by Doctor Martin Luther, Augustinian, concerning Their Fulfilling and Breaking.*[5] Very short explanatory (and frankly medieval) glosses on each commandment are followed by lengthier (medieval) examples of how one breaks the commandments, so that the First Commandment is broken by black magic, incantations, and other such supernatural machinations (including carpet riding). After this come examples of fulfilling the commandments, in which certain aspects of what will become Luther's standard interpretation of the commandments echoes more strongly. Thus, the First Commandment is about fear, love, and trust in God, the second about calling on God's name in blessing and prayer, and the third about keeping the Word and Mass. Yet, these explanations, too, have medieval and patristic roots.[6]

In a final section, the purpose of these explanations arises completely out of the late-medieval piety of private confession, as Luther proves in his conclusion,

4. Leif Grane, *Modus loquendi theologicus: Luthers Kampf um die Erneuerung der Theologie (1515–1518)* (Leiden: Brill, 1975); Gerhard Ebeling, "Die Änfänge von Luthers Heremeutik," *Zeitschrift für Theologie und Kirche* 48 (1961): 172–230; English translation: "The Beginnings of Luther's Hermeneutics, Part I . . . III," *Lutheran Quarterly* 7 (1993): 129–58, 315–38, 451–68.

5. *Die zehen gepot gottes mit einer kurtzen außlegung jrer erfullung und vbertretung von Doctor Martin Luther Augustiner gemacht* (Nuremberg: Jobst Gutknecht, 1518). It was also published at least nine times between 1518 and 1522. See WA 1:247–56.

6. For a careful exposition of this point, see Albrecht Peters, *Kommentar zu Luthers Katechismen*, vol. 1: *Die Zehn Gebote* (Göttingen: Vandenhoeck and Ruprecht, 1990).

where he discusses the attitude one should have when approaching the Lord's Supper after confession.[7] Yet precisely here, and in the same way indicated in the earlier sermons, Luther suddenly breaks medieval piety wide open. One should not approach the Supper after Confession on the strength of a good confession, prayer, and unawareness of having committed any mortal sin, all of which would result in eating judgment upon oneself by trusting in one's own works. "Instead, the ones who believe and trust that they receive grace and purity in the Sacrament [of the Altar], this faith and trust make them pure and worthy recipients, who do not trust in the above mentioned works but in the pure, true and good word and promise of Christ, who says, 'Come to me, all you who labor and are heavy-laden with sins [Matthew 11:28] and I will make you alive.'"[8] Suddenly, the point of describing the breaking and fulfilling of the commandments is not to assure people that if they do what is in them, God will not deny grace. Instead, quite the contrary, the commandments reveal the great need for God's mercy and thus drive the person to trust Christ and his gracious promise given to them in the Supper.

Von den guten Werken (1520)

With these two early contributions, Luther set the trajectory for his interpretation of the Decalogue. In 1520, in the midst of writing three treatises that would shape the course of the early Reformation—*Address to the Christian Nobility*, *Babylonian Captivity of the Church* and *The Freedom of a Christian*—Martin Luther penned another, lesser known but no less important work titled, *A Treatise on Good Works*. It was his first *major* German work on the Ten Commandments and would be followed nine years later by his far more widely read catechisms, which also included major expositions of the Decalogue. Begun at the insistence of Luther's confidant at the Saxon court, Georg Spalatin, who had suggested Luther publish a recently delivered sermon on the subject, Luther started work in February and exclaimed by the end of March that the short essay had become a book. By late May or early June the first edition was rolling off Wittenberg's presses. It was reprinted eight more times in 1520 alone and translated into Latin the following year.[9] One of Luther's first biographers, the well-respected Lutheran pastor Johann Mathesius of Joachimsthal, credited this tract with introducing Christianity to him while he was still a Roman priest.

This treatise clearly defined Luther's novel approach to the commandments. Already in the preface to Duke (later Elector) John of Saxony, Luther stated,

---

7. See Ronald Rittgers, *The Reformation of the Keys: Confession, Conscience, and Authority in Sixteenth-Century Germany* (Cambridge, MA.: Harvard University Press, 2004), and Thomas Tentler, *Sin and Confession on the Eve of the Reformation* (Princeton: Princeton University Press, 1977).

8. WA 1:255, 28–33.

9. WA 6:196–201. There were a total of fourteen printings in German and three in Latin by the end of 1521.

"this time I wanted to demonstrate how we should practice and use faith in all good works and let it be the chief work."[10] For Luther, the First Commandment was all about faith but not simply as one commandment among others but as the chief commandment and work of the Christian. For Luther, however, faith itself is hardly a work one performs to merit God's mercy; instead, it arises out of that very mercy.

What specifically do we learn from this third tract about Luther's approach to the Ten Commandments? In the very first sentence we discover what became a constant refrain in Protestant understanding of good works: they must be connected to God's command and not simply to human statutes. "First it must be understood that there is no good work outside of what God has commanded, just as there is no sin except what God has forbidden."[11] Having made this clear, Luther then moves to the "first, highest and purest good work" namely, faith in Christ.[12] This was Christ's response to the people of Capernaum in John 6:28 and following, but, far from being a simple work easily performed, this work stands at the center of the Christian's life as grounded in the certainty of divine acceptation. As David Steinmetz has noted, with Luther's Reformation it is no longer love (as even with Johann von Staupitz) but faith that defines Christian life.[13]

With Luther's third point, the reader is ushered into one of the first expositions of his understanding of Christian vocation in the world. Daily life *is* the Christian life. "If you ask them [typical medieval believers and theologians] further whether they also consider it a good work when they work at their trade or walk, stand, eat, drink, sleep, and do all kinds of work for the sustenance of their body or for the common good and whether they believe that God is pleased with them in such activities, so you will find that they say no and define good works so narrowly that only churchly prayers, fasting, and almsgiving remain. . . ."[14] Christian moralists across a wide variety of denominations may still shiver when they read these words. Whoever is born of God, Luther continues, "that is, whoever believes and trusts God does not sin and cannot sin."[15] What makes a work good or bad, in the light of Romans 14:23, is whether one is assured that it is God-pleasing, which is faith alone. This same faith makes all works equal, another direct shot at the prevailing late-medieval piety, which put vows for the monastic life and pilgrimages far above other Christian acts let alone human daily activities.[16]

Yet this "work" of faith is simply the work of the First Commandment, which Luther then paraphrases in this way, "'You should have no other gods,'

---

10. WA 6:204, 1–3. He then promised to treat faith itself, which he did in *The Freedom of a Christian* later in the same year.

11. WA 6:204, 13–15.

12. Ibid., 25–26.

13. David C. Steinmetz, *Luther and Staupitz: An Essay in the Intellectual Origins of the Protestant Reformation* (Durham, NC: Duke University Press, 1980).

14. WA 6:205, 14–19.

15. WA 6:206, 1–2.

16. At this juncture in the tract, Luther points to a marriage founded on love, where all works— large or small—are accorded the same worth. See WA 6:207, 15–26.

that is as much as to say, 'Because I alone am God, you should set all your confidence, trust and faith on me alone and on no one else.'"[17] From this one command flow all the others, Luther adds, stating a theme that he will come back to in the 1529 catechisms. With this, the rather medieval worries about witchcraft and magic carpets (the former of which at least will later come to fall under the commandment not to take God's name in vain) fade away, and Luther provides a new perspective for how a Christian fulfills the commandments: by faith alone.[18] Any act done without trusting in God's favor is an evil work. For the fulfilling of the commandment, faith, that is, inner trust, must come first, foremost, and alone.

In fact, the "work" commanded by the First Commandment[19] is so great that Luther can ask,

> Where are those who say that when we preach about faith that we teach about and perform no works? Is there not more to do in this First Commandment than anyone could do? If a person were a thousand people— or all people or all creatures—there would be enough—and more than enough—laid upon him [or her] in what is commanded: that he [or she] should live and walk at all times in faith and confidence toward God . . .[20]

This refrain that there are more works commanded than one could possibly do in a lifetime, found in other sections of this tract also finds its way into Luther's exposition of the Ten Commandments in the Large Catechism of 1529.

Thus, with the first three tracts on the Ten Commandments Luther has already set these parameters for interpretation. The chief function of the commandments is to reveal sin—not just cognitively but in experience—and thus to put to death the sinner. This revelation of sin, however, is not designed to make better, more moral people but—using Luther's later language—to drive to Christ and his promises of forgiveness and comfort. The core sin, and hence the core of the Ten Commandments, revolves around the First Commandment, which reveals unbelief and demands faith. All other commandments must be interpreted in light of it. Since Christianity is about *God's* commands and not human regulations and since God's commands focus on faith not merit, there is no better, less carnal Christian way of life. Instead, everyday life—with its mundane activities and relationships—is the Christian life. Faith alone makes everyone equal and fulfills the entire law before anyone has done anything, leaving human beings to concentrate on their trades and offices, on

---

17. WA 6:209, 25–27.

18. Luther supports his contention (WA 6:210, 3–5) with a (surprising) reference to Augustine, who argued (in *On the Spirit and the Letter*, 36 [64]), that the First Commandment was fulfilled through faith, hope, and love. For Luther, love and hope are simply different aspects of faith.

19. Luther here and elsewhere always understands that faith is a "work" in the sense that it is a human activity (trust) but not in the sense that human beings perform it to merit salvation. Indeed, faith is a work of God (subjective genitive) performed by the Holy Spirit who works through the Word to destroy human unbelief and create faith.

20. WA 6:212, 23–31.

walking, standing, and sitting. Monasticisms of all sorts can no longer boast a special set of commands (called counsels) or a higher moral good. Indeed, faith presents so many opportunities for works that there really is no time to be busy with "self-chosen spirituality," to use Luther's standard translation of Colossians 2:23.

REFINING REFORMATION INSIGHTS: 1522–1535

Luther's early work served not only the informed reader but also commoners, as is clear from the fact that they originated in sermons and were published in or translated into German. The Decalogue was not simply the stuff of classroom lecture but of life. Here, too, Luther worked hardest at delivering his insights, so exciting to the likes of Oecolampadius and Mathesius, so that simple folks could understand and use (or, better, experience) the commandments as well. This practical application of Reformation insights remained with Luther throughout his career. Thus, in "mid-career," to use Heinrich Bornkamm's apt phrase for it, Luther produced a prayer book (1522), two catechisms (1529), and an instruction on how to pray (1535)—all of which were written for the laity and applied Luther's basic theological insights to the Decalogue.[21]

Das Betbüchlein (1522)

The first of these practical pamphlets, *The Personal Prayer Book*, came out in 1522 and represented simply a collation of earlier tracts, except that Luther added important prefatory remarks.[22] Here he not only expresses his conviction that the law convicts of sin and puts to death but he then connects this function directly with the function of the gospel, represented in this booklet by the Creed, which Luther viewed as the concatenation of all God's promises. His way of stating the law and gospel's functions shows both medieval roots (in using an Augustinian metaphor of healing) and the Reformation's basic hermeneutic with the centrality of faith and God's grace.[23]

> Three things people must know in order to be saved. First, they must know what to do and what to leave undone. Second, when they realize that they cannot measure up to what they should do or leave undone, they need

21. See Heinrich Bornkamm, *Luther in Mid-Career, 1521–1530*, ed. Karin Bornkamm, trans. E. Theodore Bachmann (Philadelphia: Fortress, 1983).

22. Volume 43 of *Luther's Works* (American edition), 55 vols. (Philadelphia: Fortress and St. Louis: Concordia, 1955–86) (henceforth cited as LW), used this translation, which is somewhat misleading. It is simply *The Prayer Booklet* (*Betbüchlein*).

23. Here, however, grace is still defined as a power. Only under the influence of Erasmus's translation of *charis* in his Latin translation as *favor Dei* and Melanchthon's use of this definition beginning in 1521 did Luther himself begin to define grace not as a power or infused disposition but as God's undeserved mercy. Here it is still "medicine."

to know where to go to find the strength they require. Third, they must know how to seek and obtain that strength. It is just like a sick person who first has to determine the nature of his sickness, then find out what to do or to leave undone. After that he has to know where to get the medicine which will help him do or leave undone what is right for a healthy person. Third, he has to desire to search for this medicine and to obtain it or have it brought to him. Thus the commandments teach human beings to recognize their sickness. The Creed will teach and show them where to find the medicine—grace—which will help them to become devout and keep the commandments. The Creed points them to God and his mercy, given and made plain to them in Christ. Finally, the Lord's Prayer teaches all this, namely, through the fulfillment of God's commandments [by faith] everything will be given them.[24]

With this three-fold movement, from diagnosis to prescription to a call to the apothecary, Luther not only set the order of his catechetical instruction but also placed the commandments within the larger work of God's saving work in Christ as the person moves from sickness to healing, that is, from death to resurrection or from unbelief to faith through the Holy Spirit by the power of God's Word alone.

This movement from law to gospel or commands to promises stays with Luther throughout his career. The thirty or more printings of this prayer booklet all include this preface—a further indication of just how profoundly defining law by its uses affected Luther's interpretation. "When they realize they cannot measure up" stands as an early attempt to bring this central insight into the fiber of a developing evangelical piety. "The law only shows sin." The letter kills!

In this same period of time, beginning in 1521 in an exchange of letters between Luther in the Wartburg and his colleague Philipp Melanchthon still in Wittenberg, Luther also comes to define more clearly the difference between God's work in this world and God's proclamation in Christ of the world to come, what he sometimes calls the twofold righteousness of God or the two hands of God. In this world, reason and the law have their proper place to maintain order in the world and help the neighbor. Luther applies this insight directly to the law in his sermon helps on the appointed gospels and epistles for the Christmas season (the so-called *Weihnachtspostil* [1522]), specifically in a sermon on the Epistle for New Year's Day, Galatians 3:23–29. There, borrowing a discussion in Nicholas of Lyra's commentary that the Jews used the law in four different ways, Luther takes two of Lyra's categories and universalizes them. God uses the law, in the first place, to maintain order and restrain evil (the so-called civil use of the law). In the second place, God chiefly employs the law (in its theological use) to show sin and drive to Christ.[25] In subsequent works, both he and Melanchthon explore how this insight functions in evangelical theology and practice.

24. LW 43:13–14, with slight changes. See WA 10/2:376–77.
25. WA 10/1/1:452–58.

The Large and Small Catechisms (1529)

Preliminary Observations

The classic Lutheran exposition of the commandments comes in two of the most popular and influential writings of Martin Luther: the Large and Small Catechisms, published in 1529 and, in 1580, included in the premier collection of Lutheran confessions, *The Book of Concord*. The Large Catechism, based upon Luther's catechetical sermons to his Wittenberg congregation in 1528, clearly influenced Melanchthon and many subsequent Reformers, including (in its flowery Latin translation) John Calvin. Here we discover the mature Luther's interpretation of the Decalogue. At the same time, however, several aspects of his thought are more assumed than expressed, so that there is no separate discussion of the law's uses or even of how it convicts the sinner. Yet, sketched on the background of the preceding analysis, one can easily perceive how these categories continue to structure Luther's thought.

The convicting function of the law becomes clear most easily by recalling Luther's comment to Erasmus in *The Bondage of the Will* that an "ought" in Scripture never implies a "can." Thus, when he begins each commandment in the Small Catechism with the words, "We *are to* [*sollen*]," Luther is *not* saying that human beings do these things. This becomes explicit in the Large Catechism, when he writes against the medieval distinction between commandments and counsels that placed monastic life on a special, higher level and saw the Ten Commandments as an easy first step in Christian righteousness.

> Just think: is it not a devilish presumption on the part of those desperate saints to dare to find a higher and better way of life and status than the Ten Commandments teach? They pretend, as we have said, that this is a simple life for an ordinary person, whereas theirs is for the saints and those who are perfect. They fail to see, these miserable, blind fools, that no one is able to keep even one of the Ten Commandments as it ought to be kept. Both the Creed and the Lord's Prayer must come to our aid, as we shall hear later.[26]

Luther does not mention Jesus Christ or the Holy Spirit in his exposition of these commands but only refers to God. The commandments may drive to Christ, but they are not the same as salvation; the commandments may demand faith, but they are not the means by which the Holy Spirit creates faith. As Luther later notes in his exposition of the Creed, the commandments, written on every human heart, are for all people. The Creed, which reveals and confesses the true God, is what makes people uniquely Christian. Others may worship God, but they do not know or believe that God is gracious toward them and hears their cries for mercy.

---

26. The Large Catechism, trans. James Schaaf, Ten Commandments, par. 315–16 (henceforth cited as LC, Ten Commandments), in *The Book of Concord*, ed. Robert Kolb and Timothy J. Wengert (Minneapolis: Fortress, 2000), 428 (henceforth cited as BC 2000).

The first or civil use of the law is also not explicitly referred to in the catechisms, and yet the notion that, in addition to God's working faith through the
gospel, God works in this world by maintaining good order and restraining evil
comes to full expression in his exposition of "Honor your father and mother."
Indeed, from the special place of this commandment, one sees that de facto
Luther actually leaves behind the division of the commandments into two tablets and replaces it with three. The commandments to have no other gods, not
to take God's name in vain, and remember the Sabbath form the first part; the
commandment to honor parents a second; and the remaining commandments
a third grouping. Moreover, Luther's call for obedience to parents and others in
authority also reflects his discovery that daily life of ordinary people *is* the Christian life, this in sharp contrast (again) to the monastic *status perfectionis*, which
Luther views as having no direct command from God and thus representing an
uncertain way to please God.

> If this could be impressed on the poor people, a servant girl would dance
> for joy and praise and thank God; and with her careful work, for which she
> receives sustenance and wages, she would obtain a treasure such as those
> who are regarded as the greatest saints do not have. Is it not a tremendous
> honor to know this and to say, "If you do your daily household chores, that
> is better than the holiness and austere life of all the monks"? Moreover, you
> have the promise that whatever you do will prosper and fare well. How
> could you be more blessed or lead a holier life, as far as works are con-
> cerned? In God's sight it is actually faith that makes a person holy; it alone
> serves God, while our works serve people.[27]

The Fourth Commandment also reveals that Luther views the commandments hierarchically. The first defines all of the other commandments (see
below). The commands not to use God's name in vain or profane the Sabbath
are further expositions of the relation to God, involving prayer and worship.
The command to honor parents is, however, normed by the first three. Thus,
Luther writes, "If God's Word and will are placed first and are observed, nothing
ought to be considered more important than the will and word of our parents,
provided that these, too, are subordinated to God and are not set in opposition to the preceding commandments."[28] Similarly, the Fourth Commandment
stands over the remaining practical commandment not to kill, commit adultery,
steal or bear false witness, so that the parent or government official, when fulfilling his or her office, does not sin in punishing a person, in ending a marriage, in
collecting taxes, or in speaking ill of a person in a judicial process.

As he had already stated in the *Treatise on Good Works*, Luther also remarked
at how many works the commandments demanded—giving people no time to
make up extra works of "self-chosen spirituality."

27. LC, Ten Commandments, 145–47, in BC 2000, 406.
28. Ibid., 116, in BC 2000, 402.

It seems to me that we shall have our hands full to keep these command-ments, practicing gentleness, patience, love toward enemies, chastity, kind-ness, etc., and all that is involved in doing so. But such works are not important or impressive in the eyes of the world. They are not uncommon and showy, reserved to certain special times, places, rites, and ceremonies, but are common, everyday domestic duties of one neighbor to another, with nothing glamorous about them. Those other deeds captivate all eyes and ears. For when a priest stands in a golden chasuble or a layperson spends a whole day in the church on his or her knees, that is considered a precious work that cannot be sufficiently extolled. But when a poor servant girl takes care of a little child or faithfully does what she is told, this is regarded as nothing. Otherwise, what should monks and nuns be looking for in their cloisters?[29]

Before turning to Luther's exposition of individual commandments, we must also clarify the fact that Luther did not think that he was explaining the texts of Exodus or Deuteronomy themselves. Thus, despite the fact that later Lutherans (to say nothing of other groups) often added the so-called Prologue ("I am the Lord your God . . .") to their versions of the Decalogue, Luther himself assumed that the interesting historical and biblical setting of the commandments was unimportant for explaining the law written on each person's heart. The bibli-cal texts were simply the best and clearest expression of this law, but even they showed clearly marks of its peculiar Israelite context that did not apply to other human beings. This fact had several consequences. First, it meant that Luther could eliminate discussion of what the Reformed tradition has universally called the Second Commandment, the prohibition of graven images. It was simply a special case of the First Commandment given specifically for the Israelites but not applicable to others. Thus, there was no iconoclasm among Lutherans. Second, Luther also was quick to point out how certain commandments did not apply literally to Christians. On the Sabbath day, Luther wrote in the Large Catechism, "As far as outward observance is concerned, the commandment was given to the Jews alone. They were to refrain from hard work and to rest, so that both human beings and animals might be refreshed and not be exhausted by constant labor."[30] Luther not only allows that servants in his day also ought to be given a day off, but he also expands the commandment (according to ancient models) to include especially the preaching and teaching of God's Word. But he also takes Christ's breaking of this commandment seriously, rejecting the notion that Christians simply moved the Sabbath from Saturday to Sunday and insisting instead that God has made every day holy (not just Saturday) and that the command requires that the day become holy for us, not by our works but through the Word of God.

For different reasons, Luther also emphasizes, in the first instance, the Jew-ish nature of the commands not to covet. So that the Israelites did not restrict the commands not to kill, commit adultery, steal, or bear false witness to mere

29. Ibid., 313–14, in BC 2000, 428.
30. Ibid., 80, in BC 2000, 397.

actions, God included explicitly commands aimed at the heart. Christians already know this through Jesus' exposition of the commandments in the Sermon on the Mount.[31] Moreover, Luther also argues that the command presupposed an Israelite context in which wives and servants were chattel, an understanding that did not apply to his sixteenth-century hearers.

> Moreover, every man had the power to put away his wife publicly by giving her a bill of divorce and to take another wife. So there was a danger among them that if any man craved another's wife, he might find some sort of reason to put away his own wife and to alienate the other man's so that he might legally take her for himself. These commandments were especially needed because under the Jewish government menservants and maidservants were not free, as now, to earn a wage as long as they wanted. Rather, with their body and all they had they were their master's property, just the same as his cattle and other possessions.[32]

At the same time, Luther expands the original commandments far beyond their literal meaning but quite in line with traditional Christian exposition of them. Thus, both the command to keep the Sabbath and the commands not to covet have application to the Christian, demanding that the Word and its preaching not be despised and that all manner of coveting (especially the kind that leads to lawsuits) be avoided. Moreover, the Fourth Commandment, which literally only involves one's biological parents, Luther expands to include the heads of households, governmental officials and rulers and even pastors in the church. He even expands this commandment further by adding at the end an exhortation to parents and others in authority not to abuse their authority. Here one glimpses a canonical slant to Luther's method of interpretation.

> In addition, it would also be well to preach to parents on the nature of their responsibility, how they should treat those whom they have been appointed to rule. Although their responsibility is not explicitly presented in the Ten Commandments, it is certainly treated in detail in many other passages of Scripture. God even intends it to be included precisely in this commandment in which he speaks of father and mother. For God does not want scoundrels or tyrants in this office or authority; nor does God assign them this honor (that is, power and right to govern) so that they may receive homage.[33]

---

31. Ibid., 293, in BC 2000, 425. "These two commandments, taken literally, were given exclusively to the Jews; nevertheless, in part they also apply to us. The Jews did not interpret them as referring to unchastity or theft, for these were sufficiently forbidden in the previous commandments. They also thought that they were keeping all the commandments when they outwardly did precisely the works commanded and did not do the ones forbidden. God therefore added these two so that people would also think that coveting a neighbor's wife or property, or desiring them in any way is sinful and forbidden." See also, Susan E. Schreiner, "Martin Luther," in *The Sermon on the Mount through the Centuries: From the Early Church to John Paul II*, ed. Jeffrey P. Greenman, Timothy Larsen, and Stephen R. Spencer (Grand Rapids: Brazos, 2007), 109–27.

32. Ibid., 293–94, in BC 2000, 425.

33. Ibid., 167–68, in BC 2000, 409.

As mentioned above, the First Commandment, which commands especially trust in God, permeates all the others, because Luther views all Christian theology from the perspective of faith, demanded by that very command in his eyes. In his conclusion to all of the commandments in the Large Catechism, Luther, reflecting on how the conclusion to the First Commandment ("I the Lord your God am a jealous God . . .") applies to all of them, explains this connection as follows,

> Thus the First Commandment is to illuminate and impart its splendor to all the others. In order that this may be constantly repeated and never forgotten, therefore, you must let these concluding words run through all the commandments, like the clasp or hoop of a wreath that binds the end to the beginning and holds everything together. For example, in the Second Commandment we are told to fear God and not take his name in vain by cursing, lying, deceiving, and other kinds of corruption and wickedness, but to use his name properly by calling on him in prayer, praise, and thanksgiving, which spring from that love and trust that the First Commandment requires. In the same way, this fear, love, and trust should impel us not to despise his Word, but learn it, hear it gladly, keep it holy, and honor it.
>
> Again, throughout the following commandments, which concern our neighbor, everything proceeds from the power of the First Commandment: We are to be subordinate to, honor, and obey father and mother, masters, and all in authority, not on their own account but for God's sake. For you dare not respect or fear father or mother, doing or neglecting to do things simply in order to please them. Rather, pay attention to what God wants of you and what God will quite surely demand of you. If you omit that, you have an angry judge; otherwise, you have a gracious father.
>
> Again, you are to do your neighbors no harm, injury, or violence, nor in any way hurt them in regard to their person, spouse, property, honor or rights (according to the order in which these things are commanded), even if you had the opportunity and occasion to do so and no one would reprove you. On the contrary, you should do good to all people, help them and promote their interests, however and wherever you can, purely out of love to God and in order to please God, in the confidence that he will repay you richly in everything. Thus you see how the First Commandment is the chief source and fountainhead that permeates all others; again, to it they all return and upon it they depend, so that end and beginning are completely linked and bound together.[34]

In a similar way, Luther begins the explanation of the First Commandment in the Small Catechism with the words, "We are to fear, love, and trust in God above all things," and each subsequent commandment with the words, "We are to fear and love God."

One final general comment involves the structure of the explanations in the Large and Small Catechisms. With only a few exceptions in the Small Catechism, every commandment includes both a negative and positive side. In this

---

34. Ibid., 326–29, in BC 2000, 430.

way, too, Luther expands the commandments to include both "thou shalt not" and "thou shalt." In the Small Catechism he divides nearly every explanation with the strong adversative *sondern* (but instead). (The two exceptions are the First and Sixth Commandments, where only the positive is expressed.)[35] In the Large, Jesus' expositions of the commandments, not only in the Sermon on the Mount but also in the case of the command not to kill in Matthew 25, come into play. Thus, using that commandment as an example, Luther argues that the commandment is broken not only by harming the neighbor bodily but also by neglecting to help the neighbor in need. This doubling of the commandments' meaning reflects Luther's exposition of Scripture in general where he often interprets a text through antitheses.

Specific Explanations of the Commandments

What specifically did Luther say about the commandments in his catechisms? To begin with, and not surprisingly, he spent by far the most time on the First and Fourth Commandments. Indeed, his exposition of the First Commandment begins with one of the most famous quotes of Luther, used (among other places) by Ludwig Feuerbach to support his social construal of all religion. Luther, however, had something far different in mind.

> "You are to have no other gods." That is, you are to regard me alone as your God. What does this mean, and how is it to be understood? What does "to have a god" mean, or what is God? Answer: "god" is the term for that to which we are to look for all good and in which we are to find refuge in all need. Therefore, to have a god is nothing else than to trust and believe in that one with your whole heart. As I have often said, it is the trust and faith of the heart alone that make both God and an idol. If your faith and trust are right, then your God is the true one. Conversely, where your trust is false and wrong, there you do not have the true God. For these two belong together, faith and God. Anything on which your heart relies and depends, I say, that is really your God.[36]

Luther's explanation now puts front and center what some of the earlier expositions left in the background. For him, human life in relation to God is always (and only) about trust, that is, faith. Even when he uses an expanded definition involving fear and love or fear and trust or, as in the Small Catechism, fear, love, and trust, even these other words are permeated by faith. Luther then considers how one breaks this command and names the usual idolatrous suspects: money, fame, learning, power, family, honor, and the like. He even shows how in late-medieval practice the saints themselves became objects of trust, idols, not unlike the gods of the ancients. Finally, he considers works righteousness itself.

35. The Small Catechism, trans. Timothy J. Wengert, par. 2 and 12, in BC 2000, 351 and 353. "We are to fear, love and trust in God" and "We are to fear and love God so that we live chaste and decent lives in word and deed and each love and cherish their spouse." The latter demonstrates Luther's general reticence (like others of his age) to speak about specific sexual sins.
36. LC, Ten Commandments, 1–3, in BC 2000, 386.

There is, moreover, another false worship. This is the greatest idolatry that we have practiced up until now, and it is still rampant in the world. All the religious orders are founded upon it. It involves only that conscience that seeks help, comfort, and salvation in its own works and presumes to wrest heaven from God. It keeps track of how often it has made endowments, fasted, celebrated mass, etc. It relies on such things and boasts of them, unwilling to receive anything as a gift of God, but desiring to earn everything by itself or to merit everything by works of supererogation, just as if God were in our service or debt and we were his liege lords. What is this but to have made God into an idol—indeed, an "apple-god"—and to have set ourselves up as God? But this reasoning is a little too subtle and is not suitable for young pupils.[37]

What was the highest good work in 1520, namely faith, becomes, on the reverse side of the same coin, the central sin: lack of trust in God. Thus, for Luther and the Lutherans, faith cannot be a work or decision of human beings but only what God the Holy Spirit works in the hearing of the gospel—a point Luther will make explicitly in his exposition of the third article of the Creed ("I believe in the Holy Spirit"). Otherwise, a person ends up trusting him- or herself and his or her works and decisions.

Luther then considers what it means to trust that God provides every good thing and concludes that even those good things people receive from their neighbors are actually from God, who uses the neighbor (beginning with the mother nursing a child) as "the hands, channels, and means through which God bestows all blessings."[38] This ought to lead to thanksgiving to God, a theme to which he will return in his explanation to the first article of the Creed ("I believe in God . . . Creator of heaven and earth").

The Second Commandment deals with the misuse of God's name, which for Luther is a logical progression from the first. "Just as the First Commandment instructs the heart and teaches faith, so this commandment leads us outward and directs the lips and tongue into a right relationship with God. For the first things that burst forth and emerge from the heart are words."[39] Luther begins his description of sins against this commandment with perjury but sees the larger problem as people using God's name to cover up all manner of wickedness. But he also insists that this command also demands the proper use of God's name in prayer, praise, and thanksgiving. Luther encourages pastors to teach children to pray by employing simple prayers such as "Lord God save me" or "Help, dear Lord Christ." Luther defends such child's play by concluding, "When we preach to children we must talk baby talk."[40]

In addition to showing that the Sabbath commandment applied literally only to the Jews, Luther ties this commandment, as had the tradition, first to having a day of rest and second to the hearing of the Word of God. Thus, one moves

37. Ibid., 22–23, in BC 2000, 388–89.
38. Ibid., 26, in BC 2000, 389.
39. Ibid., 50, in BC 2000, 392.
40. Ibid., 77, in BC 2000, 396.

from a command to trust God, to the command to pray to God, to the command to hear God's Word. Indeed, Luther turns this commandment into an outline of evangelical liturgy, which centers in justifying the sinner.

> Note, then, that the power and force of this commandment consists not in the resting but in the hallowing, so that this day may have its special holy function. Other work and business are really not designated holy activities unless the person doing them is first holy. In this case, however, a work must take place through which a person becomes holy. This work, as we have heard, takes place through God's Word. Places, times, persons, and the entire outward order of worship have therefore been instituted and appointed in order that God's Word may exert its power publicly.[41]

Of course, for Luther, those who break this commandment are not only those who despise Christian worship and lie dead drunk in taverns on Sunday morning but also those who think they know everything after hearing one or two sermons or who attend worship regularly but only for its entertainment value.

Luther derives the centrality of the commandment to honor one's parents from the word "honor." "Honor requires us not only to address them affectionately and with high esteem, but above all to show by our actions, both of heart and body, that we respect them very highly, and that next to God we give them the very highest place."[42] Parents, by virtue of this command, are God's representatives and worthy on earth of higher dignity. "We are indeed all equal in God's sight, but among ourselves it is impossible for there not be this sort of inequality and proper distinction."[43] There is no addiction to the democratic myth here—in households or in governments!

But there is an interesting twist in Luther's argument. After stressing the necessity to honor one's parents, Luther goes on to say,

> In the second place, notice what a great, good, and holy work is here assigned to children. Unfortunately, it is entirely despised and brushed aside, and no one recognizes it as God's command or as a holy, divine word and teaching. For if we had regarded it in this way, it would have been apparent to everyone that those who live according to these words must also be holy people. Then no one would have needed to institute monasticism or spiritual walks of life.[44]

As with the maid making beds in the household or, one might add, the person paying taxes or following civil laws, the work of obedience is not simply a burden but a blessing, an office, which God creates and in which God places human beings. Thus, for Luther (as with Melanchthon), God's left hand does not simply include the office of parent, householder, and ruler but child, servant,

---

41. Ibid., 94, in BC 2000, 399.
42. Ibid., 107, in BC 2000, 401.
43. Ibid., 108, in BC 2000, 401.
44. Ibid., 112, in BC 2000, 401.

and subject. Suddenly, the daily life of the individual becomes filled with God-pleasing works. At the same time, the "self-chosen spirituality" of late-medieval monasticism is completely rejected.

> Oh, what a price would all the Carthusians, both monks and nuns, pay if in all their spiritual exercises they could present to God a single work done in accordance with his commandment and could say with a joyful heart in his presence: "Now I know that this work is well pleasing to you." What will become of these poor wretched people when, standing in the presence of God and the whole world, they will blush with shame before a little child who has lived according to this commandment and will confess that with their entire lives they are not worthy to offer that child a drink of water?[45]

Luther is so convinced of the honor of the parental office that he imagines that if someone had no parents he or she would wish that "God would set up a block of wood or stone that we might call father or mother."[46] This commandment also forces people to acknowledge the blessing given through parents, just as the First Commandment forces them to acknowledge God. In the one exception to his reading of the Decalogue apart from its Israelite origins, Luther also takes a stab at interpreting the phrase, "that you may have long life in the land where you dwell."[47] Not only is keeping this commandment a delight to God but it also comes with rewards—long life, which Luther points out does not simply mean length of days but also happiness and prosperity. Here, on God's left hand in creation, there is room for reward and punishment and, in order to prove the truth of this promise of the law, Luther refers his readers to experience, where fine old families prosper and the wicked finally get caught.

Luther's expansion of the Fourth Commandment to include more than parents, however grounded in similar medieval and patristic connections, makes clear from the outset that these other offices (of householder or ruler) are derived from the needs of parents and thus must serve parents.

> For all other authority is derived and developed out of the authority of parents. Where a father is unable by himself to bring up his child, he calls upon a schoolmaster to teach him; if he is too weak, he seeks the help of his friends and neighbors; if he dies, he confers and delegates his responsibility and authority to others appointed for the purpose. In addition, he has to have servants—menservants and maidservants—under him in order to manage the household. Thus all who are called masters stand in the place of parents and must derive from them their power and authority to govern.[48]

Again, these higher authorities are also God's tools for providing shelter, food, peace and order to their subjects. Indeed, the language Luther used in the First

45. Ibid., 118, in BC 2000, 402–3.
46. Ibid., 125, in BC 2000, 403.
47. Ibid., 131–39, in BC 2000, 404–5.
48. Ibid., 141–142, in BC 2000, 405–6.

Commandment and will use in his expositions of the first article of the Creed and in the fourth petition of the Lord's Prayer also occur here. Because people do not connect obedience to these authorities to God's will for humanity in this world and instead view the commands as no better than the come-on of a used car salesman (literally, a street waffle vendor), Luther asserts, they only receive just punishment, where "God punishes one scoundrel by means of another."[49]

> We certainly feel our misfortune, and we grumble and complain about unfaithfulness, violence, and injustice. But we are unwilling to see that we ourselves are scoundrels who have rightly deserved punishment and are in no way better because of it. We spurn grace and blessing; therefore, it is only fair that we have nothing but misfortune without any mercy.[50]

Finally, Luther also introduces a section on "spiritual fathers," by which he means not the papacy but those in the church who distribute God's word and, thus, deserve honor according to this commandment. He bases this and the other expansions of the commandment on instances in Scripture where it uses the word "father" for householders, rulers or, in this instance, ministers (cf. 1 Cor. 4:15). He concludes with an exhortation to parents and others in authority.

Having dealt with both the "spiritual and the civil government," that is commandments about God and about parents, Luther sees a shift in the Decalogue as it now turns to a person's relation to his or her neighbor: "Therefore neither God nor the government is included in this commandment [against killing], nor is their right to take human life abrogated."[51] He explicitly refers to Jesus' own exposition of this commandment in Matthew 5. Here, the commandment not to kill includes not only avoiding all harm to the neighbor but, as mentioned above, also caring for the neighbor in need. Thus, Luther moves from Christ's exposition in Matthew 5 to the parable of the sheep and the goats in Matthew 25, linking care for the neighbor not to the gospel and faith but to the law. This commandment commands care for the neighbor not just avoidance of harm. And these neighbors include, according to Christ's exposition in Matthew 5, enemies, something that, Luther adds, is unheard of among pagan lists of virtues and ignored by the monks' spirituality.

The commandment against adultery shows all the marks of traditional interpretation with these differences. First, Luther stresses that this commandment derives from the preceding, so that, after preserving a person's life God preserves the next closest person, the spouse. Luther explains that adultery was specifically mentioned because that was a particular problem with the Jews, who married early. His German audience was far more creative in finding ways to break this commandment since "there is such a shameless mess and cesspool of all sorts of

---

49. Ibid., 154, in BC 2000, 408.
50. Ibid., 155, in BC 2000, 408.
51. Ibid., 180, in BC 2000, 410. See above for comments on the hierarchy within the commandments.

immorality and indecency among us."[52] Again, on the basis of Jesus' exposition of this commandment in the Sermon on the Mount, Luther includes the sins of the heart as well. Once again, there is a positive side to the commandment, so that "you are to defend, protect, and rescue your neighbors whenever they are in danger or need, and, moreover, even aid and assist them so that they may retain their honor."[53] Thus, chastity touches every human being and not just those who are married. As with the Fourth Commandment, that protects and honors the office of parent and its "walk of life" (German: *Stand*), so this commandment protects the office of married person. God "has established it before all others as the first of all institutions, and he created man and woman differently (as is evident) not for indecency but to be true to each other, to be fruitful, to beget children, and to nurture and bring them up to the glory of God." Medieval discussions of this lesser estate (where the higher chastity is celibacy) emphasize the begetting of children and the channeling of sexual desire. Luther mentions these but stresses instead being true to each other. He also argues that God by this commandment places this walk of life above all others (being bishop, emperor, prince, etc.), allows it throughout the world, and (with a few exceptions) makes it a natural necessity. Here, as Heiko Oberman points out, sexual desire, far from being evil, is seen by Luther as a created gift.[54] Luther concludes, "I say these things in order that our young people may be led to acquire a desire for married life and know that it is a blessed and God-pleasing walk of life. Thus it may in due time regain its proper honor, and there may be less of the filthy, dissolute, disorderly conduct that is now so rampant everywhere in public prostitution and other shameful vices resulting from contempt of married life."[55] He concludes, however, by returning to an aspect of marriage often lacking in earlier expositions of this commandment: the role of love and faithfulness. "Wherever marital chastity is to be maintained, above all it is essential that husband and wife live together in love and harmony, cherishing each other wholeheartedly and with perfect fidelity."[56] In marriage itself there is a delightful equality, mirrored in some small degree by 1 Corinthians 7.

The commandment against stealing allows a glimpse into Luther's view of economics. Instead of reducing the commandment to petty thieves and pickpockets, Luther goes after not only the lack of care taken for the property of others by laborers or the extortion of the marketplace but also the big shots (*grosse Hansen*) and armchair robbers (*Stuhlräuber*—here Luther misunderstands a Low German word for usury [*Stôhl*]): people who oppress the poor and yet are hailed as captains of industry and friends of the princes. Luther again emphasizes the positive side of the commandment (to care for one's neighbor) and, in language

52. Ibid., 202, in BC 2000, 414.
53. Ibid., 203, in BC 2000, 414.
54. See Heiko A. Oberman, *Luther: Man between God and the Devil* (New Haven, CT: Yale University Press, 1989), 272–83.
55. LC, Ten Commandments, 217, in BC 2000, 415.
56. Ibid., 219, in BC 2000, 415.

reminiscent of Deuteronomy 28, threatens divine punishment, especially of those who exploit the poor.

> The same fate will befall those who turn the free public market into nothing but a carrion-pit and a robber's den. The poor are defrauded every day, and new burdens and higher prices are imposed. They all misuse the market in their own arbitrary, defiant, arrogant way, as if it were their privilege and right to sell their goods as high as they please without any criticism. We will stand by and let such people fleece, grab, and hoard. But we will trust God, who takes matters into his own hands. After you have scrimped and saved for a long time, God will pronounce a blessing over you: May your grain spoil in the barn, your beer in the cellar, your cattle perish in the stall. Yes, where you have cheated and defrauded anyone out of a gulden, your entire hoard ought to be consumed by rust so that you will never enjoy it.[57]

In comments on the commandment against false witness, Luther, following the tradition, applies it first to the courts of law, and God's protection of the reputations of the innocent poor. Not only are the poor attacked but so are innocent preachers of the gospel. The commandment also applies to the sins of the tongue. Not only, Luther says, must one avoid maligning the neighbor, one must also avoid spreading rumors, be they true or false.

> There is a very great difference between judging sin and having knowledge of sin. You may certainly know about a sin, but you should not judge it. I may certainly see and hear that my neighbor sins, but I have no command to tell others about it. If I were to interfere and pass judgment on him, I would fall into a sin greater than that of my neighbor. When you become aware of a sin, however, do nothing but turn your ears into a tomb and bury it until you are appointed a judge and are authorized to administer punishment by virtue of your office.[58]

He likens spreading gossip to pigs rolling in their own manure. As with the Fifth Commandment, where parents and rulers may punish the disobedient by virtue of their offices and not incur God's wrath, so, too, here, Luther argues, judges may declare a person guilty, but only as a function of their office. For truth telling among neighbors, Luther recommends using Matthew 18 and preventing public scandal. Here, too, Luther applies the Golden Rule of Matthew 7 to the positive use of this commandment, especially in speaking well of despised people, such as defenseless evangelical preachers.

Luther spends far less time on the commandments not to covet. God gave these commands to the Jews so that they would know that not simply outward conformity to the commands but also the heart was involved. Luther even applauds what he calls a Jewish interpretation: that these commandments forbid "anyone, even with an apparently good pretence and excuse, to harm a neighbor

---

57. Ibid., 240–42, in BC 2000, 418.
58. Ibid., 266, in BC 2000, 421.

by intending or scheming to take away anything that belongs to this neighbor, such as spouse, servants, house and farm, fields, meadows, or cattle."[59] He views the attempt to cover up one's venal nature with the façade of virtue and legality as a constant in human nature. Thus, these commandments are not addressed to rogues but to the upright, who hide their sins under the appearance of legitimacy, especially in lawsuits and business deals.

CONCLUDING REMARKS

Luther did not stop his exposition of the commandments with the catechisms of 1529. He continued to preach on them and to refer to them in the lecture hall. In 1535, he published *A Simple Way to Pray* and, after providing a lengthy paraphrase of the Lord's Prayer, showed how he meditated on and prayed the Ten Commandments.[60] He used a monastic method of interpretation but still managed to maintain the basic distinction between command and promise in the four aspects of his meditation, as he reflected on God's demands (law), gave thanks for the blessings God gives through the commandments (promise), confessed the ways in which he broke them (the effect of the law) and prayed for their fulfilling (given by God's promised grace in the gospel alone). Thus, in the fourth part of praying the First Commandment, Luther writes,

> Oh, my God and Lord, help me through your grace so that I may daily learn and understand your commandment better and afterwards do it with hearty trust. Protect my heart so that I may not be so forgetful and ungrateful and may not seek after other gods or find comfort in any other creature on earth but remain only and always with you, my only God. Amen, dear Lord God, Father, amen.[61]

As Albrecht Peters has shown in his magisterial work on Luther's interpretation of the Ten Commandments, in catechetical works, the Wittenberg Reformer follows traditional expositions in many aspects. Whatever new insights or new combinations of old insights one finds there, the central contribution Luther makes to Christian interpretation of the Decalogue arises from the framework in which he places it. Above all, one must distinguish law and gospel, realizing that at their heart the commandments function to reveal sin and drive to the Savior. In addition, one must distinguish the righteousness of this world and creation, addressed in the commandments (especially in the so-called second table), from

---

59. Ibid., 296, in BC 2000, 425.
60. WA 38:351–75; LW 43:200–209.
61. WA 38:365, 22–27. "Ah mein Gott und Herr, hilff mir durch deine gnade, das ich solch dein Gebot muege teglich je besser lernen und verstehen und mit hertzlicher zuversicht darnach thun. Behuete ja mein hertz, das ich nicht mehr so vergessen und undanckbar werde, kein ander Goetter noch trost auff erden noch jnn allen Creaturn suche, sondern allein, rein und fein an dir, meinem einigen Gotte bleibe, Amen, Lieber Herr Gott Vater, Amen."

the righteousness that comes in Christ through the free forgiveness of sins. From the command to honor one's parents to the end of the Decalogue, these obligations are truly for this world and shared by all human beings. And because Luther interprets them not only as forbidding the evil but also as demanding the good, they especially champion the needs of the neighbor, especially the poor and oppressed. Furthermore, the Ten Commandments embrace the entirety of life, ending the need for extra counsels and commandments, and giving human beings enough to do for their entire lives and no time for self-chosen spirituality. Set within these parameters, the Ten Commandments, viewed as reflecting the law of the human heart, take on a peculiarly Lutheran appearance, one still followed by Lutheran theologians to this day.

Chapter 7

John Calvin

SUSAN E. SCHREINER

During the 1550s in Geneva the consistory, an ecclesiastical court in charge of moral discipline, charged several people for dancing at a wedding. This tribunal also dealt with people whose clothing was judged to be improper, who were overheard criticizing the city of Geneva, and who complained about any minister in the city. The consistory also found it repeatedly necessary to rebuke and penalize those who did not attend church services or who, while at these services, made noises or laughed during the sermon. It is clear that Calvin and his fellow Reformers were trying to build a godly society—not a theocracy, but a society in which the Decalogue was instilled into the hearts and minds of the citizens. This attempt was in no way unique to Calvin since Reformation churches were struggling throughout with the problem of enforcing moral discipline, a concern sometimes displayed in the need to settle the desire of many reformation pastors to require confession without it being considered a sacrament. The reformation churches and their pastors were continually concerned about the issues regarding the control of morals under the new church orders.[1]

The place of the Law, especially the moral law of the Decalogue, was a subject of debate in the sixteenth century both between Catholics and Protestants and between the different Reformers. These controversies often centered on the distinction between law and gospel as well as the role of good works in salvation. However, fierce controversies also revolved around specific commandments and their meaning for the life of the Christian churches.[2] This essay focuses on Calvin's exposition of the law which can be found in three primary places; the *Institutes, Commentaries on the Last Four Books of Moses Arranged in the Form of a Harmony,* and his sermons on the Ten Commandments found in his sermons on Deuteronomy. The importance of the law can be seen in the fact that the 1536 *Institutes* opens with the chapter, "On the Law," which discussed the Ten Commandments. His discussion on the law was essentially formulated in the 1539 edition of the *Institutes* and finds its place in the 1559 edition. The *Harmony* dates from 1563, the year before Calvin's death. In this massive work Calvin discussed the law in terms of its preface, the explanation of the Ten Commandments, the summary of the law, the use of the law, and the promises and threats contained in the law. He also provided the various supplements that pertained to each commandment.[3] The sermons on Deuteronomy are from his two hundred weekday (including Saturday) sermons and date from the year 1555 to 1556. The sermons on the Ten Commandments which derive from Deuteronomy 4:44–6:4 began on Friday, June 7, 1555, and ended in June 19 of the same year.[4] The context of these sermons is worth noting. The sermons were preached after a decade of conflicts in Geneva. These conflicts were both about

1. See Ronald K. Rittgers, *The Reformation of the Keys: Confession, Conscience, and Authority in Sixteenth-Century Germany* (Cambridge, MA: Harvard University Press, 2004); Daniel Buscarlet, *Genève, citadelle de la Réforme* (Geneva: Comité du Jubilié Calvinien, 1959); Thomas A. Brady Jr., "In Search of the Godly City: The Domestication of Religion in the German Urban Reformation," in *The German People and the Reformation,* ed. R. Po-chia Hsia (Ithaca and London: Cornell University Press, 1988); Robert M. Kingdon, "The Control of Morals in Calvin's Geneva," in *The Social History of the Reformation,* ed. Lawrence P. Buck and Jonathon W. Zophy (Columbus, OH: Ohio State University Press, 1072), 3–16; R. Po-chia Hsia, *Social Discipline In the Reformation: Central Europe, 1550–1750* (New York: Routledge, 1989). On the consistory see *Registres de la Companie des Pasteurs de Genève autemps de Calvin,* ed. Robert M. Kingdon et al., Travaux d'Humanisme et Renaissance 55, 107 (Genève: Droz, 1962, 1963, 1969) and *Register of the Company of Pastors in Geneva in the Time of Calvin,* ed. and trans. Philip Edgcumbe Hughes (Grand Rapids, MI: Eerdmans, 1966).

2. David C. Steinmetz, "The Reformation and the Ten Commandments," *Interpretation* 43, no. 3 (1989): 256–66. On the history of exegesis of the Decalogue see Paul Grimley Kuntz, *The Ten Commandments in History: Mosaic Paradigms for a Well-ordered Society,* ed. Thomas D'Evelyn (Grand Rapids, MI: Eerdmans, 2004); *The Ten Commandments: The Reciprocity of Faithfulness,* ed. William P. Brown, Library of Theological Ethics (Louisville, KY: Westminster John Knox, 2004); *I Am the Lord Your God: Reflections on the Ten Commandments,* ed. Carl E. Braaten and Christopher Seitz (Grand Rapids, MI: Eerdmans, 2005).

3. John Calvin, *Commentaries on the Four Last Books of Moses Arranged in the Form of a Harmony,* trans. Charles William Bingham, 4 vols. (Grand Rapids, MI: Eerdmans, 1950).

4. John Calvin, *Ioannis Calvini Opera quae supersunt omnia,* vols. 1–59, ed. Guilielmus Baum, Eduardus Cunitz and Eduardus Reuss, Corpus Reformatorum, vols. 29–87 (Brunsvigae: C. A. Schwetschkte, 1863–1900). The Sermons on Deuteronomy are found in vol. 26. I have used

the right of the church to enforce moral discipline as well and about theological disputes. Some residents of Geneva took exception to the strictness of the morality being imposed by Calvin. The issue was complicated by the resentment felt by the old guard to the influx of French refugees into the city. There was also tension between the city councils and the claims of authority being made by the church. The councils tried to retain much of their authority over the social and moral issues of Geneva while the church was claiming the right to impose discipline. In 1541 the city adopted the Ecclesiastical Ordinances, which required the consistory to report repeated disciplinary problems to the Little Council. The conflict crystallized around the power of excommunication, that is, the power to keep one from partaking of the Lord's Supper. The practices laid out in the Ecclesiastical Ordinances had placed the final power to ban members from the Lord's Supper to the Little Council, a power very much resented by the consistory. This controversy was resolved only on January 24, 1555, when the city councils decided it in the favor of the consistory, a decision that made clear that the right of discipline belonged to the church. Not surprisingly, Calvin repeatedly preached on the need for discipline and the demand that the Christian submit to God's word or the yoke of God.[5] However, there were theological disputes as well. Prior to the preaching of the sermons Calvin had been in a controversy over predestination. Did Calvin's doctrine of predestination and his emphasis on the sovereignty of God make God the author of sin? Jerome Bolsec's criticism was voiced by some Swiss pastors whose parishes were under the jurisdiction of Berne. The controversy came to encompass these pastors, Bolsec as well as Sebastian Castellio who was eventually banished from Geneva. These men believed that Calvin's doctrine of predestination was too harsh and speculated too much on the secret of God's decrees. The sermons reflect these criticisms as Calvin defends his doctrine of predestination while, at the same time, prohibiting too much "curiosity" into the matter. For example, in his sermon on Deuteronomy 5:8–10 Calvin declared,

> Now if we ask, 'Why is God merciful toward some and not toward others?' it is true that the first cause is unknown to us and is not open to inquiry. Why? Because it is essential here that our senses be constrained and captivated and that we confess that God has the freedom to choose those who seem good to him and reject the rest. But whatever the case, he makes this promise to the faithful that he will have pity on their children . . . he will continue to do so until the thousandth generation . . . and in contrast he threatens the unbelievers and will not only curse them but also their race and those who are descended from their line.[6]

John Calvin, *John Calvin's Sermons on the Ten Commandments*, ed. and trans. Benjamin W. Farley (Grand Rapids, MI: Baker Books, 1980).

5. A clear overview of these controversies is found in the "Introduction" to Farley's translation of the sermons on the Ten Commandments cited above.

6. John Calvin, *John Calvin's Sermons on the Ten Commandments*, ed. and trans. Benjamin W. Farley (Grand Rapids, MI: Baker Books, 1980), Sermon 3, 72ff. Hereafter any footnote "Sermon" followed by a number will refer to this volume and the specific numbered sermon found there.

And in his sermon on Deuteronomy 5:28–33 Calvin explains that God must grant the grace to obey the law. Nonetheless, God does not grant this grace to everyone. Still, Calvin warned, "But it is not a question here of our probing into God's strict counsel as to why he reforms some by [the power of] his Holy Spirit and leaves others to go astray according to their corruption without retrieving them. We must not get into that labyrinth."[7]

Calvin's various discussions of the Decalogue often reiterated thoroughly traditional principles. He distinguished between the moral, ceremonial, and judicial law. The ceremonial law was the "tutelage of the Jews" that trained them in their childhood until the "fullness of time should come and foreshadow the truth of those things which then were foreshadowed in figures." The judicial law was given to the Jews for civil government and "imparted certain formulas of equity and justice by means of which they might live together blamelessly and peaceably." Both of these ancient laws were in conformity with the rule of love and have been abrogated without abandonment of the "perpetual duties and precepts of love" or the "perpetual rule of love."[8] The Decalogue or moral law was a "testimony of the natural law and of that conscience which God has engraved upon the minds of men." The "inward law" had been engraved by God on the conscience of all people and asserts the same things that are to be learned from the two tables of the Decalogue. The Decalogue, therefore, is the written form of natural law. Calvin details why a written law was necessary. He explains, "man is so shrouded in the darkness of errors that he hardly begins to grasp through this natural law what worship is acceptable to God." Moreover, humanity is now so "puffed up with haughtiness and ambition and so blinded by self-love, that he is yet unable to look upon himself and, as it were, descend into himself and confess his own miserable condition." Accordingly, "the Lord has provided us with a written law to give us a clearer witness of what was too obscure in the natural law, shake off our listlessness, and strike more vigorously our mind and memory."[9] Calvin also taught that the mercy of God was evident in the fact that he revealed the law twice to the ancient Jews, as recorded once in Exodus and again in Deuteronomy. As he preached to his congregation, "Moses recounts that not only did [God] transmit that law on Horeb, but after completing his wanderings of forty years or thereabouts, he again instructed the people."[10]

Calvin also repeated that traditional distinction between the two tables of the law, "which contains the whole of righteousness." Lutherans and Catholics had numbered the commandments in such a way that the First Commandment included the prohibition of any graven images of God. Believing the commandants to be arranged in a most "beautiful order," Calvin placed four

7. Sermon 15 (Deut. 5:28–33), 275. Also see 273.

8. John Calvin, *Institutes of the Christian Religion* 4.10.15; ed. John T. McNeill, trans. Ford Lewis Battles (Philadelphia: Westminster, 1960). Hereafter *Institutes*.

9. *Institutes* 2.4.2; 4.20.15; *Harmony* 2:386.

10. Sermon 1, (Deut. 4:44–5:3), 38.

commandments in the first table and six in the second. He made the First Commandment verse Deuteronomy 5:6, "I am the LORD your God, who brought you out of the land of Egypt, out of the house of bondage. You shall have no other gods before me" (RSV). Calvin also explained that "there are two principal articles in the law of God: the one concerns what we owe him; the other what we owe our neighbors with whom we live."[11] The first table of the law pertains to the pure worship of God while the second concerns the duties of love that we owe our neighbors. And, finally, Calvin emphasized repeatedly that the law always had pointed forward to its fulfillment in Christ, citing Romans 4:10, "Christ is the end of the law unto salvation to every believer."[12]

Calvin explains the way in which Christ is the end of the law by his well-known threefold use of the law: (1) The first use of the law was to reveal to us our sinfulness and drive us to Christ as the sole source of our salvation; (2) the second use was to restrain unbelievers in order to protect the public community and to maintain order; and (3) the third use was the role of the law in the life of the believer. In his teachings on justification by faith the first use is dominant; humanity cannot know the depth of sin until confronted by the helplessness revealed by the inability to obey the law. Driven to despair by this recognition of sin, the unbeliever is driven to Christ as the only means of deliverance from sin and given the faith, which justifies and saves. However, as Calvin states repeatedly, "Christ justifies no one whom he does not at the same time sanctify." According to Calvin we grasp Christ's righteousness for our justification by faith alone and by that faith we are reconciled to God. But we cannot "grasp this without at the same time grasping sanctification also." Justification and sanctification are "joined together by an everlasting and indissoluble bond, so that those whom [God] illumines by his wisdom, he redeems; those whom he redeems, he justifies; those whom he justifies, he sanctifies."[13] It is in the process of sanctification that the third use of the law becomes central and thus Calvin taught, "the third and principle use, which pertains more closely to the proper purpose of the law, finds its place among believers in whose hearts the Spirit of God already lives and reigns."[14] For Calvin the principal use of the Decalogue or moral law pertained to the life of those who were already justified by faith and who must "press on" toward God's righteousness. It is this third use of the law that propels his sermons on the Ten Commandments as well as many aspects of the *Institutes* and the *Harmony*.

The emphasis on the role of the law in the life of the believer depended to a great extent on Calvin's understanding of the *simul* doctrine, particularly as it pertained to the noetic effect of sin. Although Calvin differed from Luther on the principal use of the law, he did agree with the German Reformer on the nature of the justified person. Covered by the righteousness of Christ,

11. Sermon 6, (Deut. 5:13–15), 122; *Institutes* 2.8.11.
12. *Institutes* 2.7.2.
13. *Institutes* 3.16.5.
14. *Institutes* 2.7.12.

believers remained sinful in themselves. Through one's faith in Christ and not one's inherent holiness, the believer did not need to fear the remaining presence of sin. While one strove against this sinfulness, the certainty of salvation was founded upon, and included in, the faith one had in the all-sufficiency of Christ's sacrifice on the cross and the promise that such faith alone justified the believer before God. Calvin further stressed that the mind of the believer was not sinless or completely healed and remade into the image of God. The believer was still prone to the great sin of not clinging solely to the word of God and thereby of falling into "speculation," "curiosity," and the desire to "add" to this divine word. This was of particular importance to Calvin because it endangered the most important teaching of the law; namely, the pure or "legitimate worship" of God.[15] Because of the mind's desire to add to the law, the justified person was still always in danger of falling back into idolatry. Consequently, Calvin referred not only to the unbeliever but also to the regenerate as "runaway horses" that needed to be restrained and bridled. The mind of the justified person must be "reigned in" and "bridled" so that it would be kept within the limits of revelation. The Law provided this "boundary," "limit," or "bridle" that kept the mind of the believer within the limits decreed by God. Citing Deuteronomy 4:2 (RSV)—"You shall not add to the word which I command you, nor take from it, that you may keep the commandments of the LORD your God which I command you"—Calvin endlessly reminded his hearers and readers that they must never "add anything to the law."[16] They must "be content" with the law as revealed in Scripture and not dream up new additions. The imagination was the great danger here. Even the mind of the redeemed possessed a dangerous imagination, which was always tempted to create inventions in worship and behavior that it thought would be pleasing to God. Under the best of intentions,[17] the imagination would lead the mind to invent "additions" that abandoned the clarity of God's will as revealed in the law. Calvin explained that Moses explicitly stated that "God added nothing to these ten statements." This proves that we are not to give vent to our inventions and that we are prohibited from adding anything to God's word.[18] As Calvin said to his congregation,

> Now it is admirable that God goes to such pains to teach us and further declares that he omits nothing. Nevertheless, our minds are so fickle that we always covet something better than what we can find in the Word of God. This diabolical curiosity has forever reigned in the world. And even

15. *Institutes* 2.8.1; 2.8.5; *Harmony* 2.419; Sermon 5 (Deut. 5:12–14), 104. See also sermons 1 and 2, 37–64.

16. Calvin also cited Deuteronomy 5:32 for the same purpose: "You shall observe that which the Lord your God has commanded you; you shall not turn aside to the right hand or to the left."

17. Sermon 3 (Deut. 5:8–10), 66.

18. Sermon 13 (Deut. 5:22), 242. See also sermon 13 (Deut. 5:22), 238–39; sermon 14 (Deut. 5:23–27), 268–69; Sermon 15 (Deut. 5:28–33), 278–81; *Harmony* 2:324, 397.

today we see that wherever one turns one cannot come to the end of this accursed cupidity—that men always desire to be wiser than God intends.[19]

Our minds still "wander about" and stray from the "right path," "failing to hold to the pure truth, each person turning aside after his own reveries, saying, 'it seems this way to me' or 'That is what I find good.' We must understand that that is nothing and our obligation is to come to this certainty which our Lord Jesus Christ has brought."[20] Even though God appeared in a whirlwind and in dark clouds in order to impress his authority on the law, Calvin insisted that the purpose was also "to repress men's curiosity." God spoke in unambiguous words,

> He does not engage in equivocation but has so clearly revealed his will that we can't help but be properly instructed provided we are willing to listen to him. But nevertheless it is inappropriate for us to pursue our senseless curiosities and inquire beyond what seems good to us, for we know that men are so inclined that their ears are forever twitching. . . . Thus let us learn to be God's good pupils [recognizing] that it is not necessary to yield the reins to our imagination in order to find what must be hidden to us; but let us be content to know what God tells us and to wait on the day of full revelation for knowing the rest which for now is incomprehensible.[21]

A second point to be noted is Calvin's unrelenting demand for purity, a theme not found in Luther's discussions of the life of the believer. Unlike Luther, Calvin praised Moses as the most excellent of the prophets because he was "familiar to God as a friend" and received the law directly from God without adding anything to it. Moses was the "first doctor" because all the other prophets, even Isaiah, only expounded the Law that he first delivered. He was the "prince of all the prophets" and was "to be heard above all the rest."[22] Unlike Luther, Calvin refers to the Decalogue as the "law of grace" which was revealed by God in order to instruct in proper worship and regulate the life of the believer.[23] One's election did not mean that the law had been canceled or that the elect could become indolent or careless. The world is full of dangers and the temptations of Satan and therefore the faithful must "walk in fear" before God. This is not the fear about salvation but, rather, the fear that one would dishonor God. Justification by faith, Calvin warned, does not mean that the commandments were no longer in force. As he preached, "We must walk under God's hand with greater care. Therefore [the commandments] ought to awaken us, instead of our being asleep

19. Sermon 1 (Deut. 4:44–5:3), 39.
20. Sermon 16 (Deut. 6:1–4), 302–3.
21. Sermon 13 (Deut. 5:22), 246–47.
22. Sermon 1 (Deut. 4:44–5:3), 40–45; Sermon 2 (Deut. 5:4–7), 54; Sermon 14 (Deut. 5:23–27), 268; *Institutes* 4.8.2.
23. *Institutes* 2.8.57.

and indifferent and wanting to be easily justified before God."[24] Most importantly, this "law of grace" required purity or holiness. Calvin continually spoke
of this purity by means of various biblical verses.[25]

Both the first and the third uses of the law made this holiness possible. The
law acted as a "mirror" both to reveal the righteousness of God and to show
the unbeliever the depth of his sin, "For in truth the whole law of God is like
a mirror which reflects our filth, its purpose being to confound us and make
us ashamed of our shamefulness." The law "ought to be like a mirror for us in
which we contemplate our poverty."[26]

Calvin follows this latter statement with the exhortation, "And once we have
come to perceive our duty, let us realize that we are condemned if we do not
approach the perfection to which God calls us." Following the recognition of
one's "poverty," the believer must recall that the Lord says, "it is necessary for
minds and senses to be so enclosed by his fear and aflame with a love and desire
to walk in all holiness that we may not be lured or pushed about here and
there by any evil passion . . ." This "enclosure" is precisely the third function
of the law. The law reforms human life to the "archetype of divine purity" and
instructs the faithful how to advance on the path to holiness.[27] Thus the law
restrains and bridles as much as it instructs and leads the "way" in the "race" or
"pursuit" of holiness. Just as God chose Israel to be a holy people, so, too God's
elect are to be holy and pure from all pollution.[28] In order to explain the purity
required by the law in the life of sanctification Calvin proceeds to explain the
spiritual demands of each commandment. The law, he explains, is to be understood and obeyed in a spiritual manner. The law molds the life of the Christian
"not only to outward honesty but to inward and spiritual righteousness." The
"heart" must not be aloof from obedience to the law. When Paul said in Romans
7:14 that the law was spiritual he meant that "it not only demands obedience of
soul, mind and will, but requires an angelic purity, which, cleansed of every pollution of the flesh savors of nothing but the spirit."[29] In the midst of a polluted
world, "the Lord wills to train his people in complete purity to the extent that

24. Sermon 12 (Deut. 5:21), 226.
25. Deuteronomy 7:6, "For you are a people holy to the LORD your God." Leviticus 11:44, "For
I am the LORD your God; consecrate yourselves therefore and be holy, for I am holy." Leviticus 19:2,
"You shall be holy; for I the LORD your God am holy." Numbers 15:40, "So you shall remember
and do all my commandments and be holy to your God." Hebrews 9:14 states, "how much more
shall the blood of Christ, who through the eternal Spirit offered himself without blemish to God,
purify your conscience from dead works to serve the living God." 1 Peter 15–16 states, "but as he
who called you is holy, be holy yourselves in all your conduct since it is written, 'you shall be holy
for I am holy.'" And Colossians 1:22 says that Christ, "has now reconciled in his body of flesh by his
death, in order to present you holy and blameless and irreproachable before him."
26. Sermon 12 (Deut. 5:21), 221, 232; *Institutes* 2.7.7: "The law is like a mirror. In it we
contemplate our weakness, then the iniquity arising from this, and finally the curse coming from
both—just as a mirror shows us the spots on our face." Here Calvin is speaking of the punishing
aspect of the first use of the law.
27. *Institutes* 2.8.51.
28. *Harmony* 2: 355.
29. *Institutes* 2.8.6.

those who profess to be Christian may not only abstain from evil, but insofar as possible, may equally refuse to tolerate it at all." Calvin continued,

> For we must understand that the earth is profaned when the worship of God is contaminated here and his holy name is dishonored. The ground on which [God] wants us to live is polluted and cursed and nothing will make him come to us. In any event when God gave this privilege to his children in order that they might remove idolatry from the country in which they [were to] live, it is certain that if they failed they would provoke his anger and vengeance against them. [In the same way] today if we were to ask for the abominations of the papacy to be combined here with the pure worship of God . . . thus providing them some corner in which they could perform their idolatries and superstitions, it would be like inviting God's anger against us and lighting the very fire of his vengeance.[30]

Although Calvin severely criticized the perfectionist drive of the Anabaptists and saw their separation from the world as the new Donatism, he, too, spoke about the need to be isolated from the pollutions of the world. He reminds his congregation that "in the end it will be necessary for us to recognize that the earth on which we have lived has been defiled by us and that all of the benefits which we have received, and the fact that God has increased us by his hand, are matters for which we shall certainly have to account, seeing that we have not acknowledged him who was their author in order to honor him as he deserves."[31]

True worship and obedience requires the separation from "pollution" of both the world and the self: "Thus we see quite well that we cannot be sanctified before our God, that is to say, we cannot worship him in purity, unless we separate ourselves from opposing pollutions, or until what belongs to our nature is abolished." Calvin insists that Christians cannot purely honor God "without renouncing themselves, or being separated from the pollutions of the world and of their own flesh." The commandment to observe the Sabbath gave Calvin ample opportunity to explain the separation and purity required for the Christian life. The Sabbath day is, he says, a sign that God sanctifies us and reigns in our midst. God speaks only "to the people whom he has chosen as a heritage and whom he has adopted. Therefore insofar as the Sabbath day is a sign that God has separated the faithful of his church from all the rest of the world, why is that extended to [cover] cattle and asses?" Calvin answered that the command refers to dumb animals as a sign and visible sacrament so that we might be that much "more retained for God's service." Hence, Calvin explained, "when you are separated from unbelievers, you might be a royal sacrifice to me, asking for nothing but to serve me with full integrity and pure conscience"[32]

The commandments "train in complete purity" by reforming all aspects of the human being. Calvin repeatedly warns that God does not stop with the external

---

30. Sermon 6 (Deut. 5:13–15), 130.
31. Sermon 4 (Deut. 5:11), 85.
32. Sermon 6 (Deut. 5:13–15), 99, 100, 119–20, 123–24.

action but, rather, sees the inner motives and affections. As he states in the *Institutes*, God is not an "external lawgiver." He is not satisfied with outward appearances but with "purity of heart." Consequently when God, whose eye nothing escapes, prohibits fornication, murder, and theft he is also condemning lust, anger hatred, coveting, deceit and so forth. Calvin insists that since God is a "spiritual lawgiver, he speaks no less to the soul than to the body."[33] Calvin, then, expounds the spiritual demands of each commandment, including the fact that the prohibition also includes the commandment to do the opposite. "Thou shalt not kill" means not only that the believer must not commit murder but also that he must never quarrel, feel anger or malice. "If we keep the nature of God in mind, it is no longer necessary to confine the law of God to external works, but it is fitting to conclude that when God speaks of murders, he equally speaks of all enmity, of all indignation and anger, and of all rancor that we harbor against our fellowman." Indeed, the law "does not consider what happened, but it weighs intention and attitude." Nothing is "hidden in the presence of God" and therefore the law "should test and fathom the depths of hearts." The prohibition includes the command to do the opposite. Therefore the statement, "thou shalt not kill," also means that we must help our neighbors, remembering that God intended us to live in community so that, "we should be true brothers by involving ourselves in behalf of our neighbors inasmuch as we possibly can."[34] The command that "Thou shall not steal," also applies to the purity of the conscience. This command forbids theft, fraud, pillage, and pilfering and even the overcharging by merchants. It also includes any wrong done to a neighbor who is poor. It also prohibits all avarice and any discontent with what God has given. This command also requires us to be "poor in heart" and not place any pride or confidence in our riches or use them as a means of oppression. We must also help the poor and needy. Furthermore we are hereby commanded not to rob God of his honor or permit any person to be wronged or injured. "Thou shall not commit adultery" applies both to chastity but also to all evil affections and actions. Lewdness in dress and speech are forbidden. There must be no dancing or drinking—nor too much eating. This commandment includes all forms of lust, all evil inclinations, and all thoughts of rebellion against the law. This command tells us that we must be vigilant "since God has condemned through the law every wicked thought that incites us toward evil." Paul, Calvin says, did not speak of wills alone but also "affections and thoughts."[35] Calvin continues this way throughout his sermons and expositions of the Ten Commandments. Every commandment is analyzed in three ways: (1) The explicit prohibition and all lesser included acts; (2) the virtue opposite to the vice is commanded and must be done out of the love of neighbor; and (3) the purity of the conscience is demanded so that one's feelings, motives, thoughts, and inclinations are examined for any impurity.

---

33. *Institutes* 2.8.6.
34. Sermon 8 (Deut. 5:17), 159–65; *Institutes* 2.8.49; *Harmony* 3: 20–22.
35. Sermon 5:21, (Deut. 5:21), 220–26; *Institutes* 2.8.49–50; *Harmony* 3: 186–89.

The *Institutes* make abundantly clear that justification by faith means one is saved by faith alone and not by one's inherent holiness. We are righteous by the imputation of Christ's righteousness and the nonimputation of our sins. The law cannot confer righteousness that depends solely on God's free mercy. Purity of conscience and good works never secure for us the certainty of salvation which faith requires. In the *Institutes* Calvin warns against the danger posed by the belief in perfection. Calvin refutes the Anabaptists for what he believed to be their view of spiritual regeneration. In Calvin's view, the Anabaptists taught that after baptism the believer was to be restored to the state of innocence. Fusing the Anabaptists with the Libertines, Calvin warned against a spiritualism that rejected the need for the bridle of the law. He insists that sin remains, but does not reign, in believers and cites Augustine as an authority for this belief.[36] Calvin vehemently condemns Osiander's idea of essential righteousness, because by confusing justification and regeneration, Osiander leaves the believer uncertain of salvation. If we must look to our souls for a righteousness free from sin, we are left in doubt.

> But because it is very well known by experience that the traces of sin always remain in the righteous, their justification must be very different from reformation into newness of life. For God so begins this second point in his elect, and progresses in it gradually, and sometimes solely, throughout life, that they are always liable to the judgment of death before his tribunal. But he does not justify in part but liberally, so that they may appear in heaven as if endowed with the purity of Christ. No portion of righteousness sets our consciences at peace until it has been determined that we are pleasing to God because we are entirely righteous before him. From this it follows that the doctrine of justification is perverted and utterly overthrown when doubt is thrust into men's minds, when assurance of salvation is shaken, and the free and fearless calling upon God suffers hindrance—nay, when peace and tranquility with spiritual joy are not established.[37]

In the sermons on the Decalogue, however, Calvin emphasizes the call to holiness, the life of sanctification that follows from justification. Toward the end of the sermons and in the sermon on Deuteronomy 6:4, we find relief from what, at times, seems to be an unrelenting demand for purity. Calvin tells his congregation that our salvation does not depend on this purity. No one can fulfill the law to the perfection it requires and is summarized in Deuteronomy 6:4–5, "That we should love God with all our heart, with all our mind, with all our understanding, and with all our strength."[38] The righteousness of the law is far too high for fallen human capacity. Calvin teaches his hearers that evil lusts and even mortal sins will not be charged against us; God does not "regard them." As Calvin says, "Moreover we know that all our stains have been effaced

---

36. *Institutes* 3.3.13–14.
37. *Institutes* 3.11.11.
38. Sermon 12 (Deut. 5:21), 224; *Institutes* 2.8.51.

by the blood of our Lord Jesus Christ." We are "reputed righteous in God's sight as if we possessed full integrity and perfection in ourselves to the extent that it can only be said that we have fulfilled the entire law." Nonetheless, although God overlooks these sins, the believer is never to disregard them. If we deceive ourselves and believe ourselves to be free of all wicked desires, "then that is sufficient grounds for God to call us to account." Our sins are not counted against us but they are to be examined in order both that we remember that salvation is by pure grace and that we are still in the process of striving toward holiness.[39] Only the curse of the law has been abrogated, not the necessity to fulfill it.

In sermon 15 Calvin also explains that it is the Holy Spirit that enables us to fulfill the law. In this sermon Calvin explains that we must not presume on our own strength; only the Spirit can govern us in such a way that we progress toward holiness. So, too, in sermon 12 Calvin explains that Saint Paul presupposed that the law was impossible to keep by our own strength; the law shows us what we owe God but does not give us the capacity to do God's will. That capacity belongs to the Spirit indwelling in the soul.

It is important to understand, however, that for Calvin, our union with Christ requires holiness. Moses, he says, points out the purpose of the law; namely, "to join man by holiness of life to his God."[40] In the *Institutes* Calvin makes clear that it is not our holiness that forms this bond: "When we hear mention of our union with God let us remember that holiness must be its bond; not because we come into communion with him by virtue of our holiness! Rather we ought first to cleave unto him so that, infused with his holiness we may follow wither he calls."[41] While Calvin does not contradict this teaching in the sermon, he is sometimes less careful to clarify the nature of that holiness that unites us to Christ. Preaching on the prohibition of adultery Calvin states, "In light of the fact, then, that God wants to make [believers] his own and wants to indwell them, is it not imperative for us to learn to walk in solicitude in order that no defilement or filth be committed that would result in expelling God instead of, according to his will, our becoming his residence and holy temple?"[42]

And finally, Calvin emphasizes in the sermons that God leads us into this holiness by deigning to reward our good works. This is the famous *syllogismus practicus*. For Calvin, this concept was biblically driven. Calvin opens chapter 18 of book 3 of the *Institutes* with a long list of biblical citations that refer to reward. Against his Catholic opponents, Calvin insists that the term reward cannot be equated with the idea of merit. Relying on Romans 2:6, which states that God will render to every man according to his works, Calvin explains that Paul was referring to the stages of God's mercy. First God calls, then he justifies, and then he glorifies (Rom. 8:30). God leads the believer into this glory by granting rewards to the works of sanctification. Calvin explains, "that is to

39. Sermon 12 (Deut. 5:21), 231–35.
40. *Institutes* 2.8.51.
41. *Institutes* 3.6.2.
42. Sermon 9 (Deut. 5:18), 173. Cf. sermon 5 (Deut. 5:12–14), 100.

say, [God] receives his own into life by his mercy alone. Yet since he leads them into possession of it through the race of good works in order to fulfill his own work in them according to the order that he has laid down, it is no wonder if they are said to be crowned according to their own works, by which they are doubtless prepared to receive the crown of immortality."[43] Calvin repeatedly states that in so doing God is rewarding his own works of grace. God rewards by gratuitously "accepting" our works as worthy. Therefore God "received our works, not really considering their substance, but accepting them as good and holy because of the passion and death of our Lord Jesus Christ." As he states in the *Institutes*, "Yet those good works which he has bestowed upon us the Lord calls 'ours' and testifies they are not only acceptable to him but also will have their reward."[44] Throughout the sermons and the *Institutes* Calvin insists that God "owes us nothing." Calvin teaches that we owe God everything, while God owes us nothing. God's reward, therefore, is that God "willingly obligates himself to us." For Calvin, God says, "Nevertheless, I do not want you to serve me gratuitously: I renounce my right, that is that you are obligated to do all that I command you without expecting some reward; rather I declare to you that I am ready to bless you and make you prosper when you serve me."[45] These rewards are both a solicitous way of God leading believers into holiness and are "testimonies" of one's election. Calvin refers to the reward of our works as proofs of Christ's indwelling in the soul, signs of one's calling, and a source of confidence and comfort.[46]

Throughout all of these discussions of the Decalogue it becomes clear that the most important and all-encompassing basis of Calvin's third use of the law is the theological assumption of divine immutability. The belief in God's unchangeability governs his emphasis on both the covenant and providence. Calvin always emphasized that God did not change God's "principle" use of the law. Rather he stressed repeatedly the oneness of God's plan throughout both the Old and New Testaments. This principle lies behind his detailed discussion of the similarities between the Old and New Testaments. Calvin's emphasis is always on the oneness of the divine covenant because he wants to maintain that God did not change God's mind and abandon the Old Testament or give a different covenant in the New Testament. To think in such a way was to believe that God had to react to human events in history and change God's plan accordingly. An immutable and sovereign God would not be a mere reactor to history or someone who could be made to change.[47] Divine providence ordered and governed all events according to the immutable purpose of God's plan. Only an immutable and sovereign God was a reliable God who could be trusted to keep

43. *Institutes* 3.18.1.
44. Sermon 16 (Deut. 6:1–4), 298; *Institutes* 3.15.3.
45. Sermon 15 (Deut. 5:28–33), 284–85.
46. *Institutes* 3.16.7; 3.17.12.
47. *Institutes* 10.1–23.

his promises and who would not govern the world as if it was being "aimlessly tumbled about."[48]

Since God could not have changed God's mind or purpose, the moral use of the law was its purpose from perpetuity. He tells his congregation that although they were not present when God gave the law to Moses, "nonetheless, the authority of our law must not be deprecated, for it contains the truth of God which abides forever, which never varies and which does not perish." While the ceremonial law and the curse of the law have been abrogated, the purpose of the law and its truth remain the same throughout history: "Now this truth which is neither changing nor variable is contained in the law. It is true that the law with regard to its ceremonies has been abolished, but with regard to its substance and doctrine which it contains, it always has virtue; it never decays." Consequently Moses "was speaking to us" and not simply to the multitude assembled on Mount Horeb.[49] When discussing the lightening, whirlwind, and flames that accompanied the publication of the law, Calvin instructed his congregation, "God intended that the memory of these things should endure forever and enjoy perpetual use. Consequently God displayed his glorious majesty on that one occasion in order that we might learn to receive his Word in complete fear and humility." Hence, we cannot allege that the law "is no longer binding on us."

> Now in particular, [God] wanted to write it on two tables of stone that it might endure, for it was not given [to last] for just a brief period [of time] as something transient. It is true that the ceremonies have ended, which is why the law is called temporal, but what we must keep in mind is that this order, which was established among the ancient people to serve until the coming of our Lord Jesus Christ, has now been abolished and things have become perfect, indeed to the extent that we are no longer under shadows and figures which prevailed then. In any event, the truth and substance of the law were not [confined] to any one age; they constitute something permanent which shall abide forever.[50]

This belief and confidence in the immutability of the law leaves us with a contemporary question: is the growing interest in ethics, the Decalogue, and natural law also due to the yearning for that which is immutable? It is not that we seek an immutable God so much as an immutable morality by which everything can be judged. The many books and articles arguing for natural law, many based on Calvin, reveal a search for a way to establish an unchangeable footing in a world that seems to be falling into moral relativism and chaos. One book on the Decalogue, which confronts the predicament of the modern world, is *I Am the Lord Your God: Christian Reflections on the Ten Commandments*. David Bentley Hart's essay in this collection brilliantly defines the situation of the Christian

48. *Institutes* 1.17.11.
49. Sermon 1 (Deut. 4:44–5:3), 48–49.
50. Sermon 13 (Deut. 5:22), 249.

and the Ten Commandments in a post-Christian culture. Hart argues that obedience to the Decalogue,

> . . . for us today must involve the painful acknowledgment that neither we nor our distant progeny will live to see a new Christian culture in the Western world; we must accept this with both charity and faith. We must, after all, grant that in the mystery of God's providence, all this has followed from the Holy Spirit in time. Modern persons will never find rest for their restless hearts without Christ, for modern culture is nothing but the wasteland from which the gods have departed, and so this restlessness has become its own deity; and, deprived of the shelter of the sacred and consoling myths of sacrifice, the modern person must wander or drift, vainly attempting one or another accommodation with death, never escaping anxiety or ennui, and driven as a result to a ceaseless labor of distraction, or acquisition, or willful idiocy. And, where it works its sublimest magic, our culture of empty spectacle can so stupefy the intellect as to blind it to its own disquiet, and induces a spiritual torpor more deplorable than mere despair.[51]

Just as Calvin had to address the meaning of the Decalogue in the context of his own time, with its controversies and conditions, so too Hart challenges modern Christians to reflect on the Ten Commandments in the situation of a post-Christian culture. It is no easy task.

51. Carl E. Braaten and Christopher R. Seitz, eds., *I Am the Lord Your God: Christian Reflections on the Ten Commandment* (Grand Rapids: Eerdmans, 2005), 75.

Chapter 8

John Owen

CARL R. TRUEMAN

In approaching John Owen on the Decalogue, it is necessary to address a series of interconnected issues. First, there is the nature of law within the created realm as it stands in connection with the nature of God. This establishes the general theological context for understanding the nature of the Decalogue. Second, there is the nature of the Decalogue as something specifically revealed by God. This defines the function of law within the covenant structure of Owen's theology. Third, there is the specific application of the Decalogue to two pressing issues of social and ecclesiastical significance in Owen's time: this matter is primarily concerned with the Second Commandment and its relevance for Christian worship and the Fourth Commandment and its relevance for Christian Sabbatarianism.

THE NATURE OF LAW WITHIN THE CREATED REALM

Owen addresses the nature of law within the created realm within the context of debates about the necessity of the atonement of Jesus Christ, given the reality of human sin. In 1647, in his treatise *The Death of Death in the Death of Christ,* Owen argues that Christ's atonement is purely contingent upon the decree of

135

God and that God could, had God so wished, have forgiven human sin by a mere act of God's will. To argue the contrary, that forgiveness of sin requires atonement, is an Arminian tenet, or so Owen claims.[1]

In arguing in this way, Owen places himself within an established Christian tradition that includes Reformed theologians, such as John Calvin, William Twisse, and Samuel Rutherford; indeed, the arguments on this point stretch back into the Middle Ages, and the Protestant discussion is merely an extension of this ongoing debate. While the position of Anselm arguably makes atonement necessary, Aquinas argues for the atonement on the grounds that it is better for God to atone than merely to forgive by an act of God's will; then, Duns Scotus and the later-medieval voluntarists clearly advocated the contingency of atonement; and these late-medieval arguments were cited extensively by theologians such as Twisse in their Reformed articulation of atonement theory.[2]

Underlying the argument is not so much the idea that God could have created a universe with any moral code that God chose but rather the epistemological point that God's nature and the revelation of divine law are not so connected that the latter can be read by human beings as imposing necessary limits upon the former. The atonement is contingent because the moral stipulations of earthly life, as given by God, are themselves contingent. Such is Owen's position in 1647.

By 1653, however, Owen has dramatically changed his position, though he never explicitly acknowledges that he has made such a change. In the early 1650s, Parliament commissioned him to write a work combating the perceived threat from Socinian teaching as embodied in the ministry and writings of John Biddle. Biddle was not only the translator of the standard Socinian statement of faith, the Racovian Catechism, but also author of a number of original works of his own, all of which embodied the typical antimetaphysical and literal biblicist traits of the Socinians. Thus, he rejected not only Nicene and Chalcedonian orthodoxy in favor of a Unitarian notion of God and an adoptionist Christology, but he also denied the necessity for atonement. The root of this denial was not the same as that we see in Twisse or Rutherford, where the concern is really to safeguard the distinction between God's ways and human thought; rather, it was Biddle's rejection of the notions of original sin, total depravity, and federal, representative headship. In other words, he combined a Pelagian view of humanity with a reconstruction of God's nature, which effectively mitigated the moral seriousness of sin.[3]

In the context of responding to Biddle, Owen seems to have decided that the position articulated by Twisse, Rutherford, and himself in 1647, is insufficiently

---

1. See John Owen, *Works*, 24 vols. (London: Johnstone and Hunter, 1850–55), 10, 205.
2. For detailed discussion of the historical and theological aspects of this debate, see Carl R. Trueman, "John Owen's *Dissertation on Divine Justice*: An Exercise in Christocentric Scholasticism," *Calvin Theological Journal* 33 (1998): 87–103.
3. On Biddle, see H. J. McLachlan, *Socinianism in Seventeenth-Century England* (Oxford: Oxford University Press, 1951), 163–217; on Owen's interaction with Biddle, see Carl R. Trueman, *John Owen: Reformed Catholic, Renaissance Man* (Aldershot: Ashgate, 2007).

strong to guard against Socinianism. Indeed, we might use the modern cliché and say that he came to see his earlier view of the atonement as contingent as the start of the slippery slope to a Socinian denial of the atonement as a whole. Thus, in two major works of the 1650s, *Vindiciae Evangelicae* and *A Dissertation on Divine Justice*, he makes the argument that the law is a revelation of the very nature of God, and as such has a nonnegotiable quality that reveals necessary attributes of God and can be said, from the perspective of the human knower, to place limits on how God can and will act. Thus, in *A Dissertation on Divine Justice*, he says,

> First, the justice of God, absolutely considered, is the universal rectitude and perfection of the divine nature, for such is the divine nature antecedent to all acts of his will and suppositions of objects towards which it might operate. . . . Secondly, It is to be viewed with respect to its egress and exercise. And thus, in the order of nature, it is considered as consequent, or at least as concomitant, to some acts of the divine will, assigning or appointing to it a proper object. Hence, that rectitude, which, in itself is an absolute property of the divine nature, is considered as a relative and hypothetical attribute, and has a certain habitude to its proper objects.[4]

In other words, God's justice is an absolute property of the divine nature; it finds its contingency relative to those contingent objects that are proposed to it. For example, Adam had no necessary existence other than as God contingently willed his existence; once he existed, however, he was subject to a law of justice that is absolute, nonnegotiable, and an integral part of creation.[5]

Owen goes further in his discussion of the law, arguing that the law is that which defines the Creator-creature relationship. As the law is a revelation of the divine nature, for God to act in a way that suspends or contradicts that law would require God to suspend his divinity or deny that he is God and, by the same token, to grant human beings an autonomy that denies their creaturely, dependent existence. Thus, for God to forgive sin by a mere act of divine will would be for God to deny his very essence.

Given this, Owen is able to defend the necessity of the atonement: building explicitly on the work of the Jesuit theologian, Francisco Suárez, he argues that all outward actions of God have to be consistent with his nature, a nature that is revealed in the moral stipulations of the law; thus, given the existence of human beings, and the reality of their fall in Adam, if God wishes to forgive them for their sin, he is required to act justly, in accordance with his nature, and thus to punish sin.[6]

Owen sees the natural realm as revealing God's justice. He supports this with typical metaphysical arguments drawn from Aquinas and other Thomist sources that articulate the analogy of being; however, he sets these not so much within

4. Owen, *Works*, 10, 498–99.
5. Ibid., 10, 507–8.
6. Ibid., 10, 502–3.

a strictly metaphysical context as within that of the rhetorical device of arguing from the consent of the nations. All people consent to the idea that God needs to be propitiated, thus all people consent to the idea of God's justice, and therefore God must be just.[7] Medieval metaphysics is put in the service of an argument whose force really derives from Renaissance rhetoric.[8] In this context, he dismisses the argument of Rutherford that a universal belief in the need for propitiation indicates that all peoples, at some point, must have had access to Moses' writings. On the contrary, knowledge of the law of nature is innate in human beings, however obscured that might have become as a result of sin.[9]

THE LAW OF NATURE AND GOD'S COVENANT

For Owen, the law is part of creation, part of nature itself; but it does not in itself establish a relationship between God and humanity, which can lead human beings to eternal life. At the most basic level, the problem is ontological: the infinite God is on a totally different level of being to the finite creature and cannot be put under obligation to creatures even if they perfectly obey the law. In other words, the moral structure of creation considered in the abstract places demands upon human beings but does not provide in itself a mechanism for a connection between Creator and creature whereby the latter could merit the reward of eternal life from the former. It merely defines the moral relationship between God and humanity.

The problem of connecting the infinite and the finite in Christian theology is not new in the seventeenth century. In the Middle Ages, the issue lies at the heart of the development of the notion of the superadded gift of grace whereby Adam, in the state of nature, is yet supplied with grace that raises his perfect, yet finite, obedience to a level whereby he can merit eternal life. In the later-medieval theology, this came under increasing pressure from the *via moderna*, with its emphasis on the divine *pactum* as being that which determined the nature of merit and bridged the gap between the infinite and the finite.

Against this background, Owen's Reformed theology represents in many ways a continuation of the concerns underlying medieval discussions of the relationship between nature and grace, though he does not resolve the issue by developing the concept of superadded grace but by articulating a notion of covenant. By the late sixteenth century, the pre-fall arrangement with Adam was typically being described as covenantal, while the language remained somewhat fluid

---

7. Ibid., 10, 522.

8. On the use of the "consent of nations" argument as part of the Reformed transformation of the medieval proofs, see Richard A. Muller, *After Calvin: Studies in the Development of a Theological Tradition* (Oxford: Oxford University Press, 2003), 54–55; Carl R. Trueman, "Reason and Rhetoric: Stephen Charnock on the Existence of God," in M. W. F. Stone, ed., *Reason, Faith and History: Philosophical Essays for Paul Helm* (Aldershot: Ashgate, 2008), 29–46.

9. Owen, *Works*, 10, 539.

throughout the first half of the seventeenth century, being variously a covenant of life, of nature, or of works.[10] In this arrangement, Adam's obedience, while in itself of insufficient intrinsic merit to earn eternal life, and on one level he was obliged to do as a creature made in God's image, was yet able to be meritorious through the covenant of works. His obedience to the law was, strictly speaking, no more than was required by nature; but God, in his condescension, had arranged to reward such obedience with far more than it intrinsically deserved by establishing, above and beyond the ontological relation, a covenantal relation that determined merit.[11]

It is against this background that Owen discusses the law of creation. Indeed, in this context, he makes two points of relevance. First, the law of nature, while a nonnegotiable part of creation, is not, in its very essence, covenantal and requires no covenantal relationship to establish its validity or universal application. All human beings are subject to the moral law by virtue of their status as creatures. Human beings, as possessing the image of God, are by very nature morally dependent upon God and thus obliged to the moral law. As Owen expresses it: "For it was not possible that such a creature should be produced, and not lie under an obligation unto all those duties which the nature of God and his own, and the relation of the one to the other, made necessary."[12]

Second, in actual history, human beings never existed outside of a covenantal relationship with God. The idea of human beings as bare creatures is theoretically possible but never actually the case. On the contrary, Adam was established from the very start as the federal head of all humanity; and his obligation to obey the moral law was always within the context of a covenant that determined the meritorious nature of his work. As Owen puts it:

> Man in his creation, with respect unto the ends of God therein, was constituted under a covenant. That is, the law of his obedience was attended with promises and threatenings, rewards and punishments, suited unto the goodness and holiness of God. . . . And in this case, although the promise wherewith man was encouraged unto obedience, which was that of eternal life with God, did in strict justice exceed the worth of the obedience required, and so was a superadded effect of goodness and grace, yet was it suited unto the constitution of a covenant meet for man to serve God in unto his glory. . . . Now, this covenant belonged unto the law of creation; for although God might have dealt with man in a way of absolute sovereignty, requiring obedience of him without a covenant of a reward

10. See the Westminster Confession 7.2, Larger Catechism 20, Shorter Catechism 12.

11. There is significant debate in the secondary literature on the origins and development of the covenant of works: see especially Lyle D. Bierma, *German Calvinism in the Confessional Age* (Grand Rapids: Baker, 1996); R. Scott Clark, *Caspar Olevian and the Substance of the Covenant* (Edinburgh: Rutherford House, 2005); R. W. A. Letham, "The *Foedus Operum*: Some Factors Accounting for Its Development," *Sixteenth Century Journal* 14 (1983): 457–67; Richard A. Muller, *After Calvin*, 175–89; Willem J. Van Asselt, "The Doctrine of the Abrogations in the Federal Theology of Johannes Cocceius (1603–1669)," *Calvin Theological Journal* 29 (1994): 101–16; Peter A. Lillback, *The Binding of God: Calvin's Role in the Development of Covenant Theology* 9 (Grand Rapids: Baker, 2001).

12. Owen, *Works* 19, 336–37.

infinitely exceeding it, yet having done so in his creation, it belongs unto and is inseparable from the law thereof.[13]

Thus, in creation God establishes his absolute moral sovereignty and also reveals his loving condescension, the former in the law, the latter in the covenant of which the law is a part. Interestingly, in so doing, Owen even uses the word "superadded" echoing—whether consciously or unconsciously—the medieval language of Adamic grace.

By making the law and the covenant separable, at least at a formal level, Owen can obviously maintain the continuing moral obligation of the law on all human beings even after the covenant of works has been broken, but this then raises a further question: why is the Decalogue delivered at Mount Sinai?

MOUNT SINAI

If the covenant of works is established and broken in Eden, and if the law has universal relevance simply because of the very structure of creation, not because of the covenantal arrangement into which God condescendingly enters with Adam as humanity's federal head, then what is the significance of Sinai?

Typical Reformed theology of the seventeenth century regards the Sinaitic covenant as being essentially of grace, and the law as functioning as the moral guide for the moral regulation of God's people within the context of redemption.[14] Thus, the Westminster Confession of Faith, chapter 19, states that the law of nature in the covenant of works with Adam was articulated again in the Decalogue, though this time the promises attached to it show the believer what can be expected from obedience, though not legal obedience. The Decalogue thus has positive significance for the believer. Thomas Watson, in his commentary on the Shorter Catechism, accents the fact that the Decalogue was given to the children of Israel in the context of God's deliverance of them from Egypt. As redeemed people, they thus follow the Decalogue as means of moral response to God, out of gratitude for his salvation and in order to effect their sanctification; then, given the typological relationship of the exodus to the salvation wrought in Christ, the Decalogue continues to function in the church age as a guide to the new Israel, the Christian church. Watson even goes so far as to see this as having national implications as well: as the children of Israel were rescued from an idolatrous nation, so England too has been delivered from idolatry, the implication being that the English church needs to heed the Second Commandment.[15]

Such a use of the law as moral guide is, of course, implicit in Owen's own theology of law: as the universal obligation of humanity towards God, the law is

13. Ibid. 19, 337.
14. E.g., Calvin, *Institutes* 2.7.12.
15. See his introduction to the Decalogue in *The Ten Commandments* (Edinburgh: Banner of Truth, 1965), 1–48.

regulative of all human behavior, within and without the church. Yet this status of the law as morally normative for life is independent of any covenant nor does it require any redemptive context: the believer and the unbeliever are both, as human beings and creatures, obliged to the natural law. They have no choice in the matter, whether considered in the abstract, in a legal, or in a redemptive context. The natural law defines correct human behavior. So how does Owen understand the special arrangement at Sinai? Why does God give the law again, since it is revealed in creation and the breaking of the covenant of works does not abolish nature?

In the preliminary essay on the Sabbath in his commentary on Hebrews, Owen refers to Sinai as the renewing of the law.[16] Then, in his exegesis of Hebrews 12:18–19, he clearly characterizes the giving of the law on Sinai in terms of a covenant of works. He regards the writer of Hebrews as drawing a clear contrast between the evangelical state of the church and the bondage of ancient Israel, where the law was designed to engender a spirit of bondage.[17] In examining the passage, Owen points out that the whole description of Sinai is one designed to highlight the terror and fear of the Israelites, culminating in the oral delivery of the Decalogue, a delivery that they found unbearable.[18]

From this, Owen concludes that the delivery of the law at Sinai was essentially a recapitulation of the covenant of works, a legal covenant, made necessary by the way in which the law had come to be obscured in the human mind. It is a renewing of the law not so much because the law itself has ceased to apply, or is now being given a distinctly different moral function; it is being renewed in the sense that it is being revealed again, in a clear and precise manner, in order to remind human beings of their obligations to God. Admittedly, he acknowledges that the Decalogue serves a political purpose, in giving Israel a clear legal basis for social organization, and contains certain dispensational distinctives: for example, the promises attached relative to the land in the Fifth Commandment. But its primary purpose is to recapitulate the covenant of works. As with the law of nature, it demands that obedience of human beings which is part of their created purpose; and, as with the covenant of works, it attaches promises to obedience and penalties to disobedience. In this context, the giving of the law at Sinai is, in a sense, an act of grace on God's part in that he need not have done it for human beings, even fallen human beings, had the substance of the law been written in their hearts. He did it to sharpen knowledge of sin, given the ways in which fallen human nature became dull to its moral responsibilities: "This law, for the substance of it, was written in the hearts of mankind by God himself in their original creation; but being much defaced, as to the efficacious notions of it by the entrance of sin and the corruption of our nature, and greatly affronted as unto the relics of it in the common practice of the world, God gave it in the church this becoming renovation with terror and majesty."[19]

16. Owen, *Works* 19, 345.
17. Ibid. 24, 311.
18. Ibid. 24, 320.
19. Ibid. 24, 321.

In other words, the giving of the Decalogue serves as a reminder that the law of nature remains in place, and that nobody can hope to see God who does not obey all of its demands to the uttermost. There is no abrogation of the law in its demands, because the covenant of works has been broken; and the combination of the giving of the Decalogue with the terrifying revelation of God on Mount Sinai serves to underline this fact. For Owen, the key Old Testament passage in this regard is Deuteronomy 5:24–27, in which the Israelites express the terror they feel at the declaration of the Decalogue and go on to say (vv. 26 and 27) that no one can see God and live, and therefore Moses needs to draw near to God and mediate his words to them. Here, the function of the Decalogue is to terrify sinners and to make them acutely aware of the need of a mediator. Using language that connects Israel at Sinai with the Garden of Eden, Owen writes of them being like Adam, summoned by a righteous God and having nowhere to hide themselves.[20]

In short, there seems to be, at least in the later Owen, an emphasis on the legal aspects of Sinai that set him apart from the more mainstream approach which counterbalances these aspects of the law with an emphasis on Sinai as promoting and guiding evangelical obedience. Sinai is part of a sharp law-gospel dialectic in Owen's thinking, not the ethical map for God's graciously redeemed people. In ethical practice, of course, the fact that the covenant of works is rooted in the law of nature means that the difference counts for little; but it does suggest that Owen differed from his mainstream colleagues in seeing the significance of the Israelites at Sinai as not so much a type of the church in terms of obedience required after redemption as examples of those who need to be convicted by sin in order to flee to Christ.

This raises the question of why Owen uses Sinai to make such a sharp antithesis between law and gospel in a manner that is arguably untypical of many Puritans. While he himself gives no insight into why he does this, I would suggest that it certainly helps him reinforce a clear Protestant position on justification in an era when Arminianism and the thinking of Richard Baxter on salvation were, to Owen's mind, everpresent threats. Indeed, in the years after the Great Ejection of 1662, Owen and Baxter represented the two principal leaders and intellects of the nonconformists in England, with two different visions of how Puritan theology might develop in its new circumstances. Baxter's theology represented a turn towards a more moralistic conception of the Christian life; Owen's view of Christianity defended God's grace and justification by imputation through a sharp emphasis on the antithesis of law and gospel.[21] Indeed, Owen's description of Sinai in his commentary on Hebrews finds its literary counterpart in

20. Ibid., 319.
21. On Baxter, see J. I. Packer, *The Redemption and Restoration of Man in the Thought of Richard Baxter* (Vancouver: Regent, 2003); Hans Boersma, *A Hot Peppercorn: Richard Baxter's Doctrine of Justification in Its Seventeenth-Century Context of Controversy* (Zoetermeer: Boekencentrum, 1992); Timothy Cooper, *Fear and Polemic in Seventeenth-Century England: Richard Baxter and Antinomianism* (Aldershot: Ashgate, 2001).

John Bunyan's *Pilgrim's Progress*, where the thunder and lightning on Sinai does nothing but strike terror into the heart of Christian; and Bunyan, of course, was famously influenced by reading Luther's second commentary on Galatians, with its radical law-gospel dialectic.

Fear of legalism had led to a dramatic reappropriation of Luther on law and gospel by theologians of the mid-seventeenth century, from radical antinomians such as John Eaton to figures such as Owen and Bunyan, both suspected by some of having antinomian tendencies themselves.[22] In this context, Baxter's theology was a counterweight to this, and his belief that the gospel involved the giving of a new law, and that the believer's works were constitutive of justification, could easily find support in a view of Israelite history that saw Sinai as a redemptive moment. The giving of the law becomes not so much a restatement of the covenant of works as the articulation of a works principle within the context of a redeemed people. In Owen's scheme, however, this is not possible: Sinai is a reiteration of the demands of the law, and a restatement of the law-gospel antithesis, which maintains the clarity of his position on justification. Such a view is speculative, but would seem to make sense of the evidence.

THE ISSUES OF THE SABBATH AND OF WORSHIP

In Owen's day, two commandments in particular were of wide ecclesiastical, political, and social significance: the Second Commandment against idolatry and the Fourth Commandment on the Sabbath.

To take the latter first, Sabbatarianism had become a burning issue in the early seventeenth century. In 1595, Nicholas Bound published his *The doctrine of the Sabbath planely layde forth* (London), a text which set forth what was to become a standard, and strict, position among many in England and Scotland. To counteract this trend, James I of England and VI of Scotland, published his *Book of Sports* in 1617 with instructions that it should be read from the pulpit. This was reissued by his son, Charles I in 1633, with added legal sanctions for those who refused to read it from the pulpit. Among other fun activities, which the book promoted for the Sabbath, we find archery and dancing.

Given the *Book of Sports* teaching and legal force, it epitomized two elements that were problematic to many in the Independent and Presbyterian camps: a lax view of the Sabbath and an Erastian church settlement. The stage was set, therefore, for a struggle over the Sabbath that was always more than a struggle over the Fourth Commandment; indeed, the issue was a microcosm of church tensions, and this goes some way to explaining the peculiarly strong feelings that the Sabbath aroused in England and Scotland. It was also an issue which, as Christopher Hill pointed out, was peculiarly suited to expressing the changing

---

22. See David R. Como, *Blown by the Spirit: Puritanism and the Emergence of an Antinomian Underground in Pre–Civil-War England* (Stanford: Stanford University Press, 2004), 185–86.

nature of society in seventeenth-century England, where a rapidly emerging mercantile economy left the rhythm of the church calendar, so conducive to an agrarian pattern of life, somewhat vulnerable. One does not need to be a Marxist to see the force of this argument.[23]

Thus, by the time Owen addresses the issue of the Sabbath in his commentary on Hebrews in 1667—after the Restoration—there is a significant amount of cultural and political freight associated with the issue. Indeed, Owen himself points out the irony that the day of rest had become a source of endless strife in his own times.[24] Part of the strife which Owen addresses relates to the nature of the Fourth Command, where Owen sees two major errors of those who see the essence of the commandment as lying in the stipulation that it refers to the seventh day: there are those who thus see seventh-day observance as perpetually binding; and those who see the Sabbath as completely abolished in the church age.[25] Both positions fail for Owen, because they do not distinguish the moral aspect of the command from the positive.

Owen sees the moral part of the command as establishing the principle that one day in seven should be observed, a point which rests upon his understanding of creation and his basically Thomistic understanding of natural law. Interestingly enough, as is so typical of seventeenth-century Reformed theology, he sets his essentially medieval approach within a rhetorical context, where the consent of the nations provides the most basic elements of his argument: "All men, as we have often observed, do allow that there is something moral in the fourth commandment."[26] This allows Owen to present those who wish to abolish all notions of the Sabbath in the current dispensation as arguing incomprehensibly, even, we might say, against nature or common sense.

Owen then addresses the Sabbath command as part of the Decalogue. The Decalogue, he declares, was given to Israel as a guide for political morality and as a schoolmaster to lead to Christ; but it was moral as to its perceptive principles and thus, as we have seen, eternally binding on the created realm. All of its commands are binding on all people at all times in all places because they reflect the principles of the law of nature itself. Thus, the Sabbath command is not dispensational in principle, only in disposition. It is thus a mixed command, containing both positive and moral elements.[27] The positive element locates the Sabbath on the seventh day, and this can be altered; the moral requires as an imperative built into the very nature of creation that humans rest on one day in seven; given this, the shift to the first day is established by the teaching of Christ under the new covenant.[28] Further, in commenting on Hebrews 4:10, Owen

---

23. See Christopher Hill, "The Uses of Sabbatarianism," in *Society and Puritanism in Pre-Revolutionary England* (London: Panther, 1969), 141–211.
24. Owen, *Works* 19, 266.
25. Ibid., 362–63.
26. Ibid., 364.
27. Ibid., 366.
28. Ibid. 408–10.

indicates that, just as the seventh day was based on the timing of God's rest in creation, so the first day is rooted in the timing of Christ's resurrection in the act of re-creation. The moral principle is maintained, as is the paradigmatic nature of divine action; but the positive element is changed in the new dispensation.[29]

If debates over Sabbatarianism linked issues of divine law to issues of state power, the same can be said for worship. Almost from its inception, the English church had been afflicted with controversies over worship. The struggle between Thomas Cranmer and John Hooper in 1551, over the latter's refusal to wear vestments for his consecration as bishop, had highlighted the problems that were to beset an Erastian church settlement. Even more so, the figure of John Knox, with his syllogisms on idolatry, indicated the kind of regulative principle of worship which was to develop among some of the more radical English and Scottish divines, and that in a way which could only cause deep problems in the context of the absolutist claims and moderate church policy of the Stuarts.

Much could be said about Owen's contribution to the wider politics of these debates, but in focusing on the strictly theological dimensions of his discussion, it is interesting to note that his argument for simplicity of worship via application of the Second Commandment is rooted both in the constitution of nature and in his Christology. On the issue of images and idolatry, the status of the Second Commandment, as part of the Decalogue, is also for Owen a part of the law of nature, which continues as basic and binding in the era of the church. The essence of God, being infinite, is incomprehensible to finite creatures and cannot be represented by the finite; thus any attempt to approach the infinite essence in itself requires a finite mediator. This was true at the time of creation; indeed, the covenant of works is an example of precisely the kind of condescension necessary to bridge the ontological gap between Creator and creature. In a fallen world, this incomprehensibility of the infinite God is the cause of images and idolatry, because finite human beings have a desire to approach God in a form that is comprehensible. Thus, they depict God in ways that they can grasp and, indeed, form their theology on this basis. Hence they use images, develop notions such as the mediation of the saints because all human beings know by their very nature that there can be no direct comprehension of or access to the divine essence.[30]

What is interesting is that the resolution of this problem for Owen is revelatory and christological: since God is in himself unknowable, the Bible functions as God's revealed will for correct worship, as is typical of Puritan understanding of the regulative principle; and in the incarnate person of the Lord Jesus Christ, the divine essence is manifested in a finite form that is comprehensible by finite creatures. That this humanity is unique precludes further representations of it in pictures or statues; and it focuses attention on Christ in heaven where, incidentally, even after the fulfillment of 1 Corinthians 15:24,

---

29. Ibid. 21, 335.
30. Ibid., 1, 270–71.

the humanity remains intact because of the need for ontological mediation even after the definitive consummation of all things.[31] In the meantime, worship here on earth is to be conducted in as simple a manner as possible in order to facilitate, rather than hinder, the focusing of the Christian mind on Christ's intercession in heaven. The christological underpinnings of Owen's argument at this point indicate clearly that the Second Commandment rests upon a reality that would have required something akin to the incarnation even if humanity had not fallen.[32]

THE SIGNIFICANCE OF OWEN IN DEBATES TODAY

In closing, I want to suggest a number of ways in which Owen's approach to the Decalogue is of interest today.

First, there is the historiographical point. In the remapping of the relationship between medieval theology, Reformation thought, and post-Reformation developments, Owen's connection of the Decalogue to natural law provides an obvious point of contact between his thinking and that of the later Middle Ages. While his specific applications of this may have had a distinctively Reformed dimension, as in his use of the covenant of works concept and his critique of images, these issues should not obscure the larger debt that he owes to the Western theological tradition on this point. More specifically, his heavy debt to Aquinas on issues relating to natural theology calls into question recent arguments that have tended to deny Thomist influence in Reformed thought in favor of emphasizing Scotism as the exclusive metaphysical source. A study of Owen on law and the Decalogue suggests that a more eclectic approach is necessary.

Second, Owen's assumption that creation has a moral structure to it, and the close connection he draws between this moral structure, human transgression, and the need for atonement, gives his approach to morality a profoundly theocentric dimension. This he clearly connects to the Decalogue as a recapitulation of the covenant of works and thus, in terms of its moral principles, a statement of the law of nature. For Owen, then, the Decalogue is not significant because it articulates principles that will lead to an orderly society or to prosperity; rather, as a recapitulation of the covenant of works, it serves primarily to point the children of Israel to their inadequacy and to the Messiah to come, and reminds the contemporary church of her constant need of Christ's grace. One might also add that this theocentricity means that, for him, the moral requirements of the law, whether considered simply as the natural law or as the Decalogue, are all of a piece: one cannot pick and choose which of the commands still apply for they all do, being rooted in the very nature of the creation itself, and thus of the Creator

---

31. Ibid. 1, 271.
32. For Owen on earthly worship in its connection to the heavenly Tabernacle and the resurrected Christ, see *Works* 1, 252–72.

himself, even though there are positive aspects, as with the seventh-day Sabbath or the promises relative to the land of Palestine, which have been changed or modified under the current dispensation. It is clear that a natural law theory that outlaws murder but allows for the making of images of Christ would not meet with favor from Dr. Owen; it would, rather, seem to him like a piece of eclectic moral consumerism. For Owen, natural law is theological law, and rests upon a whole catholic, Protestant, Reformed, theological system.

Chapter 9

Lancelot Andrewes

JEFFREY P. GREENMAN

LIFE AND MINISTRY

Lancelot Andrewes (1555–1626) belongs to the second generation of leading Anglican churchmen, alongside more famous contemporaries such as Richard Hooker (1554–1600), John Donne (1572–1631), and George Herbert (1593–1633).[1] In his own day, Andrewes was a celebrated preacher, renowned for his sermons at Christmas, Lent, Good Friday, Easter, and Pentecost delivered over a period of twenty years to King James I and his court. The reputation of Andrewes was championed by T. S. Eliot, who believed that these sermons ranked with the "finest English prose of their time, of any time" and that Andrewes occupies "a place second to none in the history of the formation of the English church."[2] In

---

1. Andrewes deserves a modern, critical biography. The most comprehensive source still is Paul A. Welsby, *Lancelot Andrewes 1555–1626* (London: SPCK, 1958). An excellent short introduction to Andrewes's life and writings is *Before the King's Majesty: Lancelot Andrewes and His Writings*, ed. Raymond Chapman (London: Canterbury Press, 2008).
2. T. S. Eliot, "Lancelot Andrewes," in *The Private Devotions of Lancelot Andrewes*, trans. and ed. F. E. Brightman (Gloucester, MA: Peter Smith, 1983), xi, xxii. The text reprints Brightman's standardly used 1903 translation. Hereafter cited as *PD*.

our day, he is associated primarily with his *Private Prayers* (*Preces Privatae*), which is commonly regarded as a spiritual classic.

Andrewes was born in the same year that Nicholas Ridley and Hugh Latimer were burnt at the stake in Oxford, and just a year before Thomas Cranmer met the same fate. He was a bookish child with a precocious penchant for ancient languages, whose parents and schoolmasters had to force him to play. He entered Pembroke Hall at Cambridge University in 1571, received the BA in 1575, and immediately was appointed a fellow of his college. In 1578 he took the MA and became Pembroke's Catechist. A key source for this chapter is his 110 lectures on the Ten Commandments in this role. Andrewes was ordained deacon in 1580 and received the BD in 1585. He held various administrative posts at Pembroke before becoming Master of the College in 1589, a role which he held until 1605. Andrewes also accrued a series of major ecclesiastical positions, including serving as a chaplain to Queen Elizabeth and Dean of the Collegiate Church of Saint Peter at Westminster Abbey. Andrewes was bishop successively of Chichester, Ely, and Winchester. An indication of his prominence is that Andrewes assisted with the funeral of Queen Elizabeth and with the coronation of King James; in 1626, despite failing health, he participated in the coronation service for Charles I.

According to McCullough, "Andrewes's knowledge of the Bible—in every ancient biblical language, as well as most modern ones—probably surpassed that of any Englishman of his age."[3] This proficiency enabled him to become a major contributor to the Authorized Version of the Bible, which appeared in 1611, serving as chair of the committee that translated Genesis through 2 Kings. Although during his lifetime only a slim volume of his sermons on the Lord's Prayer was published, since the mid-nineteenth century most of his writings have been available in eleven volumes in the Library of Anglo-Catholic Theology.[4]

Despite an impressive ecclesiastical career (according to Brightman, "the most notable preacher of his day"[5]) Andrewes's thought has received relatively little scholarly attention. The only monograph dedicated to his theology in the past fifty years is by Nicholas Lossky, who admits that Andrewes is "poorly known. Not only is that so for the general public, but even among students of Anglican theology there are very few for whom he represents more than an illustrious name."[6] This chapter is a contribution toward correcting this deficiency.

3. Peter E. McCullough, *Lancelot Andrewes: Selected Sermons and Lectures* (Oxford: Oxford University Press, 2005), lvi.

4. *Works of Lancelot Andrewes*, 11 vols., ed. J. P. Wilson and J. Bliss (Oxford: J. H. Parker, 1841–1854).

5. *PD*, xlii.

6. Nicholas Lossky, *Lancelot Andrewes the Preacher (1555–1626): The Origins of the Mystical Theology of the Church of England*, trans. Andrew Louth (Oxford: Clarendon Press, 1991), 1. For more on Andrewes as theologian, see A. M. Allchin, "Lancelot Andrewes," in *The English Religious Tradition and the Genius of Anglicanism*, ed. Geoffrey Rowell (Nashville: Abingdon, 1992), 145–64.

THE DECALOGUE IN ANGLICAN CONTEXT

It is important to recognize the Anglican context that shaped Andrewes's theological vision. As Stephen Sykes has argued, a central element in articulating Anglican theology is liturgy.[7] Therefore we need to notice the prominent place of the Decalogue in Thomas Cranmer's 1552 Prayer Book service of Holy Communion. The service begins with the Collect for Purity: "Almighty God, unto whom all hearts be open, all desires known, and from whom no secrets are hid: cleanse the thoughts of our hearts by the inspiration of thy Holy Spirit, that we may perfectly love thee, and worthily magnify thy holy name: through Christ our Lord. Amen." Daniel Stevick refers to the Collect for Purity to illustrate the "one immensely rich thing" that the Prayer Book as a whole has to say: "What God expects, God alone can give."[8]

Then the Decalogue immediately follows. The rubric explains, "Then shall the Priest rehearse distinctly all the Ten Commandments: and the people kneeling, shall after every Commandment ask God's mercy for their transgression of the same, after this sort." Thus, for each commandment recited by the priest, the congregation responds: "Lord, have mercy upon us, and incline our hearts to keep this law."[9]

Anglicans encountered all Ten Commandments on a weekly basis in the context of eucharistic worship. This is a simple fact with far-reaching spiritual and theological consequences. In classical Anglican liturgy, the Decalogue functions as a "mirror of sins," demonstrating the "theological" or "pedagogical" use of the moral law in Reformation theology. Recitation of the commandments is designed to bring conviction of sin and unrighteousness.

The congregation's plea for mercy acknowledges the need for divine forgiveness; pardon for sin is based on God's mercy, not personal merit. The appeal for "inclining the heart" seeks the Lord's transforming work (implicitly through the Holy Spirit) to produce a new (or renewed) capacity to obey God's commandments. Keeping the commandments is a response to grace, not its basis. More broadly, for Cranmer the gift of saving faith includes the renewal of the human will through the giving of the Holy Spirit, who reorders human desires, rekindles a love for God and neighbor and makes possible obedience to God's law.[10] Cranmer sides with Luther over Erasmus by setting into liturgical form the belief that cooperation with divine grace was a result of salvation, not its

---

7. Stephen W. Sykes, *The Integrity of Anglicanism* (New York: Seabury Press, 1978), chap. 3.

8. Daniel B. Stevick, "The Spirituality of the Book of Common Prayer," in *Anglican Spirituality*, ed. William J. Wolf (Wilton, CT: Morehouse-Barlow Co., 1982), 119.

9. An online version of this text can be found at http://justus.anglican.org/resources/bcp/1552/Communion_1552.htm.

10. Cranmer's approach has strong similarities with the mature theology of another English Reformer, William Tyndale, who speaks often of the Spirit's work in producing a believer's "love for the law." See Jeffrey P. Greenman, "William Tyndale," in *Reading Romans through the Centuries: From the Early Church to Karl Barth*, ed. Jeffrey P. Greenman and Timothy Larsen (Grand Rapids: Brazos, 2005).

precondition.[11] This theology is expressed through the logical progression of Purity: Collect-then-Commandments-with-appeal-for-mercy. This sequence frames the worshiper's engagement with the Decalogue within an overall theological trajectory that balances dependence on God's grace with seriousness about human sin and responsibility. There is nothing here to grease a slide toward antinomianism, and there is much that steers away from legalism.

Within this theology of grace, the Decalogue serves as the appointed means for the corporate self-examination, kneeling before a holy God. Reinhard Hütter, who is deeply distressed by contemporary antinomianism, argues that the liturgy is "the first and final catechesis" whereby Christians in the past have encountered the Decalogue. For Anglicans in Andrewes's era and for many centuries, eucharistic worship was the occasion through which the Ten Commandments were "heard, expounded, memorized, interiorized, and regularly reflected upon."[12] Also, it is worth remembering that worshipers' regular encounter with the Decalogue was given visual expression in English churches after the Reformation. Hütter points out that "Anglican liturgical reformers translated their catechetical intentions into church architecture, such that the two tables of the Decalogue were placed on each side of the altar, at the eastern wall of the parish churches."[13] Thus, in coming forward to the communion rail, worshipers could not have avoided seeing the Ten Commandments in front of them and above them as they received the sacrament. This practice reinforced the centrality of the Decalogue in Anglican spiritual experience.

Moving beyond the Holy Communion liturgy, we need also to be aware that Cranmer's 1549 Book of Common Prayer included a catechism for children as part of the Confirmation service. It is structured in the familiar pattern: Apostles' Creed, Ten Commandments, and Lord's Prayer, without a section on the sacraments. The catechism asks the candidates for Confirmation to recite the Ten Commandments, and then continues with three questions for which answers are required.

Four interpretive moves in the catechism are worthy of noticing here for our purposes. These moves become standard features of later Anglican teaching on the Ten Commandments. First, the Decalogue is summarized by the Great Commandment, to love God and neighbor. Second, the Golden Rule summarizes the second table. Third, both tables are interpreted as providing the spiritual terms for defining what it means for Christians "to serve God truly" in whatever "state of life" that constitutes God's calling. Fourth, obedience to the commandments is understood to depend upon "special grace" received through prayer: "you are not able to do these things of thyself, nor to walk in the

11. For more on Cranmer's theology of grace, see Ashley Null, *Thomas Cranmer's Doctrine of Repentance: Renewing the Power to Love* (Oxford: Oxford University Press, 2000), 98.

12. Reinhard Hütter, "The Ten Commandments as a Mirror of Sin(s): Anglican Decline—Lutheran Eclipse," *Pro Ecclesia* 14, no. 1 (2005): 47.

13. Ibid., 49.

commandments of God and to serve him, without his special grace, which thou must learn at all times to call for by diligent prayer."[14]

Finally, Anglicanism's confession of faith expressed in *The Thirty-nine Articles of the Church of England* (1571) makes no direct reference to the Decalogue. However, one article is quite important as it provides the framework for discussion of the Decalogue by Andrewes and others. Article 7 states, "Although the Law given from God by Moses, as touching ceremonies and rites, do not bind Christian men, nor the civil precepts thereof, ought of necessity to be received in any commonwealth, yet notwithstanding, no Christian man whatsoever is free from the obedience of the commandments, which are called moral."[15] Although distinction between the civil and moral law is conventional, it nevertheless provides an important methodological principle used in Andrewes's exposition of the Decalogue, particularly the Sabbath commandment.

THE DECALOGUE IN THE "PRIVATE PRAYERS"

The Decalogue occupies a significant position in Andrewes's famous *Private Prayers*. This collection of prayers, composed apparently in the 1590's in Greek, Hebrew, and Latin, was translated into English and published only after his death. It appears to have developed as part of Andrewes's daily routine of spending five hours per morning in prayer and study. An early biographer stated that the original manuscript was "slubbered with his pious hands and watered with his penitential tears."[16] The volume is mostly "a mosaic of quotations" drawn primarily from Scripture and the church fathers.[17]

Andrewes's volume is marked by what Brightman aptly labels "orderly completeness." Every section is highly structured and meticulously detailed. For every day of the week he compiles prayers under the following headings and in this order: commemoration, penitence, deprecation (petitionary prayer for deliverance from evil), comprecation (petitionary prayer asking for good things), faith, hope, intercession, blessing, commendation, praise, and thanksgiving.

The first material to draw to a noticeable extent upon the Decalogue is the comprecation appointed for Sunday.

> My hands will I lift up unto thy commandments which I have loved.
>> Open Thou mine eyes and I shall see, Incline my heart and I shall desire,
>> Order my steps and I shall walk
>> In the path of thy commandments.

---

14. The text of the 1549 catechism can be found online at http://www.ccel.org/ccel/schaff/creeds3.iv.xii.html?bcb=0.

15. Mark A. Noll, ed., *Confessions and Catechisms of the Reformation* (Grand Rapids: Baker, 1991), 216.

16. *PD*, xxiv.

17. *PD*, liv.

O Lord God, be Thou to me a God: beside Thee let there not be to me another, none else, nought else with Thee.

Grant unto me to adore Thee and to worship Thee
i., in truth of spirit,
ii., in comeliness of body,
iii., in blessing of the mouth,
iv., in private and in public:
v., and to render honour to them
vi., to overcome evil with good:
vii., to win possession of my vessel in sanctification and honour:
viii., to have my conversations without covetousness, being content with such things as I have:
ix., to follow the truth in love:
x., to desire not to lust, not to lust with concupiscence, not to walk after lusts.

This prayer begins by reciting selected verses from Psalms 119 as a way to express a commitment to obedience to God: "Order my steps and I shall walk in the path of thy commandments." The opening request "O Lord God, be Thou to me a God" is a reference to Exodus 20:3. It is a prayed version of the First Commandment, a plea to maintain sole allegiance and exclusive loyalty to the Lord. Next Andrewes puts forward a list of requests with ten items, which use the Decalogue as the main organizational principle. Clearly Andrewes considers the other commandments to be an elucidation of the First Commandment, a familiar move in the long history of Decalogue interpretation. The other commandments both explicate what the Lordship of God entails and demonstrate what it means to "adore" and "worship" God. Andrewes recasts the Decalogue as a set of positive prayers. Adoring God "in spirit of truth" is an allusion to John 4:24, but also reflect Andrewes's view that the First Commandment deals with the "inner" or "spiritual" dimension of worship. The prayer's references to worship "in comeliness of body and blessing of the mouth, in private and in public" also reflect Andrewes's particular way of reading the Decalogue. The Second Commandment orients the "external" aspect of bodily actions of our worship, and the Third Commandment deals with the loyalty of our "words" used in worship, both in public and in private. This is a compressed theological presentation of presenting one's whole self to God in worship, drawn from the first table of the Decalogue.

The second half of the prayer encapsulates the second table of the Decalogue. "To render honor to them that have the rule" clearly reflects Andrewes's interpretation of the Fifth Commandment to honor all superiors and to care for and provide for one's parents. "To overcome evil with good" is drawn from Romans 12, where the context is warning against revenge and appears here as the New Testament fulfillment of the Sixth Commandment prohibiting murder. "To win possession of my vessel in sanctification and honor" is the positive aspiration toward self-control in sexual matters that follows from the Seventh Commandment's prohibition of adultery. "To have my conversations without covetousness, being content with such things as I have" is the positive petition framed by the Eighth Commandment's prohibition of stealing. "To follow the truth in love" is the request suitable for those who seek to uphold the Ninth Commandment, "thou shalt not give false testimony against your neighbor." And finally, "to desire not to lust" is a clear reference to the Tenth Commandment's prohibition against coveting your neighbor's goods or wife.

Moving to Monday's prayer of deprecation, which is followed immediately by the comprecation, there is a similar pattern. The chart below displays his prayers side-by-side to show that Andrewes recasts the Decalogue as a comprehensive array of petitions, each one correlated directly to the attitudes, disposition, or behavior seen to be required by the specific commandment.

Table 1. Monday Prayers in *Private Prayers*

Deprecation	Commandment	Comprecation
Put away from me		Grant unto me
all irreligiousness and profanity all superstitiousness and hypocrisy	*No other gods*	*Godfearingness and religion*
idolatry and idiolatry[18]	*No idols*	adoration and worship
rash oath and curse	*No misuse of Lord's name*	*fair speech and faithfulness to mine oath*
withdrawal from and indecency in worship	*Keep Sabbath*	*comely confession in the assembly*
—	*Honor parents*	*kindly-affectionedness and obedience*
swelling[19] *and heedlessness*	*No murder*	*patience and friendly-mindedness*
—	*No adultery*	*purity and sobriety*
strife and wrath, passion and corruption	*No stealing*	contentedness and goodness
sloth and dishonesty, leasing[20] *and insolence*	*No false testimony*	*truth and incorruptibleness*
every evil conceit every lascivious thought every shameful lust every unseemly thought	*No coveting*	*good imagining, continuance unto the end*

18. "Idiolatry" is the worship of yourself.
19. "Swelling" refers to becoming "distended" with emotion.
20. "Leasing" is lying.

These petitions demonstrate the character of Andrewes's *Private Prayers* as a compendium of biblical spirituality. He has incorporated the Ten Commandments into his pattern of weekly prayers. These comprehensive Christian petitions for holiness consist of rewordings or paraphrases of the Ten Commandments. From this we can see that the Decalogue clearly played a central role in Andrewes's devotional life, and that those who follow this pattern in their own prayers will have an extended opportunity to interiorize and reflect on the significance of the Ten Commandments for daily life.

THE DECALOGUE IN "A PATTERN OF CATECHISTICAL DOCTRINE" AND "MORAL LAW EXPOUNDED"

The remainder of this chapter will examine Andrewes's understanding of the Ten Commandments expressed in his 110 catechetical lectures at Pembroke College, apparently begun in 1585. He delivered them in Pembroke's chapel on Saturdays and Sundays at 3:00 p.m. Reportedly they were so popular that their audience included not only members of his own college, but also students from other colleges and people from the surrounding area. An early editor of these works stated that "he was scarce a pretender to learning and piety then in Cambridge, who made not himself a disciple of Mr. Andrewes by diligent resorting to his Lectures."[21]

We will draw from two parallel sources for our interpretation. The first source, *A Pattern of Catechistical Doctrine*, dates from 1630 and is fairly readily available in the Parker Society edition of 1846.[22] This work is approximately 280 pages in the modern edition, in which the treatment of the Decalogue runs to about two hundred pages. Andrewes's teaching is presented as an expanded schematic outline. It does not use the typical question-and-answer format of catechisms. Another work, *The Morall Law Expounded*, which dates from 1642, is a prose narrative of some six hundred pages that is far less readily available and far less readable.[23] It is a "vastly expanded version" of the *Pattern*.[24] Both versions clearly reveal the typical style of Andrewes's thought. His prose is interspersed repeatedly with Greek, Hebrew and Latin phrases, laden with countless biblical references, and filled with constant quotations from the church fathers as well as frequent citation of classical authors. These sources reflect some of the earliest work by Andrewes: he would have been just thirty years old when he delivered this material. These writings are

21. Cited by Welsby, 22.

22. Lancelot Andrewes, *A Pattern of Catechistical Doctrine and Other Minor Works of Lancelot Andrewes* (Oxford: John Henry Parker, 1846). Hereafter cited as *PCD*.

23. Lancelot Andrewes, *The Morall Law Expounded* (London, 1642). Hereafter cited as *MLE*. For most scholars, this source would be most easily accessed using the Early English Books Online database.

24. Nicholas Tyacke, "Lancelot Andrewes and the Myth of Anglicanism," in *Conformity and Orthodoxy in the English Church, c. 1580–1660*, ed. Peter Lake and Michael Questier (Woodbridge, UK: Boydell, 2000), 8.

not highly polemical, at least by Reformation standards, nor are they sermonic in tone. They are academic lectures in practical divinity.[25]

Consistent with Reformation tradition, Andrewes provides an extended treatment of the Decalogue as a central part of catechetical teaching. Andrewes begins *PCD* by discussing the nature and value of catechizing, then addresses some preliminary doctrinal questions about God's existence, divine providence, the nature of Scripture as God's Word, "whether the Christian religion alone is the true religion" and "whether our religion be truly founded on God's word." Then he devotes a major section to a discussion of God's law. First, he addresses God's law in general, then Moses' law in particular. In this context, he makes a revealing statement: "In the law of Moses, who hath set down in the Decalogue a perfect pandect[26] of all the workes and duties, that God requireth at our hands. These are the true *Ethica Christiana*, Christian Ethicks, passing all other Ethicks."[27] This suggests what we will illustrate, namely, that Andrewes's treatment of the Decalogue is really an introductory course in Christian ethics or moral theology. It is the first systematic exposition of the Christian moral life undertaken in the Anglican tradition. Welsby's analysis is apt: "As a moral theologian, Andrewes was first in the line of the later Caroline churchmen, although his greatest contribution in this sphere was made during Elizabeth's reign."[28]

Another feature of Andrewes's opening apologetic section in the *PCD* sheds light on his eventual interpretation of the Decalogue. In a section arguing that Christianity "be truly founded on God's word," he claims that the antiquity of our religion shows its truth. He claims "that our religion is the same which the Jews had before Christ; for as the Law is nothing else but the old gospel, so the gospel nothing but the new Law; the Law *evangelium reconditum*, 'the gospel under veil,' the gospel *lex revelata*, 'the law unveiled;' and therefore our religion the same that the Jews had before Christ, and so the most ancient of all other religions."[29] This is a slight exaggeration since Andrewes will argue that Christians need not uphold the Sabbath commandment as did the Jews. But this affirmation of the fundamental continuity of Old and New Laws, and thus Old and New Testaments, enables him to interpret the Decalogue as being fully consistent with the Christian gospel and therefore the basis for Christian ethics.

---

25. This chapter will not discuss Andrewes's thirty small pages of paraphrase of the Ten Commandments found in *Holy Devotions, with Directions to Pray; also a brief exposition upon the Lord's Prayer, the Creed, the Ten Commandments, the 7 Penitential Psalms, the 7 Psalms of Thanksgiving: together with a Letanie* (London: A. Seile, 1663). His treatment of the Decalogue in *Holy Devotions* simply summarizes what he spells out in far more detail elsewhere.

26. "Pandect" is an archaic term for a code or system of laws.

27. *MLE*, 74.

28. Welsby, 29. Important later Caroline churchmen who contributed to Anglican moral theology would include figures such as Jeremy Taylor, Robert Sanderson, Joseph Hall and Henry Hammond. For an extended treatment, see Jeffrey P. Greenman, *Conscience and Contentment: A Reassessment of Seventeenth-Century Anglican Practical Divinity*" (Ph.D. diss., University of Virginia, 1998).

29. *PCD*, 47.

For Andrewes, the value of the Decalogue is not diminished by God's revelation in Christ, but is brought to its fulfillment.

Our study will focus on his understanding of the structure of the Decalogue, and then examine his interpretation of the First, Fourth and Fifth Commandments, ones where his distinctive methods and theological interests are particularly evident.

STRUCTURE OF THE DECALOGUE

Here is Andrewes's own schema (*MLE*, 106):

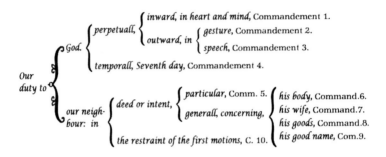

Andrewes rejects the Jewish division of the commandments into two equal tables of five, and also opposes the Roman Catholic conflation of what he views as the first two and the separation of the coveting the neighbor's house and wife into two distinct commandments. Instead, Andrewes divides the commandments into two tables that contain "our duty and piety" toward God (*PCD*, 169) in the first four and "our justice towards man" in the last six.[30] This is standard teaching: love of God and love of neighbor summarize the Decalogue.

He calls the first table "the table of holiness" and the second "the table of righteousness." The first table regulates worship, and the second table orders social conduct. He says that the two tables are "well joined together" and that "the latter dependeth well on the former" so that "the stream of justice may run along from the well-spring of piety" (*PCD*, 169). He says: "The commandments of the second table serve for the uniting of man to man, as the commandments of the first were for the unity of man to God" (*PCD*, 170). He adds that with the second table, "we depart not from the love of God, but rather love him more" (*MLE*, 363).[31]

---

30. *MLE*, 106; *PCD*, 75. On *MLE*, 70, he claims to be following the "greatest part of the Fathers" in this division.

31. Andrewes pauses in his exposition after the Fourth Commandment to offer a short treatise on the proper love of one's neighbor, in which he explains that loving one's neighbor means loving him or her "not so much as thyself, but after the same manner" (*PCD*, 173).

The First, Second and Third Commandments are classified as "perpetual" duties, whereas the fourth is called a "temporal" duty because its focus is limited to the seventh day. The First Commandment is characterized as applying inwardly to the heart and mind ("inward worship") whereas the next two apply outwardly either to gesture or "outward signs" (two) or to words and communication (three). Put differently, Andrewes sees the "manner and means of God's worship" being addressed in the Second Commandment, and the "scope" (i.e., extent or range) and "end" of God's worship in the third, which is praise.

Andrewes interprets commandments five through nine as dealing with "truth in the inward parts" (i.e., intentions) or "the actions, as they are committed before God, and man, as our neighbours." According to Andrewes, the Fifth Commandment speaks "particularly" to relationships between "man and man" but commandments six through nine speak more "generally" and "absolutely" of "duties to all." These are respect for the neighbor's own person in his very life and its preservation (sixth), "his own flesh" or wife and the preservation of wedlock (seventh), the preservation of his goods or "gifts, substance and wisdom" (eighth) and the maintenance of his "good name" (ninth). All these have to do with protection against harm or loss in temporal goods. Finally, the Tenth Commandment "restrains the first motions" (that is, intentions that are the grounds or cause of action).

So far, this seems quite straightforward. But this ordering does some important moral work for him. He says, "The first table doth bind more than the second." Why? Because the superior end of the first table over the second: "God's glory" takes precedence over "the health of ourselves and our brethren." He goes on to explain the internal logic of the order. This is a nice piece of moral reasoning. He states: "In the first Table, three Commandments are perpetual, one temporal . . . let the temporal give place to the eternal" (*MLE,* 118). This gives Andrewes a logical way to resolve conflicts between commandments. Since the requirements of the Fourth Commandment reflect a temporal order, if those requirements come into "comparison" (i.e., conflict) with one of the first three, they may be violated. "The rest of the Sabbath may be broken, that God's Name may be sanctified" (*MLE,* 118).

Similarly, there is a moral ordering principle at work in the second table, moving from what is common to what is private. "If any comes into comparison with the Fifth Commandment, it is to give place, because that is *de communi bono,* of the common good" on the basis that what is "common is to be preferred before private, general before particular" (*MLE,* 118). He adds that there is an ordering in the remaining commandments, ranking them in terms of a hierarchy of goods, yielding a moral ordering according to the severity of damage: "damage of life before damage of chastity; in chastity, before in goods; in goods, before fame" (*MLE,* 119). The Sixth Commandment comes before the others which follow "because life is dearer to us than those things which pertain thereunto, and which are spoken of in the rest of the commandments" (*PCD,* 213). When he comes to the Ninth Commandment, Andrewes argues that if any of the previous three have been breached (through murder, adultery, or theft) the matter must come before judges. And if so, then witnesses must speak the truth—hence, the importance of the Ninth Commandment's prohibition of false testimony against one's neighbor. Andrewes sums up his account of the logical ordering of the second table by saying: "We are more restrained by actions, then in word; and in word, more than in thought; life is more precious than chastity; chastity than substance; substance than fame; there can be no better order than that which God hath set down" (*MLE,* 119).

FIRST COMMANDMENT

Like many commentators on the Decalogue, Andrewes devotes a disproportionate amount of attention to the First Commandment: forty-one pages in *The Pattern of Catechistical Doctrine* and 159 pages in *The Morall Law Expounded.* He explains the First Commandment in three affirmations: "we must have a God; Him for our God; Him alone, and none else" (*PCD,* 82). These three affirmations correspond to three types of sin: profaneness, false worship, and "mingling" of religions. Andrewes explains that our worship of God is founded on God's attributes: majesty, truth, unchangeableness, will, justice, mercy, knowledge, power, ubiquity, and eternity.[32] Each attribute has a corresponding Christian virtue: God's wisdom corresponds to our knowledge; God's truth corresponds to our belief; God's justice corresponds to our fear; God's mercy to our love; and so on. Of these divine attributes, two "essential" attributes are justice and mercy, to which correspond our knowledge and love respectively. "From knowledge of God's justice and mercy come fear and humility, hope and love" (*PCD,* 84). His exposition goes on to describe in detail how fear, humility, hope, prayer, and love of God are appropriate responses to knowledge of God's attributes. He focuses far more on explaining the nature of the Christian life that follows from each attribute than to describing the attributes themselves. His primary concerns are practical, not doctrinal. In fact, the divine attributes appear almost self-explanatory, while the virtues require extensive elaboration.

With each virtue, Andrewes gives a detailed delineation that marks out this work as an example of moral theology. For example, his discussion of humility begins with a definition ("true humility is to give all glory to God"), explains the nature of true humility ("ascribing nothing to our own power; nothing to our own merit"), the "advantages" of humility, and what I would call the content of humility (to have humility of heart, "to restrain our appetite from desire of degrees of excellency," and "submission to our brethren"). This is followed by a detailed examination of pride, the contrary of humility, as consisting in five things ("in thinking we have that which we have not"; "in thinking every little good we have, greater than it is"; "to attribute that we have to our own

---

32. Andrewes has Exodus 34:6–7 in mind.

power"; "to make ourselves the end of that we do or of that we have"; and "to give more excellency to ourselves than to others"). This analysis is followed by a brief discussion of the means to pride, then some "further rules for humility" followed by four items that are the means to humility ("to consider the baseness of our metal, that we are but dust and ashes"; "to bring it into our hearts, we must consider that we are sinners, bondmen, and slaves to Satan, not having in us one good thought"; "to consider our afflictions and diseases, the forerunners of death"; "to consider the examples of humility, and especially Christ, whose birth, preaching, miracles, and death, were all in humility").[33] This section concludes with four "signs" of humility: "in speech, not to talk of high matters and proud things"; "to set ever before us . . . what is good in others, and what is evil in ourselves"; "to suffer backbiting and shame"; and "to be content to be condemned that God may have the glory."

When this same systematic approach is applied to each of the chief Christian virtues as they correlate to God's attributes, the result is a practical, comprehensive account of the Christian spiritual and moral life. These are lectures for university undergraduates in what we would now call "Christian formation." They cover a great deal of territory in conventional, orthodox teaching. His discussion of the virtue of fear discusses the distinction between the "fear of servants" (based on fear of punishment) and the "fear of sons" (based on love). Likewise, his treatment of prayer offers a typology. All prayer is categorized as either thanksgiving or petition (either for ourselves or others). His analysis of the love of God is concerned to explain why love is the greatest virtue, even above faith and hope: it has superior breadth (since it is extended even to God and enemies) and superior length (since it is continued even in heaven). The virtue of "true religion" is explained as involving several of what we would call the "spiritual disciplines" of the Protestant tradition: reading the Scriptures, prayer, giving alms, and fasting. His discussion of "thou shalt have no other gods" makes an important pastoral distinction between the Christian calling to exercise perseverance ("the tediousness of long delay") and the duty of patience ("the sorrow of bearing the cross"). What we are seeing is virtue-centered, theologically orthodox Anglican moral theology in the making.

Another feature of his treatment of the First Commandment clearly marks out his discussion as an example of moral theology. He is concerned to give a theological account of moral action. This has three parts. First, he emphasizes that "the fruit of love is obedience, whereby we conform ourselves and our wills to God's will, and willingly bear and undergo whatsoever it pleaseth Him to lay upon us" (*PCD*, 84). His point is that an authentic moral action must be in obedience to God's law, but that something more than external conformity is required for virtuous action. The interior source of obedience is love for God, a love nurtured by the core practices of Christian piety, especially prayer. Andrewes does not accept the reduction of Christian ethics to the question of

33. *PCD*, 93.

obligation. Rather, he shows how obligation to God's law forms part of the pursuit of Christian virtue.

Second, Andrewes takes up a central concern of moral theology by describing the conditions that constitute the moral goodness of actions. He states, "The law is *doctrina agendorum*; every action must be with a motion, every motion with a will, will with a desire, desire with knowledge; therefore take away knowledge, and take away all" (*PCD*, 85).[34] This somewhat cryptic statement deserves analysis. The divinely revealed moral law—here, the Decalogue and its "extensions"—constitutes "a teaching of things that should be done." There is a clear sense of moral obligation here: the law is not a list of suggestions, but the doctrine of what must be done. He assumes that good moral action in obedience to God's law is performed deliberately and freely through the agent's exercise of will and reason. From the standpoint of the agent's interiority, there must be motivation to pursue and do the good. He appears to be saying: moral action is a matter of choice, which involves the exercise of the will, which itself is oriented by the pursuit of a desire (some perceived or apparent good), which in turn is rightly determined by knowledge (i.e., knowledge of the moral good in the divine law). All of these factors—will, desire, and knowledge—must be aligned toward a good end in order for the action to be good. Moreover, there is a primacy of knowledge (rather than will) in the process of action: "take away knowledge, take away all." From the external or objective standpoint of the evaluation of the content of the action, the judgment of reason is decisive, verifying that the action conforms to God's law. Without the agent's knowledge of the law, there can be no interiority orientation of the self in conformity to its demands and no objective measure of the content of moral action. While Andrewes does not include an extended philosophical discussion of these distinctions, nor does he engage the medieval background on this topic, he seems closest to the position of Aquinas and the intellectualist tradition rather than Scotus and the voluntarists.

Third, "To our knowledge we must add practice, for as in the anatomy the veins come from the heart to the hands, so in divinity the life of that which is in the heart is practiced in the hand" (*PCD*, 86). This statement reflects a deep current in Andrewes's writings. Despite his strong emphasis on the centrality of knowing the content of the moral law, the real point is doing what it says. Knowledge of the law is meant to be practical knowledge, not speculative knowledge. Obedience to God's law is meant to arise from the harmonious interaction of the heart (our transformed desires), mind (understanding the content of God's demand) and hand (in faithful action in the world). In this way, Andrewes expresses what virtually every commentator has noticed about the Decalogue, namely, its comprehensive scope in ordering every aspect of human life by addressing itself to heart, mind, intention, speech and action. In keeping with the classical Christian tradition of exposition, Andrewes sees the Decalogue

---

34. I am grateful to my colleague Dr. Michael Graves for clarifying the Latin translation here.

as putting forward a vision of "the ideal religious person" who embodies faithfulness to God in all its varied dimensions.

FOURTH COMMANDMENT

In Andrewes's organizational scheme, the Sabbath commandment concludes the first table of the Decalogue. He emphasizes that "sanctifying is the end, and is chiefly aimed at" whereas "rest is a subordinate end, and conduceth to our sanctifying the Lord's day aright" (*PCD*, 156). Andrewes's discussion of the relationship between sanctification and rest takes us to the heart of his exposition. He reminds his readers that the Sabbath was set apart in Eden, before sin entered the world. The command comes to finite creatures, for whom "if two things are done at once, one part of our thoughts will be taken from the other, we cannot wholly intend two things at once" (*MLE*, 328). God instituted the Sabbath "for a remedy against distraction to be intended to any other use, especially in the solemn worship of the Lord; that takes up the whole man, and necessarily suffereth no distraction." The first three commandments call us to wholehearted worship of God, with mind, soul, and body, bringing all of what we are and have before God. Such worship is made possible and protected by the keeping of the Sabbath. What we need as a "remedy against distraction" is rest; the "total solemn sanctification" means ceasing entirely from daily labor, in order to focus exclusively on the Lord. He clarifies that the reason for this commandment is not that our everyday works are evil, "but onely [sic] because they distract the minde; and would not suffer the whole man, wholly to intend the workes of the Sabbath" (*MLE*, 338).

Andrewes goes on to argue for a very strict observance of the day of rest. This fact alone does not qualify him a Puritan sympathizer early in his career, yet he argues that the Sabbath is not a day for "revel or riot" (no shows, stage-plays, dancing).[35] But he makes the point that "an idle rest" is not adequate either. He asks, "is it enough that we put on our best clothing and do nothing?" Andrewes answers that this sort of attitude befits "the Sabbath of oxen and asses" and that bodily rest profits little. The right keeping of Sabbath involves prayer, diligent use of God's word (reading or hearing it privately, hearing it publicly, searching the Scriptures, pondering its truths in our hearts, and conferring with others about the Word) and thanksgiving (in corporate worship, including receiving the Eucharist). Andrewes also recognizes that "those good works which tend to the practice of holiness are to be done on the Sabbath day, and are also a part of our sanctification of the Sabbath; namely, works of mercy, outward and inward." Here Andrewes deals extensively with New Testament texts, and especially the

---

35. Contra M. M. Knappen, "The Early Puritanism of Lancelot Andrewes," *Church History* 2 (1933). It is also worth noting that Andrewes never showed any sympathy for the Presbyterian form of church government.

example of Jesus, who pointedly heals on the Sabbath. Showing his traditionalist bent, Andrewes affirms the propriety of engaging in the traditional seven works of corporal mercy (drawn from Matt. 25:34–35) and the seven works of spiritual mercy (except his discussion of prayer omits prayer for the dead).[36]

What is most important, and possibly original, about Andrewes's treatment of this commandment is his argument that the Sabbath precept is part of the moral law (and therefore permanent) rather than ceremonial law. First, he claims that the Sabbath commandment cannot be a ceremony, because it was given in Eden, before there was any sin, and so before there was any need of a Savior, or any figure of a Savior. Ceremonies have to do with salvation, yet the Sabbath commandment was pre-fall, and so must not be a ceremony. Second, he claims from Deuteronomy 6:13–14 that "the law came immediately from God, the ceremonies were instituted by Moses." That means that all the Decalogue is entirely law without any ceremonies. Third, since no one doubts that the other nine commandments are moral, why would God put one ceremonial precept in the middle of the list? Fourth, he argues: "This is a principle, that the Decalogue is the law of nature revived, and the law of nature is the image of God; now in God there can be no ceremony, but all must be eternal; and so in this image, which is the law of nature; and so in the Decalogue; whereas a ceremony is . . . 'a matter only to endure for a time'" (*PCD*, 154). It is traditional teaching that the Decalogue "revives" the natural law. Unfortunately, Andrewes nowhere elaborates extensively on this theological principle. Fifth, he argues from the New Testament that "all ceremonies were ended in Christ; but so was not the Sabbath" since in Matthew 24:20 Jesus prays that the day of their visitation would not be on the Sabbath, implying that there would still be a Sabbath after Christ's own death. Hence, it must be an enduring reality, not a ceremony. Sixth, he argues that in New Testament times "those which were ceremonies were abrogated" (by Christ's death and resurrection) and not changed, whereas "those which were not ceremonies were changed." Thus, the change of day to the Lord's Day was not the church's changing of a ceremony, but revision of the enduring moral law in a new situation.

FIFTH COMMANDMENT

Andrewes's exposition of the commandment, "Honor your father and mother," runs to forty pages in *PCD*. Perhaps surprisingly, less than two pages of this exposition actually deal with issues concerning the relations of actual parents and their children. The reason why is that Andrewes takes up a long-standing

36. The seven works of corporal mercy are to feed the hungry, give drink to the thirsty, clothe the naked, shelter the homeless, visit the sick, visit those in prison, and bury the dead. The traditional seven works of spiritual mercy are to convert the sinner, instruct the ignorant, counsel the doubtful, comfort the sorrowful, bear wrongs patiently, forgive injuries, and pray for the living and the dead.

Christian tradition of interpreting this commandment very broadly, as extended to address the whole range of Christian social relationships. On this line, the commandment is primarily about the relations of superiors to inferiors—parents and children are just one example of that wider interest. Elsewhere, he claims that the commandment states a general precept (our duty to all our elders and superiors) and a particular precept (our duty to our natural parents).[37]

In this order, he takes up rulers and ruled (in general terms, including the issue of whether obedience is required to wicked rulers); husbands and wives; parents and children; masters and servants; teachers and hearers; ministers and congregants; kings and subjects; how to relate to people of unusual "excellency" (of mind, in the form of outstanding intellect; of body, in the form of old age; or of estate, in the case of those of nobility and wealth); and, finally, benefactors and patrons.[38]

He begins with discussion of this commandment by saying, "God hath not made all men alike, but hath made some partakers of His excellency, and set them in superior place; others of a meaner degree, and set them in a lower place; that mutual society might be maintained" (*PCD*, 174). Andrewes's way of handling this commandment makes sense when located in a distinctly hierarchical conception of the social relations. The logic behind this extension of the scope of the commandment depends to a considerable extent on conceptual and verbal links with the word "father." Magistrates and others in authority are called "fathers" and so he extends the application to all forms of earthly superiors. He defines the word "father" (Hebrew, *abba*) used in the commandment as meaning "he that hath a care or desire to do good, so that he is a father by whom others are in any better estate" (*PCD*, 175). This means to honor them is to "add an excellency" or "add estimation" to them.

With this in mind, Andrewes begins in very general terms. There are two duties common to inferiors and superiors: love, and "to wish well to whom we love." Then, he addresses the duties of inferiors: to honor (with our good opinion, with outward honors such as rising up in their presence, uncovering one's head, bowing the knee, being silent when they speak, using words of submission), fear and obey one's superiors. Next he spells out the general duties of superiors: they must recognize their office as being from God and that they are God's ministers; to use their authority to "nourish and cherish those that are under them"; to maintain the social hierarchy established by God (*PCD*, 180).

Next, he turns to "the manner of their government." Here we find a richly moral conception of the use of authority. He explains that superiors must always be concerned with "walking uprightly" and being an example of their people; not to deal cruelly, but to use moderation, to avoid a "proud manner" marked by "contumelious words and tyrannous deeds." In this context he cites Psalm

---

37. Lancelot Andrewes, *Holy Devotions*, 455–457.

38. This same approach is found in the most widely used English Protestant catechism of the era written in 1570 by Alexander Nowell.

82, a chapter that speaks of the king as someone who defends the cause of the weak and fatherless, maintains the rights of the poor and oppressed, rescues the weak and needy, and delivers them from the hand of the wicked. This text is a critical part of Andrewes's moral vision of authority in all social relationships. Superiors of all kinds are morally obligated to do good for inferiors. They are to govern or rule or teach entirely for the benefit of those under their care.

A clear example is his treatment of the relationship between masters and servants. Andrewes emphasizes just treatment of servants. The master's commands must be lawful, and not only lawful but also possible. They must be given for a good purpose and must be "proportionate to time, place and person." All this is a way of saying that the vulnerability of servants must not be exploited. In addition, masters are not to be "sharp and bitter" toward them and should "provide them meat, drink, and clothes, or wages agreed upon." Similarly, Andrewes emphasizes that magistrates, as "fathers of the country" are to be "shepherds" that feed their people and protect them from harm. Likewise, a king's duty is to do justice and to be "humble and meek" in ruling.

In this context, he spells out the relations of parents and children in five highly conventional duties. Parents have the duty to reproduce; to nourish and provide materially for their children; to bring them up in the Lord, "that they may be Christians"; to set a high example and provide correction, as needed; and to pray for their children. Children have corresponding duties: to honor and serve their parents, to deal honestly with them, to receive instruction and correction, and to imitate their good example. Having said so much about the right use of authority and the right honoring of superiors, one gets the sense that Andrewes has very little left to say that applies specifically to parents, apart from their spiritual nurture of children.

By interpreting the Fifth Commandment largely in terms of a general precept to honor all superiors, it becomes a way for Andrewes to teach a fairly comprehensive Christian social ethic. Obedience to authority is the premiere social virtue. He emphasizes a highly pastoral conception of authority, wherein superiors are "shepherds" who are to care for, guide and protect inferiors, and the flock has a strong reciprocal duty of obedience toward their superiors.

CONCLUSION

Our study provides ample evidence for Chapman's judgment: "The genius of Andrewes was to combine learning and devotion in powerful teaching of the faith and its practical implications."[39] Andrewes positions the Decalogue at the center of the Christian spiritual and moral life that involves the pursuit of holiness and virtue that transcends mere conformity to God's law. His treatment

39. Raymond Chapman, introduction, in *Before the King's Majesty: Lancelot Andrewes and His Writings* (London: Canterbury Press, 2008), 8.

of the Ten Commandments emphasizes the so-called third use of God's law: guidance for Christians who seek godliness in daily life. What we have seen is traditional Anglicanism doing its characteristic work of applying a robust biblical theology to the pastoral needs of its time. His famous *Private Prayers* incorporates the Decalogue into the regular pattern of personal confession and petition, and his catechetical lectures interpret the Ten Commandments as "the true *Ethica Christiana*, Christian Ethicks, passing all other Ethicks" (*MLE*, 74). Moreover, his interpretation of the Decalogue is the first systematic exposition of the Christian moral life undertaken in the Anglican tradition, a pioneering and foundational document for the development of Anglican moral theology by writers of subsequent generations.

Chapter 10

John Wesley

D. STEPHEN LONG

In 1789, toward the end of his life, John Wesley wrote straightforwardly against the Enlightenment humanism he saw making vast inroads in European culture. His explicit rejection of such humanism should have produced much more reticence if not explicit denials that Wesley was a modern, Enlightenment thinker. Alas, the guild of Wesley studies continues unabated to make him one of the first modern theologians whose work is readily accessible to us because it is, or can be made, relevant to Enlightenment thought.[1] I find this unconvincing. In fact, Wesley may actually share something in common with certain postmodern thinkers: antihumanism. But this is not because like them he fears that humanism is one more metanarrative that seeks a metaphysical closure by replacing God with another objective signifier, this time "humanity." Wesley would agree that "humanity" cannot take the place of God, but this is not because he feared metanarratives. The reason Wesley cannot be rendered relevant to Enlightenment humanism is because of his interpretation of the Ten Commandments.

1. For example, see Kevin Twain Lowery, *Salvaging Wesley's Agenda: A New Paradigm for Wesleyan Virtue Ethics* (Eugene, OR: Pickwick Publications, 2008), Ronald H. Stone, *John Wesley's Life and Ethics* (Nashville: Abingdon, 2001), Theodore Runyon, *The New Creation: John Wesley's Theology Today* (Nashville: Abingdon, 1998).

Any humanism that truly advocates love of neighbor cannot be successful without love of God; the two sets of duties in the Ten Commandments, duties to God and duties to neighbor, are inextricably linked. One set could not be satisfied without observing the other. For Wesley, you cannot love your neighbor with a genuine humanism if you do not love God; for God is the neighbor's true end. For this reason, theology and ethics are inseparable.

In 1789 as he rightly discerned the emergence of western secular humanism, he diagnosed it based on his interpretation of the Ten Commandments, and found it more than wanting. He wrote,

> . . . how great is the number of those who allowing religion to consist of two branches, our duty to God and our duty to our neighbour, entirely forget the first part and put the second part for the whole, for the entire duty of man. Thus almost all men of letters, both in England, France and Germany, yea and all the civilized countries of Europe, extol "humanity" to the skies, as the very essence of religion. To this the great triumvirate, Rousseau, Voltaire and David Hume, have contributed all their labours, sparing no pains to establish a religion which should stand on its own foundation, independent on any revelation whatever, yea, not supposing even the being of a God. So leaving him, if he has any being, to himself, they have found out both a religion and a happiness which have no relation at all to God, nor any dependence upon him. It is no wonder that this religion should grow fashionable, and spread far and wide in the world. But call it "humanity," "virtue," "morality," or what you please, it is neither better nor worse than atheism. Men hereby willfully and designedly put asunder what God has joined, the duties of the first and the second table. It is separating the love of our neighbour from the love of God.[2]

For Wesley then, the rise of secular humanism results from failing to heed the wisdom of the Ten Commandments. Humanism without God fails because it cannot adequately account for love of neighbor. Interestingly, Wesley here anticipates arguments made after the triumph of humanism, albeit much less polemically, by Henri de Lubac and Charles Taylor.[3] They, too, argue that an exclusive humanism too easily loses the very thing it seeks to preserve by closing itself off from any transcendent source. Like them, what Wesley shares in common with postmodern antihumanism is at best minimal: nothing more than a recognition of the failure of an exclusive humanism. They would all share a sensibility that "exclusive humanism"—love of neighbor—cut off from something beyond itself, fails finally to serve humanism itself. But this should not imply that Wesley, or de Lubac or Taylor, would then give up on a Christian version of the humanist project.

    2. John Wesley, Sermon 120, "The Unity of the Divine Being," §20, in *The Works of John Wesley*, vol. 4, ed. Albert C. Outler, (Nashville, Abingdon, 1987), 69. All references hereafter to Wesley's sermons come from this Outler edition and will be designated as *Works* with volume and page number.
    3. See Charles Taylor, *A Secular Age* (Cambridge, MA: Harvard University Press, 2007). Henri de Lubac, *The Drama of Atheist Humanism* (San Francisco: Ignatius Press, 1995).

Wesley polemicized against anyone who would seek humanism without God. He wrote, "We know that as all nature, so all religion and all happiness depend on him; and we know that whoever teach to seek happiness without him are monsters and the pests of society."[4] To seek happiness in the human without God creates a monstrous and pestilential society. Perhaps Wesley saw something that was coming, the horrors that this kind of humanism produced in the next few centuries. But if the two tables of the Law are kept in relation to each other, a genuine humanism—love of neighbor for the neighbor's sake—can be preserved. Wesley also had a place for this kind of humanism. He stated, "From this principle [love of God] springs real, disinterested benevolence to all mankind . . ."[5] The relation between the two tables of the Ten Commandments preserves the possibility for a true love of neighbor. We love God so that we can love humanity. Love of humanity, if it is true, will direct us to love God.

This Christian humanism found in Wesley's interpretation of the Ten Commandments not only brings together the two tables of the Decalogue, it also brings into close proximity the Law and the gospel. In fact, as we shall see, Wesley does not shy away from equating Jesus and the Torah. This entails a strong anti-Lutheran and anti- (late) Scholastic impulse in his theology. The anti-Lutheranism is found in his rejection of the law/gospel distinction. As he put it in a sermon on the Sermon on the Mount, "there is no contrariety at all between the law and the gospel; that there is no need for the law to pass away in order to the establishing of the gospel. Indeed neither of them supersedes the other but they agree perfectly well together."[6] The anti-Scholastic impulse is found in his rejection that the Ten Commandments are a natural law known universally albeit independently of the gospel. For Wesley the Ten are the *revelation* of the natural law all creatures should know but no longer do because of sin. They are a revelation that illumines what our nature should be and brings it to perfection. He refers to the Ten as a "light." But in order to be properly illumined by this light the revelation in Jesus will also be necessary.

Wesley, like many of the church fathers and medieval theologians, juxtaposes two mountains: Mount Sinai where God gives the Law to Moses and the mountain where Jesus brings the Law to fulfillment in his sermon. These two mountains must be seen together or we will not see God well. For Wesley, to bring these two mountains together and set the latter over the former like a palimpsest, is the essence of religion. He asks, "What is religion?" and answers, "it is love which 'is the fulfilling of the law,' 'the end of the commandment.'"[7] The blessed life Jesus pronounces on the mountain fulfills the law God gave Moses. But this account of "true religion" raises two important questions. If religion is love fulfilling the law, what does he mean by law and how is it fulfilled? We will examine each in turn.

4. *Works*, 4:70.
5. Ibid.
6. Ibid., 1:554.
7. Ibid., 3:189.

WHAT IS MEANT BY "LAW"?

First, what does he mean by "law"? This is not easily determined. He does not mean the specific statutes in the Old Testament, whether they are ten or 613 specific commandments. These commandments are not to be neglected, and Wesley offers extensive commentary on them. But he is no restorationist seeking a literal return to Old Testament law. We can gain insight into what Wesley meant by "law" through observing how he interpreted the act of creation in Genesis 1, the giving of the Law in Exodus and Leviticus, and the article of Religion on the law found in the Anglican and Methodist articles.

Law: the Light of Creation

For Wesley, the Law is present in God's act of creation as "Light." He writes, "The first of all visible things which God created was *light*, the great beauty and blessing of the universe. Like the firstborn, it does, of all visible beings, most resemble its great parent in purity and power, brightness and beneficence."[8] Now when we recognize that both the Ten Commandments and Jesus are interpreted as "light," this interpretation of Genesis 1 becomes truly significant. For this reference to *light* as the "firstborn" as that which "resembles its parent" is a Trinitarian reference. The "Light" on the first day of creation is the image of the Second Person of the Trinity that illumines all of God's creative activity.

When Wesley explains the light created on the first day, we are compelled to see it in christological terms. "He said, *Let there be light*. He willed it, and it was done; *there was light*. Such a copy as exactly answered the original in the eternal mind. *God saw the light, that it was good*. It was exactly as he designed it; and it was fit to answer the end for which he designed it."[9] This, of course, is no reference to the sun, which was not created until the fourth day. It is something other than that. The expression, "the original idea in the eternal mind" was how medieval theology described the "eternal law" in which the "natural law" was a "participation." The essence of the natural law was "do good and avoid evil." The eternal law, as the "original idea in the eternal mind," was usually considered to be a christological reference. So the natural law was understood to be a participation in the eternal law, who is Christ. The "Light" in Genesis 1 then is best understood within this christological context of the relation between the eternal and natural law. The light, because it is made, cannot be Christ, but it is the "law" that illumines all of creation and should help us discern the difference between good and evil. It is a copy of the "original" in the divine mind.

We see this confirmed when Wesley comments on the other creation story in Scripture, John 1. He states that Jesus is the "light" who is "the giver of life

---

8. John Wesley, *Wesley's Notes on the Bible*, G. Roger Schoenhals, ed. (Grand Rapids, MI: Zondervan Publishing House, 1987), 21. This source will be referred to hereafter as *Wesley Notes* along with the page number.

9. *Wesley Notes*, 21.

to all that lives . . . the fountain of wisdom, holiness and happiness to man in his original state."[10] The expression "holiness and happiness" is Wesley's moral teleology; for they are the ends for which creation exists. In the "original state," before the fall, Jesus is the light that gives wisdom, holiness and happiness, which are the human creatures' *teloi*. Wesley states that this light is "vulgarly termed 'natural conscience.'" It "[points] out at least the general lines of good and evil. And this light, if man did not hinder, would shine more and more to the perfect day."[11] Note then what the light does. It differentiates good from evil.

Wesley then reads Genesis 1 and John 1 together. The light in John 1 is Jesus, and in Genesis it is a copy of him that should have allowed creatures to discern good from evil and attain the end for which they were created, happiness and holiness. So far this much should be clear. But how is this light related to the Ten Commandments? To see that we will need to examine Wesley's interpretation of the giving of the law to Moses; for it, too, is an image of the "Light."

Giving of Law in Exodus

For Wesley the commandments are tacitly present in creation itself via the "Light" created on the first day. Sin then obscures this "Light" and the Ten Commandments are the revelation that first seeks to reinstate it and illumine our lives so that we might discern good and evil. In an important sermon entitled, "The Original, Nature, Properties, and Use of the Law," Wesley once again makes reference to this "Light," relating it to creation, Christology and the Ten Commandments. The argument is straightforward. The light given in creation to Adam and Eve should have sufficed. But sin eclipsed it. Wesley states, "But notwithstanding this light, all flesh had in process of time 'corrupted their way before him' . . ." So what does God do? God "chose out of mankind a peculiar people, to whom he gave a more perfect knowledge of his law. And the heads of this, because they were slow of understanding, he wrote on two tablets of stone which he commanded the fathers to teach their children through succeeding generations. And thus it is that the law of God is now made known to them that know not God."[12]

For Wesley, the Ten Commandments given to Moses and Israel are not coextensive with the law; they are "the heads," law written on two tablets of stone. What is the "law" then? The law is fundamentally God's self-expression by which God enters into covenant with creation, with his chosen people and with the church. The law is a divine communication by which we can "communicate" or participate in and with God. It is the light that is to illumine God's creation as the exact imprint of the triune procession of the Son.

10. Ibid., 454.
11. Ibid.
12. *Works*, 2:7–8.

Most important to Wesley's interpretation of the Ten Commandments is what inaugurates them in Exodus 20:1, "God spoke all these words," on which Wesley comments,

> The law of the Ten Commandments is a law of God's making, a law of his own speaking. God has many ways of speaking to the children of men by his Spirit: conscience, providence; his voice in all which we ought carefully to attend to. But he never spoke at any time upon any occasion so as he spoke the Ten Commandments, which therefore we ought to hear with "the more earnest heed." This law God has given to man before, it was written in his heart by nature. But sin had so defaced that writing that it was necessary to revive the knowledge of it.[13]

Wesley then focuses less on the content of the Ten Commandments, as important as that is, and more on the fact that this is God's speech. God's speech also created, so we should have known how to live into God simply by our created nature illumined by the light of God, but this did not suffice. The Ten are given as a form of revelation or illumination, another mode of God's speech to clarify what we have lost. But that also did not suffice. In order to clarify or illumine God's communication completely he reveals the Son, the transfigured illumination of God's own glory who, like the "Light" on the first day, illumines our way to know the good and avoid evil.

In his sermon "The Original, Nature, Properties, and Use of the Law," Wesley explains the gift of the Ten to Moses in startling christological terms. "Now this law is an incorruptible picture of the high and holy One that inhabiteth eternity. . . . It is the face of God unveiled. . . . Yea, in some sense we may apply to this law what the Apostle says of his Son—it is 'the streaming forth' or out-beaming 'of his glory, the express image of his person.'"[14] Here we see the same language used to explain the Law as we saw used in his commentary on Genesis 1 to explain the "Light" on the first day of creation. Now the Law is said to be "in some sense" the Son himself. Wesley goes on to explain this more fully:

> The law of God is all virtues in one, in such a shape as to be beheld with open face by all those whose eyes God hath enlightened. What is the law but divine virtue and wisdom assuming a visible form? What is it but the original ideas of truth and good, which were lodged in the uncreated mind from eternity, now drawn forth and clothed with such a vehicle as to appear even to human understanding.[15]

The law has taken a "visible form." Jesus is the Torah. If we are to see the law, we must look to him.

This is far from any Lutheran law/gospel dialectic. Wesley draws on themes readily found in patristic and medieval sources. Jesus does not overcome the Law;

---

13. *Wesley Notes*, 77.
14. *Works*, 2:9.
15. Ibid., 2:9–10.

he fulfills it. The Law is not primarily negative. It is not prohibitive; it is permissive. It was not only given as a response to sin. The commandments order our lives even in innocence. In fact Wesley finds evidence of the commandments in creation long before the sin of Adam and Eve. So in his commentary on Genesis 2 he wrote, "The sabbath and marriage were two ordinances instituted in innocency; the former for the preservation of the church, the latter for the preservation of mankind."[16] The relation between Adam and Eve prior to sin already form two social relations by which we commune with God and that are found in the two different tables of the Law. The church is present in Adam and Eve as they rest on the Sabbath Day and observe an essential commandment from the first table that orders their love toward God. They keep the Sabbath. Their sexual fidelity fulfills an essential commandment from the second table that orders their love toward each other and extends it outwards to all of humanity. The "law" is God's own self-communication; first given to Adam and Eve. It is originally intrinsic to nature, to creation, then disclosed to Moses and made manifest to anyone who has been "enlightened" in Jesus. So what does this say about the specifics of the Law?

LAW IN THE ARTICLES OF RELIGION AND GENERAL RULES

For Wesley we are not to observe all the commandments found in the Old Testament, but neither are we to violate them at will. How do we know which ones we are to observe and which to abandon? I think we find two ways Wesley helps us discern which laws are binding and which are not. The first comes from Scripture as it is interpreted through the Anglican Articles of Religion. The second is unique to the Wesleyan movement and is found in the General Rules.

In the seventh Article, titled "Of the Old Testament," the Anglican church taught,

> The Old Testament is not contrary to the New; for both in the Old and New Testament everlasting life is offered to mankind by Christ, who is the only Mediator between God and man, being both God and Man. Wherefore they are not to be heard who feign that the old fathers did look only for transitory promises. Although the law given from God by Moses as touching ceremonies and rites doth not bind Christians, nor ought the civil precepts thereof of necessity be received in any commonwealth; yet notwithstanding, no Christian whatsoever is free from the obedience of the commandments which are called moral.[17]

This same article was retained in the twenty-five articles binding on the Methodists.

16. *Wesley Notes,* 26.
17. Mark A. Noll, ed., *Confessions and Catechisms of the Reformation* (Grand Rapids: Baker, 1991), 216.

It makes a threefold distinction in the Law that can also be found in Calvin and Aquinas: the Law is ceremonial, civil, or moral. There are those laws that touch on ceremonies, such as what you should eat and what you shouldn't, and whether or not males should be circumcised. These ceremonial laws are no longer in effect for Christians. Peter's vision in Acts 10 and Paul's mission to the Gentiles led to a rereading of these obligations. Christians are permitted to eat all things, and they need not be circumcised. In fact, baptism replaces circumcision as the "ceremonial" obligation imposed on Christians

There are also "civil precepts" that provide legal obligations for how God's people should love such as Sabbath observance or the jubilee year in Leviticus 25. These civil precepts may still be obligatory for Christians, but they are not to be imposed any particular nation or state. We need not force the Ten Commandments on the nation-state's judicial system. But the moral laws, the laws that allow us to discern good and evil, will lead to happiness and holiness and they are to be observed.

Wesley used this threefold distinction when he commented on Leviticus 27:34, "These are the commandments, which the Lord commanded Moses for the children of Israel in mount Sinai" (KJV). Wesley wrote,

> This has reference to the whole book. Many of these commandments are moral; others ceremonial and peculiar to the Jewish economy; which yet are instructive to us who have a key to the mysteries that are contained in them. Upon the whole we have cause to bless God that we are not come to Mount Sinai, that we are not under the shadows of the law, but enjoy the clear light of the gospel. The doctrine of our reconciliation to God by a Mediator is not clouded with the smoke of burning sacrifices, but cleared by the knowledge of "Christ and him crucified.[18]

The reference to Mount Sinai and the "shadow" of the law is a reference to Hebrews 12. The theophanic light on Mount Sinai was so overwhelming that it occluded vision. It was a terrifying light, which is nonetheless God's gracious communication. For that reason even the ceremonial laws and those "peculiar to the Jewish economy" are "instructive," but now they are so in "the clear light of the gospel." It does not supersede them, but helps us read them properly. Jesus is the key that helps us discern these mysteries. For Wesley, Jesus does this in the Sermon on the Mount. The "Beatitudes" fulfill the law by demonstrating to us what a blessed life, a life of wisdom, happiness and holiness, is. The Beatitudes do not render the law void; they complete it. For this reason, Wesley gave to the Methodists "General Rules."

The General Rules of the Methodist people are the first precept of the natural law. They are: "do no harm," "do good" and "attend upon the ordinances of God." Each of these rules has contained within it a subset that helped the Methodist people discern what laws remained binding upon them. Some of these are

---

18. *Wesley Notes*, 112–13.

repetitions of the Ten Commandments, such as "do no harm such as the taking of the name of God in vain," or "such as profaning the day of the Lord, either by doing ordinary work therein or by buying or selling."[19] Still others can be understood as more specific interpretations of the commandments. Given the practice of slavery in Wesley's day, the general rule for Methodists to do no harm such as "slaveholding: buying or selling slaves" could certainly be understood as a practical observation of the Sixth (or Fifth) Commandment: "Thou shalt not kill." Other rules come from the Gospels. What is interesting is that Wesley gave Methodists these rules and then called them, "the righteousness of a Pharisee" as well as "the religion of the world."[20] What did he mean by this? These rules were what the Pharisees and those who were observant should know. The Methodists were to obey them, but they were not ends in themselves. The bare observance of the Law did not make one a Christian. The Law, like the General Rules, was a means not an end. The end was "the religion of the heart." It fulfilled the law.

HOW IS THE LAW FULFILLED?

The law is fulfilled by faith produced in Christ's body—the church—the religion of the heart. It is not some warm-hearted existential experience. It is not an "internal" matter separate from the externals of the Law. The religion of the heart is the life Jesus pronounced as blessed, a life determined by the Beatitudes. For this reason, the key to the Law is in the Sermon on the Mount. Here Jesus is presented to us in a manner very similar to Moses. As Moses was receiving the Law on the mount, so Jesus is giving the purpose of the Law on the mount. For Christians, these are not two distinct events that can be divided from each other. The Law given to Moses is God's mediation of God's wisdom and will to creation. In the Sermon on the Mount, Jesus faces toward us giving us the fulfillment of the Law in a life of blessedness. That he faces us rather than turns away from us as Moses did, bears witness to who Jesus is.

Before he begins to explain the importance of the religion of the heart as disclosed in the Sermon on the Mount, Wesley states the importance of recognizing who it is that is speaking: "Let us observe who it is that is here speaking that we may 'take heed how we hear'. . . . It speaks the Creator of all—a God, a God appears! Yea, [the One Who Is], the being of all beings, Jehovah, the self-existent, the supreme, the God who is over all, blessed for ever."[21] God spoke at creation, mediated through the light. That light became obscured. God spoke to Moses, whose face was veiled because of the light of God's glory. But now, God speaks in Jesus, who is the very glory of God, Light of Light, true God of

---

19. The General Rules are found in the *United Methodist Book of Discipline* where they are theoretically, albeit not in practice, binding upon Methodists to this day.

20. *Works*, 1:565–67. For a fuller discussion of this see D. Stephen Long, *John Wesley's Moral Theology* (Nashville: Kingswood, 2005), chap. 4.

21. *Works*, 1:474.

true God, the one who bears the Name. In so doing, God speaks and gives us the purpose of the Law. It is found in "beatitude" or happiness. In the Sermon on the Mount, Jesus pronounces certain ways of life blessed. These are the eight Beatitudes. Throughout the Christian tradition, these Beatitudes were correlated with the gifts of the Holy Spirit to give us a sense of what the Christian life should look like.

The Beatitudes are: poverty of spirit, meekness, mourning, righteousness, mercifulness, purity of heart, peaceableness, and persecution for the sake of righteousness. The gifts are fear, piety, knowledge, fortitude, counsel, understanding, and wisdom. Many great theologians of the church, such as Augustine and Thomas Aquinas, correlated the first seven Beatitudes with the first seven gifts. Wesley did something quite similar. This helps us understand why these good works are the "fruit" of the Holy Spirit. They are not first and foremost our own works; we cannot produce them by ourselves. They are the "fruit" of our communication with God and our neighbor, a communion the Holy Spirit effects in our lives and that fulfills the Law.

In the Sermon on the Mount, Jesus shows us the goal of the Christian life. This is the form of life he will bless on the Last Day. It was not prohibitive— a mere "thou shalt not" that always assumed we secretly desire something to which God as the pleasure police says "No!" The Law is there to communicate God's life to us. It takes visible form in Jesus. We see this also in Wesley's commentary on Matthew 5 where he wrote,

> To bless men, to make men happy, was the great business for which our Lord came into the world. And accordingly he here pronounces eight blessings together, annexing them to so may steps in Christianity. Knowing that happiness is our common aim, and that an innate instinct continually urges us to the pursuit of it, he in the kindest manner applies to that instinct and directs it to its proper object. Though all men desire, yet few attain happiness, because they seek it where it is not to be found.[22]

Law directs human acts to the blessedness of the Sermon on the Mount. The Beatitudes show us what the law intended.

True faith then lives the law and in so doing "sanctifies" God's name on earth. This is our most basic prayer, "Our Father, who art in heaven, hallowed be your Name." To hallow God's name is to sanctify it. This is done by living in accordance with God's wisdom and will. It is obedient love, which is "to love God with all our hearts and to walk in his holy commandments blameless" as the Methodist article on sanctification states. I think this is why Wesley ordered his sermons as he did. Before he gave us three sermons on the law, he wrote thirteen discourses on the Sermon on the Mount. They set forth "the religion of the heart" and allow us to discern how the law still binds. In fact, when Wesley explains why he wrote and published his sermons, he gave us a key for

---

22. *Wesley Notes*, 407.

understanding how to relate the Law and the gospel. In the 1746 preface to his Sermons he stated,

> And herein it is more especially my desire, first, to guard those who are just setting their faces toward heaven (and who, having little acquaintance with the things of God, are the more liable to be turned out of the way) from formality, from mere outside religion, which has almost driven heart-religion out of the world; and secondly, to warn those who know the religion of the heart, the faith which worketh by love, lest at any time they make void the law through faith, and so fall back into the snare of the devil[23]

"Mere outside religion" is the religion of the world, or the righteousness of a Pharisee. It is the bare observance of the commands as if they were ends in themselves or primarily prohibitive. This is one concern Wesley had during his day. He guarded against a "formality" in the Christian life. This would be pure ceremony where we think that the mere outward observance of the law is sufficient. We could refrain from violating it and yet still fail to fulfill it. This would be insufficient; nothing but a "mere" observance, a religion of the world. But nor is it sufficient to think that once we have the religion of the heart, we can do without the Law. Thus Wesley has a second concern that those who claim to know the religion of the heart do not "make void the law through faith, and so fall back into the snare of the devil." The freedom of a Christian did not mean that the Law was now void. Instead it is a necessary albeit insufficient means to the end, the end being the life of blessedness that happiness and holiness characterizes.

On the one hand, we should not make the commandments ends in themselves and follow them literally or slavishly. Then we have mere formality. On the other hand, we should not think that once we have the religion of the heart we no longer need law and are free to disregard it.

Let me conclude with an example as to how faith fulfills the law. Imagine I have a difficult neighbor, and I wake up every day debating whether or not I should kill my neighbor. I do a cost-benefit analysis weighing the benefits I would receive from the costs. If I kill my neighbor, he will no longer be able to annoy me. But there will be costs. I might be sent to jail, which would end my career as a professional religious person. So after weighing the costs against the benefits I decide not to kill my neighbor. Then the question arises, Have I kept the Law? Have I kept the Sixth Commandment—"Thou shalt not kill?" The answer is yes and no. Yes, I kept the law in a purely formal manner. I did not do the thing I wanted to do. I did not kill my neighbor. If someone decided to keep the law only in this purely formal manner and chose not to kill me, then I would nonetheless be grateful. Such mere external observances are better than the alternative. In fact, the Methodist General Rules explicitly state that we are to keep the rules irrespective of some inner disposition of our heart. We are to "trample

---

23. *Works*, 1:106.

under foot that enthusiastic doctrine that 'we are not to do good unless *our hearts be free to it.*'" Yet I have not truly kept the Law. I have not observed what matters most. I am not yet enlightened, summoned by God's own presence, God's Light or Law, to love my neighbor as I should. If I am truly illumined, then it would not even occur to me to do a cost-benefit analysis as to whether or not I should kill my neighbor. If I have the "religion of the heart" and then claim that I can go about breaking the law because it no longer has a hold on my life, then I have "made void the law through faith." This is not the purpose of creation, the giving of the Light that allows us to know what is good and true. Nor is it consistent with the republication of that Light in the revelation to Moses. Finally, it is Christ, the Light who comes into the world but who also already illumined it, whose life makes possible a blessedness, a happiness and holiness that renders the Law fulfilled. For Wesley, Christ is the Law and the Light.

Chapter 11

Christina Rossetti

TIMOTHY LARSEN

The third edition of *The Norton Anthology of English Literature*, published in 1974, declared that Christina Rossetti (1830–1894) was "perhaps the finest" of all of England's women poets.[1] Since that time her reputation has risen even higher, with current assessments emphasizing the superiority of her poetry to that of male poets whose achievements were once deemed greater. Poetry itself, of course, does not have the place in society today that it did in the nineteenth century, but those who attend to poems are likely to be familiar with Rossetti compositions such as "When I Am Dead, My Dearest," "Up-Hill," "Goblin Market," and "My Heart Is Like a Singing Bird." Her delightfully playful poem, "No, Thank you, John," can be seen as the original "Dear John" letter, ending, of course, with the obligatory consolation prize that they can still be friends ("Here's friendship for you if you like; but love, — / No, thank you,

An earlier version of this chapter was published as Timothy Larsen, "Christina Rossetti, the Decalogue, and Biblical Interpretation," *Zeitschrift für Neuere Theologiegeschichte* 16:1 [2009] and is reprinted by permission of De Gruyter. www.degruyter.com.
    1. M. H. Abrams et al., eds., *The Norton Anthology of English Literature*, vol. 2, 3rd ed. (New York: W. W. Norton and Co., 1974), 1481.

John").[2] Even those impervious to poetry may still know Rossetti's work through her Christmas carol ("In the Bleak Midwinter"), with its popular last stanza:

> What can I give Him,
>   Poor as I am?
> If I were a shepherd
>   I would bring a lamb,
> If I were a Wise Man
>   I would do my part,—
> Yet what I can I give Him,
>   Give my heart.[3]

The devotional sentiment expressed in that carol leads to the observation that Rossetti's relationship with God through Jesus Christ was the central core of her life. Her resolute Christian identity found its particular home and expression in the Anglo-Catholic wing of the Church of England. Always devout Anglicans, the Rossetti women (Christina, her mother, and her sister Maria) joined the Tractarian revival when Christina was just entering her teen years. For Maria, this led on to her becoming a Sister in one of the new Anglican religious orders, All Saints.[4] Christina Rossetti's devotional life included daily private prayer, leading the household in corporate prayer in both the morning and the evening, and being highly active in the congregational life of her church, including receiving the sacrament twice a week (on Thursdays and Sundays).[5] Her agnostic brother, William Michael Rossetti, although a champion of Christina's literary reputation, was baffled and repelled by her spiritual fervor and spoke rather dismissively of "her perpetual church-going and communions, her prayers and fasts, her submission to clerical direction, her oblations, her practice of confession."[6] When William's infant son was dying he humored Christina's request to be allowed to baptize him, reflecting on this sacramental moment: "I doubt whether any act of her life yielded her more heartfelt satisfaction."[7] Rossetti refused to marry the two main suitors that came to her in life because of religious incompatibly, the first because he was a Roman Catholic and the second because his personal faith was underdetermined. She died of breast cancer in 1894. When Rossetti became too infirmed to leave home, her priest came

2. William Michael Rossetti, ed., *The Poetical Works of Christina Georgina Rossetti* (London: Macmillan and Co., 1904), 349.

3. Rossetti, *Poetical Works*, 246–47.

4. For Maria's influence on Christina, see Mary Arseneau, "Recovering Female Community: Frances, Maria, and Christina Rossetti," *Journal of Pre-Raphaelite Studies* 12 (2003): 17–38.

5. Mackenzie Bell, *Christina Rossetti: A Biographical and Critical Study* (London: Thomas Burleigh, 1898), 162–65.

6. Rossetti, *Poetical Works*, lv.

7. Rossetti, *Poetical Works*, lvii.

once a week to administer the sacrament. Too ill to speak, she died moving her lips and body in inarticulate prayer.

Christina Rossetti was profoundly immersed in Scripture and her commitment to the Bible was resolute and rigorous. Dinah Roe has observed, "It could be said that Rossetti's poetry is in fact constituted by exegesis. She refers to the Bible, either by quotation or allusion, in nearly every poem."[8] Nilda Jiménez compiled a concordance of the scriptural references in Rossetti's poems.[9] It is 258 pages long and follows a trail across the whole canon, with references to almost every book in the canon. Moreover, Rossetti's primary engagement with Scripture is to be found in the six works of devotional prose, which were published during her lifetime. Indeed, her last book was, fitting, a commentary on the last book of the Bible.[10] Far from being a slap-dash project, Rossetti spent seven years of her life working on this 552-page long devotional exposition of the Revelation of St. John the Divine.[11]

There has been a long history of scholars finding Rossetti's Christianity repulsive. Repeatedly, critics have been unable to forgive her for allowing her religious scruples to result in a life of celibacy when it is a matter of public record that at least two men were willing to hazard all on the theory that there was something exciting beneath her prim, drab, and determinedly unfashionable clothes.[12] Notably, Virginia Woolf pronounced Rossetti's love of God life-denying,[13] and this became the standard view (it being, I suppose, just plain bad manners to wonder whether Woolf was really the more life-affirming figure by introducing the wholly irrelevant fact that she committed suicide). A contemporary scholar in this trajectory is Germaine Greer. Her animosity to Rossetti's faith looms so large that it drives her critique into absurdities and even incoherence. When Rossetti is credited with having a genuine faith, then she is described as a "bigot" given over to "sectarianism."[14] Constructing an artificial division, Rossetti's "religious" poems are explicitly contrasted with her "literary" ones and condemned as lacking merit, while her devotional faithfulness is derided as a willful wasting of her life. No attempt is being made here to answer these charges systematically,

8. Dinah Roe, *Christina Rossetti's Faithful Imagination: The Devotional Poetry and Prose*, Houndsmills (Basingstoke: Palgrave Macmillan, 2006), 9.

9. Nilda Jiménez, compiler, *The Bible and the Poetry of Christina Rossetti* (Westport, Connecticut: Greenwood, 1979).

10. Christina Rossetti, *The Face of the Deep: A Devotional Commentary on the Apocalypse* (London: Society for Promoting Christian Knowledge, 1892).

11. Georgina Bottiscombe, *Christina Rossetti: A Divided Life* (London: Constable, 1981), 196.

12. Diane D'Amico has well observed, "Freudian theories of repression, tend to pity, even to condemn her for such choices." Diane D'Amico, "'Choose the stairs that mount above': Christina Rossetti and the Anglican Sisterhoods," *Essays in Literature* 17 (1990): 204–21 (here 208).

13. Virginia Woolf, *The Common Reader: First and Second Series* (New York: Harcourt, Brace, and Company, 1948), 257–65; Anne Olivier Bell, ed., *The Diary of Virginia Woolf, Volume 1: 1915–1919* (New York: Harcourt Brace, 1977), 178–79 (entry for 4 August 1918).

14. Germaine Greer, *Slip-Shod Sibyls: Recognition, Rejection and the Woman Poet* (London: Viking, 1995), "The Perversity of Christina Rossetti," 359–89.

but it is worth pointing out as an aside that far from being a bigot, Rossetti was a good friend with the celebrated poet, A. C. Swinburne, whose militant atheism made him notorious in Victorian society. Moreover, Swinburne could so readily discern artistic achievement in Rossetti's religious poems that he declared of one of them that "nothing more glorious in poetry has ever been written."[15] Even this harsh perspective of dismissing Rossetti's religion as corrosive bigotry, however, is to allow her Christianity too much space, so Greer even attempts to deny the very reality of Rossetti's faith. This more fundamental attack is focused on reading Rossetti's love of God as a "perverse" expression of incestuous desire for her brother, Gabriel Dante Rossetti (a speculation unencumbered by a single piece of evidence), and ends with one, final, desperate lunge, which bizarrely compares Rossetti's work to "a Satanic mass."[16]

Another strand of scholarship has sought to recover Rossetti's religious writings by mangling them to make them appear to conform to the sensibilities of critics today. It has become something of a clichéd convention to say that Rossetti's attitude toward women's suffrage was "ambiguous." In a slight variation, Roe has stated that Rossetti's attitude toward women's social equality was "cautious." This is usually the best that can be done, given Rossetti's clear and public opposition to votes for women. Bottiscombe, however, in a deceptive account, in presenting a key letter, does not quote Rossetti's rejection of the cause which is the context for what follows, but only some playful comments she made thereafter as "some startlingly advanced views" on women's rights, omitting also what follows, a reference to women in the military, as it is by that time all too apparent that she is offering this a *reductio ad absurdum*.[17] In fact, Rossetti was so unequivocally opposed to women's suffrage that she even signed a petition against it![18] Moreover, it is telling for the purpose of this study that she objected to it specifically because of her commitment to Scripture: "Does it not appear as if the Bible was based upon an understood unalterable distinction between men and women, their position, duties, privileges?"[19] Perhaps the most egregious coopting of Rossetti is an article by Frederick S. Roden. If one has not read Rossetti's devotional writings, it would be impossible to gain from this article even a general impression of what they actually contain. Instead, random phrases are pressed into serving Roden's own preoccupations. For example, when Rossetti expresses a desire to be "open" to God's mercy, this is construed as representing a sexually "receptive state."[20] At its nadir, Roden finds a challenge

15. Bottiscombe, *Rossetti*, 113.

16. Greer, *Slip-Shod Sibyls*, 389.

17. Bottiscombe, *Rossetti*, 171.

18. Jan Marsh, *Christina Rossetti: A Writer's Life* (New York: Viking, 1995), 466.

19. Anthony H. Harrison, ed., *The Letters of Christina Rossetti: Volume 2: 1874–1881* (Charlottesville, VA: University Press of Virginia, 1999), 158 (Christina Rossetti to Augusta Webster, undated [c. 1878]).

20. Frederick S. Roden, "The Kiss of the Soul: The Mystical Theology of Christina Rossetti's Devotional Prose," in *Women's Theology in Nineteenth-Century Britain: Transfiguring the Faith of Their Fathers*, ed. Julie Melnyk (New York: Garland Publishing, 1998), 37–57 (here 48).

to "hegemonic patriarchal and heterosexist religious frameworks" in a pedestrian remark about the bond between Ruth and Naomi—this widow and her mother-in-law being recast as an example in Rossetti's work of "same-sex affectional pairings."[21] Another work in this vein is Lynda Palazzo's recent monograph, *Christina Rossetti's Feminist Theology* (2002). What is controlling Palazzo's analysis is amply revealed in the introduction which is focused on the thought of the contemporary post-Christian feminist theologian, Mary Daly and, remarkably, fails to even mention Rossetti herself. Far from appreciating Rossetti's Christianity on its own terms, three times on one page the Tractarian zeal of her church is described as "hysteria."[22] Instead, readers are reassured that Rossetti can be observed, for those who have eyes to see, "moving towards a position" similar to Mary Daly and "re-imagining God" in "endlessly" expanding ways.[23] Fortunately, there have also been a handful of scholars who have attended sympathetically and carefully to Rossetti's Christian thought on its own terms, notably Diane D'Amico, Mary Arseneau, Amanda W. Benckhuysen, and, most notably for the purpose at hand, Dinah Roe.[24]

Meanwhile, conservative biblical scholars have their own bias with which to contend. Often, when the notion of hearing the biblical interpretations of diverse voices such as those of women is raised, they respond with a catch–22: if these voices say something different from what the standard white, Western, male, professional interpreters have expounded, then it just proves that they were not pursuing their exegesis accurately, while if they say something similar, then it demonstrates that there is no need to attend to such figures because their contribution is redundant. This chapter will demonstrate that Rossetti's commentary on Scripture successfully evades this catch–22 by readings and emphases that are both faithful and different from traditional male ones. The recovering of women interpreters of the Bible is currently a vibrant, promising, and growing field. A pioneering study was a work by Marla J. Selvidge, but, using contemporary sensibilities as a control, she intentionally included only women from the past whose works could be seen as in an unfolding trajectory leading to current feminist thought as she admires it.[25] In recent years, however, a substantial effort, with Marion Taylor at its center, has been made to recover nineteenth-century women interpreters of the Bible on their own terms.[26] Nevertheless, this emphasis has yet to be integrated into wider studies. A recent account, *Anglican*

21. Ibid., 39, 49.

22. Lynda Palazzo, *Christina Rossetti's Feminist Theology* (Houndmills, Basingstoke: Palgrave, 2002), 3.

23. Ibid., 2, 88.

24. Some of the works of all these scholars are cited in other notes, but I also wish to acknowledge here the following one: Mary Arsenseau, *Recovering Christina Rossetti: Female Community and Incarnational Poetics* (Houndmills, Basingstoke: Palgrave Macmillan, 2004).

25. Marla J. Selvidge, *Notorious Voices: Feminist Biblical Interpretation, 1500–1920* (New York: Continuum, 1996).

26. Marion Ann Taylor and Heather E. Weir, eds., *Let Her Speak for Herself: Nineteenth-Century Women Writing on the Women of Genesis* (Waco, TX: Baylor University Press, 2006); Christina de Groot and Marion Ann Taylor, eds., *Recovering Nineteenth-Century Women Interpreters of the Bible*

Approaches to Scripture: From the Reformation to the Present, for example, ignores the contributions of Anglican women altogether.[27] To focus on the chronology at hand, the chapter on the nineteenth century has five men named in the titles of its subsections and not even a passing reference in the main text to even one of the famous Anglican women from that century who wrote extensively and insightfully on Scripture such as Hannah More, Florence Nightingale, Josephine Butler, and Christina Rossetti, let alone the more obscure ones who did significant work that has recently been recovered. A related bias, which has hindered the rediscovering of women interpreters, has been the assumption that critical biblical scholarship is all that needs to be attended to in the nineteenth century. In contradiction to such an assumption, it is readily apparent that most of the engagement with Scripture then (and now) is devotional, ecclesial, and sermonic, rather than critical, and some of this material is intellectually serious and spiritually insightful and therefore itself deserving of critical attention.

Rossetti's most substantial reading of the Decalogue was her book *Letter and Spirit: Notes on the Commandments* (1883).[28] This volume was not only published by the Anglican Society for Promoting Christian Knowledge, but specifically under the direction of its tract committee. This committee was composed entirely of Anglican priests. Moreover, in order to ensure strict and entire orthodoxy, books were only published under its imprint, which had gained the approval of five bishops who acted as external readers.[29] In other words, Rossetti's commentary on the Decalogue comes as close as one can realistically imagine to being episcopally sanctioned, authorized Anglican biblical exposition.

Marion Taylor and Heather Weir have taught us to read women interpreters of Scripture with the question in mind, "What does she see that a man might not see?"[30] This approach pays considerable dividends when applied to *Letter and Spirit*. Rossetti is extraordinarily attentive to the women of Scripture. To observe that in a commentary on the Decalogue she refers on more than one occasion to Eve, Mary and Martha, Ruth and Naomi, Esther, Rachel, the Virgin Mary, Lot's wife, Deborah, Rebekah and Delilah, is to just get started. To these names need to be added her references to Elisabeth, Miriam, Hannah, Leah, Sarah, Priscilla, Rahab, Abigail, Sapphira and, in good Victorian manner, a suitably coy allusion to Lot's daughters. Moving into more advanced territory of biblical literacy, Rossetti also mentions Orpah, the five daughters of Zelo-

---

(Atlanta: Society of Biblical Literature, 2007). See also an older book with a wider chronological sweep, Patricia Demers, *Women as Interpreters of the Bible* (New York: Paulist Press, 1992).

27. Rowan A. Greer, *Anglican Approaches to Scripture: From the Reformation to the Present* (New York: Herder and Herder, 2006).

28. Christina G. Rossetti, *Letter and Spirit: Notes on the Commandments*, published under the direction of the Tract Committee (London: Society for Promoting Christian Knowledge, n.d. [c. 1883]).

29. Lorraine Janzen Kooistra, *Christina Rossetti and Illustration: A Publishing History* (Athens, Ohio: Ohio University Press, 2002), 144–45.

30. Taylor and Weir, *Let Her Speak*, 18.

phehad, Jephthah's daughter, Manoah's wife, Peninnah, Vashti, and Naaman's wife's "little maid." I must confess to having been stumped myself by Jehosheba, and I took perverse pride when even an Old Testament scholar was not able to recognize Rossetti's reference to "the King's Daughter" (which, as it turns out, is unmistakably an allusion to Psalm 45:13–14). Other texts, which refer to unnamed women gestured at in this way, include the married woman and the virgin (1 Cor. 7:34–38); the "prophetesses of Israel" whom Ezekiel rebukes (Ezek. 13:17–23); and "the virgin, the daughter of Zion" (Isa. 37:21–29).

Moreover, Rossetti treats many of these biblical women with more sympathy and respect than male commentators have usually done. Several scholars have explored Rossetti's preoccupation with Eve.[31] In *Letter and Spirit*, Rossetti builds upon the Genesis narrative in which Eve is tempted by the arguments of the serpent while Adam is tempted by his wife. In a striking inversion of Victorian gender stereotypes, Rossetti reads this as the woman being led by her "mind" and the man by his "heart."[32] Rossetti delights in arguing that, when it comes to couples of the Bible, the wife is often the more impressive one of the pair. Of Deborah, she observes wryly, "although she is defined as 'wife of Lapidoth,' after-ages only know of his existence as husband of Deborah."[33] Again, "between Manoah and his wife, the wife appears the quicker-sighted in matters spiritual," and, when it comes to Esther, it is not hard to spot "the husband's essential inferiority."[34] In a detail traditional male commentators overlook, Rossetti reads Matthew 12:50, "For whosoever shall do the will of my Father which is in heaven, the same is my brother, and sister, and mother", as her Lord making a gender inclusive statement: "Christ deigns to claim each obedient disciple as His own 'brother and sister.'"[35] She even adapts Luke 14:28–30, which uses male pronouns, so that the example figure becomes a Christian patroness: "She 'considers' a field before buying it, and counts the cost before beginning to build Church or Hospital, or (far behind these) her own house (see Luke xiv. 28–30)."[36]

To move on to the primary text being examined, Rossetti notices and does not evade a gender issue in the Decalogue itself: the Tenth Commandment (coveting) is written as if the hearer or reader is male. She explains playfully: "The precept is constructed explicitly for men, implicitly for women; were it not so, to covet a neighbour's *husband* would become defensible!"[37] There is another difficulty, however, which once again Rossetti faces squarely. Does it not appear that his wife is listed as one of a husband's possessions? Rossetti set up readers

---

31. For a prime example, see Diane D'Amico, *Christina Rossetti: Faith, Gender, and Time* (Baton Rouge, LA: State University Press, 1999), 118–46.
32. Rossetti, *Letter and Spirit*, 18.
33. Ibid., 57.
34. Ibid., 57–58.
35. Ibid., 45.
36. Ibid., 123.
37. Ibid., 190–91.

to hear her solution to this challenge brilliantly. As will be shown, throughout the commentary Rossetti heightens the significance and implications of the commandments and biblical words and phrases, teasing out entailments that magnify their scope. Therefore, the reader is not surprised, let alone suspicious, when she does this with the word "house" in the Tenth Commandment: "Thou shalt not covet thy neighbour's house." Rossetti interprets this word as signifying more than just a building, but rather a person's standing and thus their status, their reputation, their public self. Having quietly set this up, she is then able to argue that "wife" coming next after "house" in the list does not mean that she is being cataloged as a mere thing her husband owns. "House" stands for his very identity and thus "obviously she ranks with the man himself."[38] She may be seen as his most valuable possession, but only to the extent that he equally is her dearest possession, Rossetti avers. To clinch the argument that no ontological gender inequality is being taught in the Decalogue, the poet observes that the wife is not mentioned in the Fourth Commandment, but rather it is assumed that "she is wholly at one with her husband."[39] Moreover, no ontological inequality is being asserted regarding servants and maids either: "the Fourth vindicates their essential equality of person and rights: the Tenth implies their accidental and temporary inferiority."[40]

Having entered Rossetti's commentary through an interest in how the issue of gender is handled therein, it is time to gain a more comprehensive view of her reading of the Decalogue. Rossetti's approach is a biblical theology, one in which the witness of the entire canon is freely drawn upon in order to illuminate each commandment. She explains: "since all Holy Scriptures were given for our learning, we do well to study each subject throughout the Bible."[41] Therefore, Rossetti frequently provides the reference for specific biblical passages and, in this way, all but thirteen of the sixty-six books of the Bible are cited in *Letter and Spirit*. Many of them are drawn upon frequently. To take the first and last books of the two testaments as examples, Genesis is cited twenty-one times, Malachi three, Matthew thirty, and Revelation five. Sometimes entire pages are filled with just scriptural quotations. For example, the Ninth Commandment (false witness) prompts a wide-ranging discussion of the right and wrong uses of speech, which includes a stretch of over three pages, which contains exclusively germane biblical texts.[42] The vast cast of women biblical characters is the result of Rossetti's technique of searching the Scriptures for figures whose lives illustrate either breaking or keeping the commandment under discussion. This biblical theology approach arises from Rossetti's high doctrine of Scripture. She is convinced that even the very phrases of biblical texts need to be attended to with care and reverence as the word of

38. Ibid.
39. Ibid., 192.
40. Ibid., 193–94.
41. Ibid., 137.
42. Ibid., 154–57.

God: "Since not one jot or one tittle shall in any wise pass from the Law till all be fulfilled, we may do well to ponder the individual form assumed by each Commandment, such doubtless being the perfect form wherein to embody the particular precept."[43]

Another way to emphasize this feature of the commentary is to observe that Rossetti is deeply committed to the unity of Scripture. One way she expresses this is by using verses from one part of the canon as a lens through which to read a passage from another. *Letter and Spirit* begins in the manner of sermon with three texts written out in full: Mark 12:28–30; Matthew 22:39–40; and Exodus 20:3–17. That is, Rossetti frames the entire book as a reading of the Decalogue through the perspective of Christ's teaching on the greatest commandment. The first table is a fleshing out of the greatest commandment, while the commandments of the second table likewise all come under the umbrella of Christ's second, which is like unto it. This lens approach is particularly striking in her exposition of the Seventh Commandment (adultery). Victorian propriety underlined her conviction that a multitude of words on such a subject would be apt to result in sin. Her solution is to recommend that the Seventh Commandment be approached fleetingly and through New Testament passages on purity, notably "Blessed are the pure in heart" (Matt. 5:8) and "unto the pure all things are pure" (Titus 1:15).[44] In this same vein, *Letter and Spirit* ends with a kind of appendix offering bonus material for the hard-core fans. It is a harmony in which the marks of love given in 1 Corinthians 13 are correlated with passages from the Gospels, which show Jesus of Nazareth exemplifying them in his behavior.

There are repeated references to the Sermon on the Mount in *Letter and Spirit* and my own view is that this is a primary lens through which Rossetti reads the Decalogue. Referring to the Seventh Commandment, Jesus proclaims: "Ye have heard that it was said by them of old time, Thou shalt not commit adultery: But I say unto you, that whosoever looketh on a woman to lust after her hath committed adultery with her already in his heart" (Matt. 5:27–28 KJV). Christina Rossetti learned from her divine Master that the way to expound the commandments for spiritual growth is to drive home that they are even more radical and comprehensive than one would assume. Her instinct is always to heighten the demand of a commandment and to tease out entailments that the reader has not discerned. The First Commandment (no other gods), for example, plumbs our inmost reality and exposes our wickedness even when all is well in our behavior. Balaam violated it to the point of being a notorious sinner even though "his conduct is such that it becomes difficult, if not impossible, to prove him in fault at any given moment."[45] You can bear false witness without even speaking: Judas violated the Ninth Commandment with a kiss. The Fifth Commandment does

43. Ibid., 88–89.
44. Ibid., 101.
45. Ibid., 31.

not just refer to our immediate, biological parents. Adam and Eve are parents of us all and to mistreat their children would be to dishonor them, thus this commandment demands that we treat all human beings with respect. Instead, of honoring our elders, however, we too often actually underrate them: "they speak and we wish they would be quiet; their manners are old fashioned, their taste is barbarous, their opinions are obsolete, their standard is childish, they know nothing available, they do not even aim at knowing any person or any thing worth knowing."[46]

The Sixth Commandment (murder) entails thoughts against God as well as people. Clearly, Rossetti assumed rightly that most of her readers were already keeping up with respectable Christian standards of behavior as monitored by polite society and therefore she wanted to unsettle them and thereby call them to a higher state of holiness. She still wants the Seventh Commandment to prompt conviction and repentance even if adultery is not one's besetting sin: "The Seventh Commandment forbids by analogy, though not verbally, the over-indulgence of any bodily appetite; thus, gluttony and drunkenness range under this Commandment."[47] You can be dutifully participating in a Sunday morning church service but still breaking the Fourth Commandment by allowing your mind to wander to matters of business. Nevertheless, Victorian values and Rossetti's own passion for her work are on display in her emphasis that the Sabbath comes after one has labored hard for six days. In one of her more delightful heightenings, Rossetti pronounces all bad theology as a violation of the command not to take the Lord's name in vain: "To misrepresent God Almighty either as to His essence or His character, constitutes a breach of the Third Commandment; it is to call by His Name a something other than Himself."[48] God takes our words seriously: Zacharias was struck mute for saying the wrong thing even though there was not even another human being present to be negatively influenced by his statement. Rossetti even claims that all flippant words are a breach of the third command: "all profane speech, including light or unmeaning blessings, and exclamatory invocations, falls under the ban of the Third Commandment."[49] (As Charlie Brown would say, "Good grief!") A reviewer aptly wrote of "Miss Rossetti's severity."[50] The poet also warns nineteenth-century Britons that their sin means that they have good reason to fear a coming judgment of God upon the nation. Amanda W. Benckhuysen has emphasized that in *Letter and Spirit* Christina Rossetti "unabashedly adopts an authoritative voice as a prophet."[51] Still, this severity was balanced by her own

---

46. Ibid., 67.
47. Ibid., 106.
48. Ibid., 137.
49. Ibid., 135.
50. *The Academy*, 9 June 1883, 395–96, (Review of *Letter and Spirit* by G. S. Simcox).
51. Amanda W. Benckhuysen, "The Prophetic Voice of Christina Rossetti," in de Groot and Taylor, *Recovering*, 165–80 (here 175). Likewise, Jan Marsh discerned a new level of confidence in Rossetti in *Letter and Spirit*, describing it as her taking on the "manner of any preacher": Marsh, *Christina Rossetti*, 503.

joyful anticipation of the delights of the coming Kingdom. Here is one of the more radiant passages from *Letter and Spirit*:

> For the books we now forbear to read, we shall one day be endued with wisdom and knowledge. For the music we will not listen to, we shall join in the song of the redeemed. For the pictures from which we turn, we shall gaze unabashed on the Beatific Vision. For the companionship we shun, we shall be welcomed into angelic society and the communion of triumphant saints. For the amusements we avoid, we shall keep the supreme Jubilee. For the pleasures we miss, we shall abide, and for evermore abide, in the rapture of heaven. It cannot be much of a hardship to dress modestly and at small cost rather than richly and fashionably, if with a vivid conviction we are awaiting the "white robes" of the redeemed.[52]

Moreover, Rossetti also gave positive instructions on what to pursue as well as what to shun: notably, prayer is an act of keeping the Third Commandment that one should cultivate, and one can learn to obey the Tenth Commandment by fostering the virtue of contentment.

Rossetti's belief in the unity of Scripture also leads her to expect to find connections and patterns. For example, at one point she suggests that the four commandments of the first table can be correlated with the four parts of ourselves with which we love God: heart, soul, mind, and strength.[53] The main structural core of *Letter and Spirit* is based on Rossetti's efforts to uncover connections between the individual commandments of the Decalogue. The First Commandment is the root one, corresponding to Christ's greatest commandment, and the second through fourth fall underneath it; likewise, the Fifth Commandment of the Decalogue corresponds to Christ's Second Commandment and the sixth through tenth come under its scope. In another way, the Second Commandment (graven images), because it refers to a sensual temptation to create physical idols can be seen as an overarching one under which the sixth, seventh, and eighth find their place. Notably, the theme of idolatry as adulterous behavior in Israel's covenant with the Almighty which recurs in the Old Testament gives warrant for finding a parallel between the second and seventh commandments. The Third Commandment has a "marked correspondence" to the ninth as the first addresses speech that disrespects God and the latter speech that injures one's neighbor.[54] The Fourth Commandment (Sabbath) is connected to the tenth (coveting) as both are about accepting our lot and not chafing against it: "Well, I think, may we speak of the "circle" of both Will and duty; the Fourth and Tenth Commandments lead us back to the starting-point of a holiness spiritual and, so to say, immaterial; our strength will in great measure be to sit still; or as Moses

---

52. Rossetti, *Letter and Spirit*, 104.
53. Ibid., 15.
54. Ibid., 141.

bade Israel in all the haste of the Exodus, to stand still and see the salvation of the Lord."[55]

The Fifth Commandment has particular resonance in relationship to Rossetti because her own life was devoted to honoring her parents, especially her mother, who survived her father by thirty-two years. Rossetti nursed her father when he was dying, and then spent the next three decades living with and looking after her mother until she could care for her in her final illness as well. In that curious way in which the Victorians all seemed to know each other, there is a powerful photograph of an adult Christina Rossetti leaning against her mother taken by Lewis Carroll (C. L. Dodgson) of *Alice in Wonderland* fame. They are even immortalized together in art, because her brother, Dante Gabriel Rossetti, the celebrated Pre-Raphaelite painter, used Christina and their mother as the models for the Virgin Mary and her mother, Anne, in his famous picture "The Girlhood of Mary Virgin".[56] The dedication page for *Letter and Spirit* reads, "To My Mother in thankfulness for her dear and honoured example." As fitting as it is for a book that expounds the Fifth Commandment to be dedicated to her mother, it was purely accidental. With two special exceptions, Rossetti dedicated all her books—a good shelf full—to her mother. Her first book, a collection of verses privately published by her grandfather when she was just seventeen years old, was dedicated to her mother, as was her very last one, her commentary on Revelation, even though her mother had been dead for six years by that time. Indeed, the first poem that Rossetti ever wrote was when she was twelve years old and it was composed to honor her mother on her birthday.[57] As grown women living together, Rossetti unfailingly composed a poem for her mother every Valentine's Day.[58] When the fellow poet Thomas Gordon Hake praised Rossetti's commentary on the Decalogue, she replied deferentially: "Thank you for welcoming 'Letter and Spirit'. My Mother's life is a far more forcible comment on the Commandments than are words of mine."[59]

Letter and Spirit also reflects Christina Rossetti's identity as a loyal member of the Church of England. Tellingly, it would seem that all the sources she cites are Anglican ones. These include two bishops of Calcutta, Reginald Heber and Robert Milman, and the bishop of Salisbury, George Moberly. Rossetti also relates a charming anecdote in order to illustrate that recreation, in its place, is needful, Christian, and good: a bishop, when asked by a house guest what he would do if he knew the Day of Judgment was just an hour a way, replied that he would continue playing his game of chess. Most of the references in *Letter and Spirit*, however, are to material in the Prayer Book, notably repeated ones

55. Ibid., 162–63.
56. Bottiscombe, *Rossetti*, 48.
57. Bell, *Rossetti*, 191.
58. Bottiscombe, *Rossetti*, 194.
59. Anthony H. Harrison, ed., *The Letters of Christina Rossetti: Volume 3: 1882–1886* (Charlottesville, VA: University Press of Virginia, 2000), 118, (Christina Rossetti to Thomas Gordon Hake, 14 May 1883).

to the Catechism and the Athanasian Creed. Indeed, as the Ten Commandments are themselves included in the Church of England Catechism, the very
subject matter of this volume flows fittingly from her Anglican spiritual formation, which had included her mother teaching her the Catechism. Aptly for a
study of the Decalogue, Rossetti also evokes a prayer from the Litany: "From
contempt of Thy word and commandment, Good Lord, deliver us."[60] Rossetti's
Anglican faith can repeatedly be glimpsed shaping the conversation. Putting her
theological instincts on display, Rossetti's commentary begins with a section in
which she explores the meaning of the oneness of God as declared in the *Shema*
(Deuteronomy 6:4) in the light of the doctrine of the Trinity. Rossetti pronounces that the Ninth Commandment condemns all oaths on trivial occasions
"at the very least."[61] It would seem that her heightening instincts might have
been tempting her to move in the Anabaptist direction of forbidding all oaths,
but the last of the Thirty-nine Articles necessitated a less absolutist position. On
the other hand, a High Church sense of the Christian tradition meant that Rossetti did not think there was any need to become unsettled by the Sabbath having gravitated from Saturday to Sunday: "this has been settled for us ages ago by
Catholic consent."[62] At one point, she discusses the commandments in the light
of the seven deadly sins. There are also recurring references to the sacraments.
Rossetti observes that our disobedience as human beings is such that when we
were told in the garden of Eden not to eat something we ate it and now that
we have been commanded to eat something ("*Do this* in remembrance of me")
people generally neglect it.

As to biblical interpretation, Rossetti is comfortable approaching the text typo-
logically. She identifies in the course of her commentary Joseph as "the typical
brother," David as "the typical king," Eve as the "typical woman," and Abraham
as "the typical Father."[63] She is also aware of the history of biblical interpretation,
justifying allegorical readings on the grounds that they are established "by ancient
interpretation" and observing when "tradition" has identified figures in various
Gospel texts as the same person.[64] Her confidence that allegorical readings are
appropriate may be amply illustrated by a particularly infelicitous one, which she
offers. Hiel who, defying the curse pronounced by Joshua, rebuilt Jericho, and
paid the penalty of the deaths of his first and last sons (1 Kgs. 16:34), is spiritual-
ized as representing God the Father. A reviewer, who liked *Letter and Spirit* overall, conceded that many readers would find that particular reading repellent.[65] So
far from seeing them as an example of "same-sex affectional pairings," Rossetti's

60. Rossetti, *Letter and Spirit*, 113.
61. Ibid., 130.
62. Ibid., 174–75.
63. Rossetti, *Letter and Spirit*, 54, 64, 17, 47. For Victorian culture and typological readings of
the Bible, see George P. Landow, *Victorian Types, Victorian Shadows: Biblical Typology in Victorian
Literature, Art, and Thought* (Boston: Routledge and Kegan Paul, 1980).
64. Rossetti, *Letter and Spirit*, 50, 33.
65. *The Academy*, 9 June 1883, 395–96.

allegorical reading of Ruth's good treatment of Naomi is that it is a picture of how Christians should behave to the "Jewish race."[66]

Fascinatingly, there is a surprising amount of reflection on the task of biblical interpretation itself in *Letter and Spirit*. Rossetti reacts defiantly to those who might find her biblical theology approach naïve: "Old fashioned it certainly is to search the Scriptures (*see* Acts xvii. 10–12) for our examples and warnings; but surely the dread of appearing old fashioned is one form of that Disinclination in which already we have thought to discern a breach of the First Commandment!"[67] On the other hand, she cautions herself that her approach could easily slip into irreverence: "It is a solemn thing to write history. I feel it a solemn thing to write conjectural sketches of Scripture characters; filling up outlines as I fancy, but cannot be certain, may possibly have been the case; making one figure stand for this virtue and another for that vice . . ."[68]

Rossetti finds a lens for her interpretive task in Proverbs 24:17–18 ("Rejoice not when thine enemy falleth, and let not thine heart be glad when he stumbleth. . . ."). In other words, we endanger incurring the displeasure of the Almighty if we expose the failures of biblical characters in a callous or high-handed manner. Rossetti explores at some length two ways in which the reader may go astray in biblical interpretation. The first is by allowing idle inquisitiveness to mute the force of the main point of the passage. For example, on the account of the fall, "[t]he question of mortal sin shrinks into the background while we moot such points as the primitive status of the serpent: did he stand somehow upright? Did he fly? What did he originally eat? How did he articulate? Or again, man's overwhelming loss ceases to be the chief concern, when at the gate of Paradise our eyes light upon the flaming sword."[69]

So we go on through the canon: "Clear up the astronomy of Joshua's miracle. Fix the botany of Jonah's gourd." The second error in biblical interpretation dovetails well with Rossetti's desire that the full demands of the text be understood. She warns that in an effort to evade the radical nature of a passage one can end up actually inverting its message. Rossetti mocks playfully the way that preachers try to drain the force from Christ's words to the Rich Young Ruler: "It does not, we are assured, by any means require us to sell all; differences of rank, of position, of circumstances are Providentially ordained, and are not lightly to be set aside; our duties lie within the decorous bounds of our station. . . ."[70]

This goes on until the congregation leaves with an impression as if the text was, "be not righteous overmuch" (Eccl. 7:17), rather than "sell whatsoever though hast, and give to the poor" (Mark 10:21). In short, Christina Rossetti believed that our inability to interpret Scripture correctly is primarily rooted in our sinful desires such as *curiositas* and disobedience.

---

66. Rossetti, *Letter and Spirit*, 54.
67. Ibid., 43–44.
68. Ibid., 158.
69. Ibid., 85.
70. Ibid., 28.

While this chapter has focused on *Letter and Spirit*, it is worth observing in conclusion that Rossetti's engagement with the Decalogue was life long. Her commentary on Revelation, for example, contains numerous references to the Ten Commandments.[71] In another of her devotional books for the Society for Promoting Christian Knowledge, *Time Flies*, Rossetti tells of how impressed she once was with the "courageous reverence" of someone who refused to look at William Blake's illustrations of the book of Job for fear that it would be a breach of the Second Commandment.[72] Rossetti even retitled one of her longer poems after a phrase from the Second Commandment: "The Iniquity of the Fathers upon the Children." She had originally titled it, "Under the Rose," but later decided that a biblical phrase was more fitting given the solemnity of the theme. This poem was prompted by her experience doing voluntary Christian work with the Anglican sisters who ran a home at Highgate for what the Victorians called "fallen women," that is, it existed to help women out of a life of prostitution and probably as a shelter for unwed mothers and mistresses abandoned by their partners. Rossetti eventually volunteered there for ten years, writing this poem in 1865, in the middle of that decade of service. What she heard at Highgate increased Rossetti's awareness of the dangers that girls and women face. One result was that she became active in political campaigns to raise the age of consent and to make more severe the penalties for violating it. Another lesson was that the man was usually more culpable, but the girl or woman was the one whose life was ruined. "The Iniquity of the Fathers upon the Children" is told from the perspective of an illegitimate daughter. Her mother, although wealthy and aristocratic, never marries. The iniquity of her father was a transgressing of the Seventh Commandment (even if he was not married, it would still be this in Rossetti's heightened reading of its entailments). The man was a sexual predator who had taken advantage of a girl who was "scarce sixteen." The "fathers" of her biblical text thus happened to be gender specific in a way that Rossetti thought was particularly apt. The poem concedes that such cruel circumstances make it hard for a girl to keep the Fifth Commandment:

> I love my dear old Nurse
> Who loved me without gains;
> I love my mistress even,
> Friend, Mother, what you will:
> But I could almost curse
> My Father for his pains;
> And sometimes at my prayer
> Kneeling in sight of Heaven
> I almost curse him still:

71. For some instances, see Rossetti, *Face*, 62, 64, 271–72, 396–97, 399.

72. Christina Rossetti, *Time Flies: A Reading Diary* (London: Society for the Promoting of Christian Knowledge, 1885), 71. Bell reveals that the prints were by Blake and that it was her sister, Maria: Bell, *Rossetti*, 61.

> Why did he set his snare
> To catch at unaware
> My Mother's foolish youth;
> Load me with shame that's hers,
> And her with something worse,
> A lifelong lie for truth?[73]

In the narrative of the poem, the girl's mother takes her to live in her house, but lies about the true nature of their relationship, thus living continually in breach of the Ninth Commandment.

Finally, Christina Rossetti even wrote substantial notes on the entire book of Exodus and the book of Genesis as well, possibly with the intention of writing a full commentary.[74] These notes underline her reverent approach to Scripture. A comment that she wrote in the Exodus section of this private manuscript may serve to express Christina Rossetti's general attitude toward her work as a biblical commentator: "All this I write down craving pity & pardon of God for [Christ's] sake if I err."[75]

73. Rossetti, *Poetical Works*, 41–47 (here 47).

74. Diane D'Amico and David A. Kent, "Christina Rossetti's Notes on Genesis and Exodus," *Journal of Pre-Raphaelite Studies* 13 (2004), 49–98.

75. D'Amico and Kent, "Notes," 81 ("Christ's" is written as a contraction: "Xt's".)

Chapter 12

Karl Barth

GEORGE HUNSINGER

Karl Barth wrote no extended treatment of the Ten Commandments in his *Church Dogmatics*. He once surveyed the significance of the Ten Commandments in general,[1] and some commandments are included as part of a wide-ranging discussion of ethics in his doctrine of creation.[2] By taking up the Sabbath Day, parents and children, man and woman, and respect for life, Barth was obviously alluding, if somewhat selectively, to the Fourth, Fifth, Sixth and Seventh Commandments. Moreover, his critique of modern industrial capitalism might be taken as a meditation on the Eighth Commandment, "You shall not steal"; while his reflections on the theme of honor pertained to the Ninth Commandment on not bearing false witness against one's neighbor. But this was still less than the whole Decalogue, and not much was said about Commandments One, Two, Three, and Ten.

---

1. Karl Barth, *Church Dogmatics*, II/2 (Edinburgh: T. & T. Clark, 1948), 683–86. (Hereafter cited as *CD*). Barth argues that the Decalogue does not represent an independent ethical teaching. It cannot be detached from the grace of the covenant and therefore from the Lordship of God. It forms the broad framework within which the Lord God more specifically guides and commands God's people.
2. Ibid., III/4.

Yet even if Barth's ethics of creation were entirely devoted to the Ten Commandments, attempting to summarize his seven-hundred-page treatise in a brief paper would make little sense. In any case, the Ten Commandments entered into the argument only partially and unsystematically. An obligation to say something about Barth's view of the Decalogue, therefore, would seem to land his commentator in a quandary.

There was at least one commandment, however, namely, the First, to which Barth repeatedly turned. Moreover, as this volume as a whole reveals, Barth is standing in a long and rich tradition of interpretation in which many figures have focused primarily on the First Commandment as the fountainhead of the Ten Commandments. Here again, the First Commandment was not discussed comprehensively so much as under a particular aspect. Barth regarded his well-known strictures against "natural theology" as a matter of nonnegotiable obedience to the First Commandment. He interpreted "You shall have no other gods before me" as an axiom of theological epistemology. Like Calvin and many others, he was interested not simply in what the Commandment ruled out, but also in what it might properly rule in. Yet Barth's famous *No* to natural theology was unfortunately louder than his accompanying *Yes*.

This chapter proposes to reconsider Barth's position on "The First Commandment as a Theological Axiom." That was the title he gave to an essay from the fateful year 1933, and it will be worth our while to examine it. What did Barth think the First Commandment prohibited regarding our knowledge of God, and more importantly for our purposes, what did he think it properly required and allowed? In light of the First Commandment, was Barth's rejection of natural theology, or at least of natural revelation, as sweeping as is commonly assumed?

Barth has not always been well understood on these matters for several reasons. His views were at once quite simple and yet highly complex: they used dialectical modes of thought that are unfamiliar and counterintuitive, they were not always fully set forth, and they were innovative in history of theology. Barth proposed to rethink the question of the knowledge of God by adopting a new conceptual framework. The root metaphor for this framework was not that of a fragment to be completed by a larger whole, as a vase might complete a potsherd, nor that of an ellipse with two foci, which implied a method of systematic correlation. It was rather the metaphor of a circle with its center and circumference (or periphery), a metaphor that appeared regularly throughout Barth's writings. To make the meaning of this metaphor clearer, it might be expanded into that of a sphere rather than a circle, and in fact into a series of concentric spheres with a common center at the core, as will be explained.

SOME BASIC PREMISES

Barth proposed to rethink the problem of natural theology by developing the meaning of revelation according to the insights of the Reformation. The basic principles for Barth were "Christ alone" (*solus Christus*), "grace alone" (*sola gratia*), and "faith alone" (*sola fide*). These principles derive from "Scripture alone" (*sola Scriptura*). Grace alone has sometimes been called the "material principle" of the Reformation, while Scripture alone has been named the "formal principle." Grace alone provided the content, for which Scripture functioned as the decisive source and norm. The Reformation applied these principles mainly to matters of salvation and the will (like matters of "faith and works" or "grace and merit"). Barth proposed to apply the same principles to the doctrine of revelation and the perceiving mind, something he thought the Reformation did not always successfully do. Thus, in his 1934 essay against Brunner, titled "No!"[3] Barth wrote:

> If we really wish to maintain the Reformers' position over against that of Roman Catholicism and Neo-Protestantism, we are not in a position today to repeat the statements of Luther and Calvin without at the same time making them more pointed than they themselves did. . . . They did not feel themselves called upon to clarify the problem of the *formal* relation between reason with its interpretation of nature and history on the one hand and the absolute claim of revelation on the other. (p. 101)

Barth intended to think with the Reformation while also going beyond it. Natural theology needed to be reconsidered, he urged, in light of revelation's "absolute claim." It was a claim he saw embedded in the First Commandment.

The First Commandment as a Theological Axiom

The lengthy opening section to Barth's similarly titled essay from 1933 focused on clarifying the term "axiom."[4] The exercise was important to Barth, because it showed that even such an apparently innocuous term as "axiom" could not be taken over by theology without further ado. Before it could be used, it had to be dismantled and reassembled to bring it into conformity with basic theological convictions. It had, so to speak, to be sanctified or purged of impurities in light of God's uniqueness and disruptive grace.

Barth's approach to this term would prove to be emblematic. It signified something crucial about how he understood the epistemological relevance of the First Commandment. All our earthly terminology and all our benighted thinking needed to be melted down and reminted in light of God's Lordship and his exclusive claim: "You shall have no other gods before me." Since we were all in the thrall of other gods, there could be no direct continuity between the things of this world and the things of Christ.

---

3. John Baillie, ed., *Natural Theology* (London: The Centenary Press, 1946). The volume includes Brunner's essay "Nature and Grace" along with Barth's reply "No!" Page numbers are cited in the text.

4. Karl Barth, "The First Commandment as an Axiom of Theology" in *The Way of Karl Barth*, ed. H. Martin Rumscheidt (Allison Park, PA: Pickwick Publications, 1986), 63–78.

If Barth had had nothing more to say than merely No, if he had been no more than a theologian of discontinuity, then his approach to theological language would have been apophatic or at least "sectarian" in H. Richard Niebuhr's Christ-against-culture sense. Barth, however, was neither apophatic nor sectarian in theological epistemology. Nor, to stay with Niebuhr for a moment, was he accommodationist (Christ of culture), synthetic (Christ above culture), or dualistic (Christ and culture in paradox). He was rather deliberately "conversionist" (Christ transforming culture), and the paradigm of transformation that guided him was the resurrection of Christ from the dead.

Therefore, although the First Commandment could not be subsumed under the term "axiom," the term "axiom" could be subsumed under the First Commandment (p. 63). It was not nature that mediated access to grace, but grace that mediated access to itself through a critical appropriation of nature. "Axiom" in the normal or dictionary sense stood as a marker for nature, while the First Commandment stood as a marker for grace. The term could be subsumed for theological use only through a critical appropriation.

Unlike ordinary axioms, the First Commandment was encountered as something written in an authoritative document. The Commandment was therefore "not perceivable in a direct, immediate or general way" (p. 65). It could only be perceived indirectly as mediated through the particularity of the scriptural text.

Secondly, the Commandment was given through a "report about an *event in time*, namely as words addressed by one person to another" (p. 65). Rooted in an event, the Commandment had a certain contingency setting it apart, again, from any ordinary axiom, while this distinctiveness was only heightened because the Commandment was a matter of personal address and personal encounter. We might say that Barth saw the First Commandment as an axiom embedded in an actualistic and personalistic context: "I am the LORD your God. You shall have no other gods before me." This was an I-Thou encounter, which took place once and for all, but which then continued to become contemporary again and again. Better, it was not so much that the event became contemporary to Israel as that Israel was continually made contemporary to it. The Commandment could not properly be abstracted from these personalistic and actualistic aspects, for it was never independent of them (pp. 65–66).

Finally, the First Commandment could be used as an axiom only if taken seriously as a Commandment. As a Commandment, it signified God's "factual lordship" (p. 67). "God not only *designates* himself as the Lord," wrote Barth, "but *acts* as such by demanding, commanding and forbidding" (p. 67). As a Commandment, it needed to be not only understood but also obeyed. Yet as a Commandment, it also belonged to the covenant of grace. "The general meaning of 'axiom,'" wrote Barth, "fails here completely. What should the truth and knowledge of a logical and mathematical axiom have to do with divine election, covenant making, grace and forgiveness of sin?" (p. 69). The concept of an axiom could certainly not be stretched to include the affirmation that Jesus Christ died and was raised, and yet it was finally Christ's death and resurrection by which the covenant had been underwritten and fulfilled. The First Commandment was not something "abstractly discernible" in creation, but could be apprehended only in the covenant of grace. As an axiom of theological knowledge, the First Commandment's covenantal context was for Barth a matter of signal importance. He summarized up the significance of the First Commandment as follows:

> The Commandment does not state simply that those other gods have no reality. On the contrary, it assumes that they do have a definite reality just as it assumes that there are peoples who have them as gods, who give their hearts to them. Precisely where that occurs there are gods . . . God reveals himself as the sole god. God reveals all other gods as nothings. Their reality fades away before God's revelation. Only in giving God and God alone fear, love and confidence do those people know God as the sole god and all other gods as nothings, despite their reality (p. 70).

What inferences did Barth draw from this analysis about the First Commandment as a theological axiom? How did he think the Commandment pertained to our knowledge of God? His conclusions were essentially two.

First, the Commandment implied that all things must be measured by the norm of Scripture. Scripture was the norm that had no norm. As the norm that normed itself, it could not be normed by anything outside itself. It was therefore the *norma normans non normata*. Though Barth did not use that term, it captures meaning he saw in *sola Scriptura*. It belonged to the grammar of the Christian faith to affirm Scripture as the norm of norms (p. 73).

Barth's second conclusion was a corollary to the first. Other things had to be interpreted according to revelation and not the other way around. Neither natural theology nor cultural phenomena like nationhood could be allowed to compete with or compromise Scripture. In themselves all natural and cultural phenomena were caught up in the fallenness of the world. Whatever might be valid within them could only be discerned and critically appropriated on the basis of Scripture alone (p. 74). That was the final conclusion of Barth's essay on the First Commandment as a theological axiom. However, many questions were still left unanswered. In particular, it remained less than clear what exactly Barth thought was ruled in with regard to extra-scriptural sources and norms. More light was shed on that question by some of his other writings to which we now turn.

Jesus Christ as the One Revelation of God

Barth argued that there was only one revelation of God, not two (or more). It was, however, one revelation that included a diversity of aspects within itself. Everything revealed in other forms was somehow included in Jesus Christ and determined by him. All of the diverse aspects were dependent on Christ as the one revelation at the core. He himself was the revelation of God. The various aspects were always completely—not just relatively—dependent on the absoluteness of revelation in him. As secondary expressions of the core, they had no relative independence. They were not presuppositions that were logically prior to Jesus Christ at the center of the sphere, nor were they material foundations that were external to or separate from him, nor were they semi-independent sources or norms that might exist alongside him or apart from him. As manifestations of Christ at the center, any diverse aspects at the periphery, or on the outer surface, so to speak, of the sphere, were always logically and materially dependent on the centrality of Christ. They were always somehow expressions of the central christological core, not existing independently of it.

The Theological Declaration of Barmen (1934)[5] was meant to reject all sources and norms of revelation alongside or apart from Jesus Christ. It was meant to reject the logic of the ellipse in favor of the logic of the circle (or sphere). Here are its introductory words to its first major claim:

> In view of the errors of the "German Christians" and of the present Reich Church government which are devastating the Church and are also thereby breaking up the unity of the German Evangelical Church, we confess the following evangelical truths:
>
> 1. "I am the way and the truth and the life; no one comes to the Father but by me." (John 14:6) "Truly, truly, I say to you, he who does not enter the sheepfold by the door but climbs in by another way, that man is a thief and a robber. . . . I am the door; if anyone enters by me, he will be saved." (John 10:1, 9)
>
> Jesus Christ, as he is attested to us in Holy Scripture, is the one Word of God whom we have to hear, and whom we have to trust and obey in life and in death. We reject the false doctrine that the church could and should recognize as a source of its proclamation, beyond and besides this one Word of God, yet other events, powers, historic figures and truths as God's revelation.

Idolatry had taken a political turn and was widely embraced in the church. Nationalism, militarism, and anti-Semitism had taken the German Christians into their deadly grip. These cultural forces had become authoritative sources and norms apart from and alongside Jesus Christ. "Whatever your heart clings to, that properly is your god," said Luther.[6]

NO SYSTEMATIC COORDINATION

Barth argued that the logic of the ellipse was a logic of systematic coordination. This kind of coordination meant that something alongside and apart

5. The Barmen Declaration, which has been widely reproduced, can be found in the appendix in *Reformed Confessions of the Sixteenth Century*, ed. Arthur C. Cochrane (Louisville, KY: Westminster John Knox, 2003), 332–36.
6. Martin Luther, Large Catechism, in *The Book of Concord*, ed. Theodore G. Tappert (Philadelphia: Fortress, 1959), 365.

from Christ was accorded a normative status that would qualify, condition, and restrict the affirmation of "Christ alone." It was in effect a matter of epistemological Pelagianism or semi-Pelagianism—Pelagianism of the mind as opposed to Pelagianism of the will. Whether openly or secretly, blatantly or subtly, it introduced a second source of revelation and a second norm for establishing revealed truth alongside and apart from Christ. Systematic coordination meant that this second source and norm of revelation was not only judged in light of Christ, but Christ was also judged in light of it.

Barth argued that this kind of logic pervaded Roman Catholic theology and modern liberal Protestantism ("Neo-Protestantism"), because they both involved "the systematic coordination of nature and grace" (p. 96). Brunner's interpretation domesticated Calvin's views by neatly "surveying"[7] them and systematically coordinating "God and [humankind], nature and grace, reason and revelation" (p. 99). By calling "natural revelation" a "preparation" or a "presupposition" of the divine revelation in Christ, "pre-Christian knowledge of God" was coordinated systematically with "Christian knowledge of God"— "with the result that [the former] becomes the framework and secret law of the latter" (p. 102).

Barth believed that the ellipse was inherently unstable. It always openly or secretly resolved itself into a new circle in which the second source and norm usurped the center that belonged exclusively to Christ. Christ himself was effectively relegated to the periphery. No matter how much he might be officially honored and praised, he was no longer the exclusive source and norm, the sole object and content, the true controlling center, of revelation. He had instead become like a satellite rotating around a different planet.

For Barth, the opposite of "systematic coordination" was not a complete absence of coordination; it was rather the total subordination—sometimes systematic, sometimes ad hoc—of all other secondary expressions of revelation as they might appear in culture, nature, or history. Barth did not deny that there were such expressions, but he wanted to interpret them christocentrically.

A TRINITARIAN LOGIC

As we continue to explore the contours of Barth's thought arising from his use of the First Commandment of the Decalogue as a theological axiom, the next question that needs to be addressed is, How was Jesus Christ as the one revelation of God to be understood in relation to all the diverse aspects that Barth believed were actually intrinsic to it and included within it? For Barth, revelation in Christ was exclusive as a source and norm, but inclusive in the wide diversity

---

7. I have revised the translation to replace the translator's use of "overlooks" which is confusing. Barth's meaning here is more akin to "looks over" than "fails to see."

of its many secondary and dependent expressions and manifestations in nature, culture and history.

If we think in terms of a sphere and its center, then revelation in Christ would be one and indivisible at the core, while still allowing for a diverse and abundant variety of expressions—an "almost confusing richness" of forms—projected outward from the core, and appearing, so to speak, on the surrounding surface of the sphere (*CD* II/1, 317). In all its forms, revelation in Christ was always one and unvarying. Although it was diversely manifested at the periphery, it was still always the same, and nowhere a different revelation. Revelation in Christ included an infinite richness within itself.

Three points need to be noted about how the one and the many, Christ the center along with secondary forms at the periphery, were related in revelation. First, the whole was, so to speak, always in the part. The material content at the core was always manifested *as a whole* in any of its diverse forms or aspects out at the surface of the sphere. Strictly speaking, the content of revelation was one and indivisible. It was never manifested only partially, though it could be and was manifested under particular aspects, and these different aspects could and did coexist simultaneously. (In this sense revelation was something like a hologram.)

An implicitly Trinitarian logic was at work here. In the doctrine of the Trinity, the reality of God (God's *ousia* or being) was seen as indivisible. It was not composed of three parts that added up to a larger whole. Quantitative modes of thinking could not be used in this case. Each "person" (or *hypostasis*) of the Trinity was in fact the one being of God as a whole. As we read in the Athanasian Creed: "The Father is God, the Son is God, and the Holy Spirit is God, and yet there are not three gods but one God." That was the mystery of the Holy Trinity in a nutshell. God's simple and indivisible being was internally complex, but it was not composite, in the sense of being composed of "parts."

Barth applied something like this "logic" to his idea of revelation. In Jesus Christ God's self-revelation to us was internally complex, but it was not composed of "parts." Each diverse form of its secondary manifestation, out there on the surface of the sphere, was somehow, even if indirectly, an expression of the whole as given in Christ at the central core.

Another analogy for this peculiar logic might be seen in the Lord's Supper. In the view of Aquinas, the whole Jesus Christ was present in the Eucharist under the forms of the consecrated elements. The bread and wine had been mystically converted into his body and blood. But his body and blood were not detached from the real presence of the living Christ as a whole person. The whole Christ was present under a particular form or aspect. The presence of the whole Christ under the particular forms of his body and blood was known as Aquinas's doctrine of "concomitance." Concomitance meant that there was a real union of the whole in and with the part or aspect under which it appeared. The whole was implicit and really present in and with the aspect.[8]

Barth made a similar move in thinking about the logic of revelation. Revelation could assume many different secondary aspects or forms in the world, but they were always forms (not parts) of its one indivisible content. Again, this was essentially a Trinitarian logic. It was a matter of one indivisible whole as being present and implicit in a diversity of forms or expressions or manifestations. In this sense revelation in Christ was like a great crystal with many facets. Each facet offered a different point from which to apprehend the whole.

A Hierarchy of Forms

Second, and quite unlike the persons of the Trinity (who are coeternal, coequal and coexistent), the secondary and dependent forms assumed by God's unitary revelation in Christ, as understood by Barth, were ranked in a hierarchy (see *CD* II/1:319). They did not all exist on the same level or with the same significance. A memorable remark may illustrate this. "God may speak to us," Barth wrote, "through Russian Communism, a flute concerto, a blossoming shrub, or a dead dog. We do well to listen to him if he really does. But . . . we cannot say that we are commissioned to pass on what we have heard as independent proclamation" (*CD* I/1:55). Note the key word "independent." Such manifestations of God, Barth insisted, were not normative in themselves, nor were they regular or standard. They had no independent validity. They were entirely ad hoc, occasional, and unpredictable. Other forms, however, might be more normal or standard, like God's self-manifestation through the order of nature—which Barth did not reject *simpliciter* but only *secundum quid*, that is, not absolutely or unconditionally but only in a certain, if rather crucial, respect. What he rejected was the utility of natural revelation apart from faith.[9]

In light of the First Commandment as a theological axiom, Barth thought that "natural revelation" through the order of the cosmos (1) could only be properly discerned in light of God's revelation in Christ and (2) that it was a *secondary and dependent form* of what is revealed in Scripture about creation as a work of the triune God in which Christ himself plays a central and decisive role (e.g., John 1:3; 1 Cor. 8:6; Col. 1:16). Revelation in Christ made explicit what was implicit in this cosmological form of revelation, but we could not

---

8. I must assume here without argument what I take to be the case, namely, that "concomitance" can be affirmed without entailing "transubstantiation." For "transelementation" (*metastoicheosis*) as an alternative to transubstantiation, see George Hunsinger, *The Eucharist and Ecumenism: Let Us Keep the Feast* (Cambridge: Cambridge University Press, 2008). In any case no tradition that upholds the real presence of Christ in the Eucharist, regardless of how it may be defined, believes that Christ is merely "partly" present. Rather, the whole Christ is conceived as present in a sacramental mode.

9. See especially Barth, *The Christian Life: Church Dogmatics IV/4: Lecture Fragments* (Grand Rapids: Eerdmans, 1981), 120–21.

know that it was implicit apart from revelation in Christ. Furthermore, apart from Christ natural revelation in the cosmological sense can only be apprehended improperly at best, and is in fact, under the conditions of the fall, always entangled in idolatry.

Note that making something explicit that was previously implicit is not the same as adding one thing on to another in an external or supplementary way. It may be noted in passing that revelation as it took place in the covenant with Israel was seen as an anticipation of revelation in Christ, so that it too was implicitly Christ-centered in a way that could not be apprehended apart from revelation in Christ. An example might be seen in Paul's statement in 1 Corinthians 10:4 that "the rock was Christ," where this truth could only have been known in retrospect. In any case, for Barth, all revelation, regardless of its form and manifest content, was implicitly or explicitly christocentric (by definition). "There are," Barth wrote, "strictly speaking no Christian themes independent of Christology, and the church must insist on this in its message to the world" (CD II/1:320). But whatever these diverse forms might be, some of them—like Scripture and the preaching based on it—were necessarily regular, normative and standard forms of revelation.

In Barth, Jesus Christ, Scripture, and preaching were all referred to as the Word of God, but they were not all the Word of God in the same way. There was one threefold Word of God, Barth taught, but these three forms were ranked in relation to each other. Jesus Christ was the one Word of God in the strict and proper sense. Scripture was God's Word in a secondary and dependent sense, and preaching was then tertiary and dependent on Scripture. Scripture and preaching were said to be indirectly identical with the Word of God (Jesus Christ) (See CD I/1:88–124).

Another illustration, besides the sphere and its central core, might be a tree with its trunk and its branch-work, extending even out to the twigs. This metaphor also has its limits but it gets at the idea of a hierarchy of forms existing in an ordered relation to one another. God's revelation in Christ, as Barth sees it, was manifest and variously implicit in a whole hierarchy of diverse forms, all of which had a very definite center in Christ, who was the sole norm and source, as well as the direct or indirect object and content, of them all. Again, some of these forms were regular and constant while others were occasional and temporary. Revelation in Christ was infinitely rich and diverse without ceasing to be unitary and indivisible. All the secondary and immanent forms of God's presence in the world, Barth stated, derive from Jesus Christ, "attesting him, serving and leading to him, as in fact disclosed to our sight and hearing in God's revelation" (CD II/1:318).

The idea that there was a hierarchy of forms all of which had a common center might best be illustrated not simply by a sphere with its central core (in which everything was in principle contained), and an outer surface, but rather by several concentric spheres, in which aspects of the center were made manifest in a ranked and ordered way. The innermost sphere would indicate those closer to the center while more remote aspects would appear at the surface of the outer spheres.

A One-Way Relationship of Absolute Dependence

Finally, the one and the many in revelation were governed by a relationship of absolute dependence. All the diverse forms of revelation were completely dependent on Christ at the center. Christ himself, on the other hand, the Lord of Revelation, was in no way dependent on them.[10] Christ and the secondary revelatory forms were related (1) by a pattern of unity-in-distinction and (2) by a one-way relationship of absolute dependence. It was they that were tested, criticized, and validated by Christ, not he by them.

In light of the First Commandment as a theological axiom, there was no way from them to him, but there was a way from him to them. In light of Christ at the Center, it became possible to apprehend something of the various forms of his presence and revelation in a hierarchy of expressions and significance. (Russian Communism, the flute concerto, etc. would be like the twigs. Word and Sacrament would be like the first big outgrowths of the main trunk.) Further out in the branch-work, somewhere in-between, would be natural revelation through the order of the cosmos.

Formally, the center and the periphery, Christ and the secondary forms, were related by what might be called the Chalcedonian pattern: "without separation or division," "without confusion or change," and asymmetrically, in a one-way relationship of absolute dependence. It was the Christ-centered pattern of an ordered unity-in-distinction. Christ was related to the forms, and they to him, in terms of both correspondence and coinherence, within the ordered scheme determined by Christ at the center.

How Nature and Grace Are Related: *Aufhebung*

For Barth there could be no simple continuity between nature and grace. Grace always meant both the judgment and the transformation of nature. Borrowing a term from Hegel (and redefining it), Barth saw this process of judgment and transformation as one of *Aufhebung*. The process involved three stages.

Stage 1. Something is posited or given: (+)

Stage 2. It is negated: – (+)

Stage 3. The negation of the negation: – [– (+)]

---

10. "There is a way," wrote Barth, "from Christology to anthropology, but there is no way from anthropology to Christology" (*CD* I/1:131).

The first stage was like the incarnation: (+); the second stage, like the crucifixion: [– (+)]; and the final stage, like the resurrection: – [– (+)]. If Christ took sin and death to himself on the cross in order to negate them from within, then his resurrection might be seen as God's "negation of the negation" in which Christ himself was delivered, validated and reconstituted on a higher plane.

For Barth, nature and grace did not exist on the same plane, nor did they differ merely by a matter of degree. The transformation of nature—especially in its fallen, corrupted state—by grace was not a gradual matter such as we would find in the relative transition from illness to health. On the contrary, it was a miraculous, drastic transformation. It involved a moment of severe judgment (stage two), in which the judgment was not partial but total. It was then followed by a miraculous restitution in which it was reconstituted to a new and higher state than it enjoyed before. Think, for example of Christ's risen body. It was still a body: (+); it bore the marks of the cross: – (+); but it was now a "spiritual body," that was somehow heavenly, luminous, mysterious and not subject to ordinary natural laws: – [– (+)]. It had been affirmed, negated and reconstituted on a higher, transcendent plane.

Resurrection, not a relative and gradual process like being healed from illness, was the model Barth used for thinking about how nature was transformed by grace. Nothing natural could ever be appropriated by grace, so that it found its proper place in relation to Christ the center, apart from a revolutionary process that moved from affirmation, through negation, and finally to a negation of the negation.

When Barth spoke about "miracle" in his "No!" to Brunner, he was presupposing this revolutionary process of dialectical transformation. It was a matter of miracle, not of merely repairing the old, broken-down human being by restoring it to its original unfallen condition (p. 94).

> The fact that we become hearers and doers of the Word of God signifies the realization of a divine possibility, not one that is inherent in our human nature. Freedom to know the true God is a miracle, a freedom of God, not one of our freedoms. (p. 117)
> The Holy Ghost, who proceeds from the Father and the Son, and is therefore revealed and believed to be God, does not stand in need of any point of contact but that which he himself creates. Only retrospectively is it possible to reflect on the way in which he "makes contact" with [the human being], and this retrospect will ever be a retrospect upon a *miracle*. (p. 121)

The transformation was not a matter of simple continuity, but of continuity in the midst of drastic discontinuity, or rather it was a matter of "the divine miracle" in which the "continuity" of our very existence was negated, retrieved and reconstituted on a higher plane, only as we were made to die and rise again in union with Christ by grace through faith (p. 92). There was no point of contact between a wholly corrupted human nature: – (+), and the advent of grace:

– [– (+)], except for the miracle of Christ's resurrection as made present and applied to us here and now in the power of the Holy Spirit through God's Word.

CONCLUSION

Consider a statement from Calvin. He rejects as "Pelagian" the idea that our sinful obtuseness about God needs nothing more than teaching and guidance from God's Word. Even David, he says, asked that "his eyes be opened to contemplate the mysteries of [God's] law" (Ps. 119:18). Calvin then states, "By this expression [David] evidently means that the sun rises upon the earth when God's Word shines upon [human beings]; but they do not have its benefit until he who is called the 'Father of lights' (James 1:17) *either gives eyes or opens them.* For wherever the Spirit does not cast his light, all is darkness."[11]

Calvin's main point is that even the Word is ineffectual without the Spirit to illumine our hearts and minds. But there is a significant difference in how this illumination may be accomplished. Would there not be a difference between actually being *given* eyes and merely having them be *opened?* Would not the first seem more radical than the second? There is a subtle ambiguity here that can be taken to point to an important difference between Barth and Brunner. The negation of the negation would imply that we get new eyes; the point of contact, that they simply needed to be corrected and opened.

> Whenever we meet with heathen writers, let us learn from the light of truth, which is admirable displayed in their works, that the human mind, fallen as it is, and corrupted from its integrity, is yet invested and adorned by God with excellent talents. If we believe that the Spirit of God is the only fountain of truth, we shall neither reject nor despise the truth itself wherever it shall appear, unless we wish to insult the Spirit of God.[12]

As I have shown in my essay on "Secular Parables of the Truth," much the same stance was strongly reaffirmed by Barth in a less pneumatological, but a more christocentric idiom.[13]

What Barth took away from nature with one hand, he gave back with the other by grace. He did so, in effect, on the basis of the First Commandment as a theological axiom. What that Commandment was thought to rule out was any independent sources and norms of revelation alongside biblical revelation as

---

11. John Calvin, *Institutes of the Christian Religion* 2.2.21; ed. John T. McNeill, trans. Ford Lewis Battles, LCC (Philadelphia: Westminster, 1960), 1:280–81, emphasis added.

12. John Calvin, *Institutes of the Christian Religion*; trans. John Allen, 6th American ed. (Philadelphia: Presbyterian Board of Publication and Sabbath-School Work, 1921), 1:246–247.

13. For a discussion of how this christological point was elaborated by Barth, see George Hunsinger, "Secular Parables of the Truth," in *How to Read Karl Barth* (Oxford: Oxford University Press, 1991), chap. 7.

it was centered and fulfilled in Christ. No systematic coordination was permitted between other supposed sources and norms and God as revealed in Christ. Nevertheless, the *No* to independent sources and norms as well as to systematic coordination—a *No* necessary because of the First Commandment—did not rule out but in fact included a corresponding *Yes*.

It was a *Yes* grounded in grace alone and apprehended by faith alone. It was, we might say, a faith-based *Yes*, a self-norming *Yes*, and a critical *Yes*. It involved elements of hierarchical ranking, correspondence, coinherence, and *Aufhebung*. It was an attempt to rethink the doctrine of revelation from a thoroughgoing christocentric standpoint. In revelation as in everything else, Barth believed, "[Christ] is before all things, and in him all things hold together" (Col. 1:17). But it did not take more for faith to discern, with proper caution and care, the operations of divine grace and revelation *extra muros ecclesiae*—outside the walls of the church, in various forms throughout nature and culture.[14]

14. I would like to thank Paul Molnar, Keith Johnson, and W. Travis McMacken for helpful comments on a previous version of this essay.

Chapter 13

John Paul II and Benedict XVI

WILLIAM E. MAY

Before presenting the teaching of Popes John Paul II and Benedict XVI on the Ten Commandments, it is advisable to note differences in the numbering and identification of the Ten Commandments in the Catholic and Protestant traditions. In the Catholic tradition they are numbered and identified as follows in the *Catechism of the Catholic Church,*

1. I am the Lord your God; you shall not have strange gods before me.
2. You shall not take the name of the Lord your God in vain.
3. Remember to keep holy the Lord's Day.
4. Honor your father and your mother.
5. You shall not kill.
6. You shall not commit adultery.
7. You shall not steal.
8. You shall not bear false witness against your neighbor.

9. You shall not covet your neighbor's wife.
10. You shall not covet your neighbor's goods.[1]

According to this tradition (also followed in the Lutheran tradition), the first three commandments, which have to do with our obligations to God, were inscribed on the "first tablet" that Moses brought down from Mount Sinai according to Exodus or Horeb according to Deuteronomy, whereas the final seven, which concern our obligations to our neighbor, were inscribed on the second of these tablets.

In the Protestant/Anglican tradition, the first four commandments are concerned with our relationship to God, and the second half of the First Commandment in the Catholic tradition was numbered as the Second Commandment, with subsequent renumbering of the other commandments, so that those pertaining to God have as the Fourth Commandment the hallowing on the Lord's Day, and those concerning our neighbors begin with honoring father and mother as the Fifth Commandment.

KAROL WOJTYLA/JOHN PAUL II

I will briefly consider John Paul II's treatment of the Ten Commandments when, as Karol Wojtyla, he served as professor of philosophy at the University of Kraków, and then examine his teaching of the commandments as Pope John Paul II.

Love and Responsibility

In 1960 Wojtyla wrote an exceptionally thoughtful work for his students focusing on the love meant to exist between man and woman, *Love and Responsibility*. In it he was very concerned with the Sixth and Ninth Commandments ("you shall not commit adultery" and "you shall not covet your neighbor's wife"). He viewed them through the prism of his "personalistic norm," and addressed the responsibilities of husbands and wives not only to themselves but to God, the author of marriage who has given it its internal structure and significance. In treating these responsibilities Wojtyla was at pains to show that adultery, covetousness, and an unwillingness to accept the gift of human life (linked to the Fifth Commandment, "You shall not kill") when engaging in the conjugal act, violated the personalistic norm. This norm in its negative aspect, states that the person is the kind of good which does not admit of use and cannot be

---

1. See *Catechism of the Catholic Church with Modifications from the* Editio Typica (New York: Doubleday Image, 1997), 551–52, where this way of naming and numbering the Ten Commandments is described as "A Traditional Catechetical Formula."

treated as an object of use and as such the means to an end. In its positive aspect the personalistic norm confirms this: the person is a good toward which the only proper and adequate response is love.[2]

According to Wojtyla there is a relationship between the personalistic norm and the "love commandment" of the New Testament that "demands from man love for others, for his neighbors—in the fullest sense, then, love for persons. For God, whom the commandment names first, is the most perfect personal Being."[3] Wojtyla does not provide a reference to any New Testament text concerning love for neighbors, but he undoubtedly had in mind a text such as Matthew 22:36–40 (and parallel texts in Mark 11:28–31 and Luke 10:25–28) in which Jesus speaks of the two great commandments: love of God above all things and love of one's neighbor as oneself.

In the fourth chapter of *Love and Responsibility* ("Justice toward the Creator"), Woytyla considers monogamy and the indissolubility of marriage. He argues that the personalistic norm requires monogamy and the indissolubility of marriage. After noting that Jesus dealt with this question decisively and indicating that attempts to justify the polygamy of the Old Testament patriarchs because of the desire for a numerous progeny do not really succeed (p. 213), Wojtyla argues (pp. 14–15) that the personalistic norm requires that marriage be monogamous and indissoluble once it has come into being despite subsequent desires on the part of husband and wife, because human choices, made in the light of the truth (cf. p. 214), *determine* the self, and that in choosing to marry a man and woman freely give themselves the identity of husband and wife, committing themselves henceforth to be utterly faithful to one another: the personalistic norm leads them to the irrevocable gift of self, to the full affirmation of the personhood of the other. Marriage thus embodies and demands observance of the Sixth and Ninth Commandments.

The Encyclical Veritatis Splendor

John Paul takes up the normative requirements or truths of natural law in his presentation of the essential link between obedience to the Ten Commandments, which the Catholic tradition has always recognized as requirements of natural law, and eternal life. Here he makes it clear that the primordial moral requirement of natural law is the twofold love of God and of neighbor and that the precepts of the second tablet of the Decalogue are based on the truth that we are to love our neighbor as ourselves.

He begins by noting that our Lord, in responding to the question posed to him by the rich young man, "Teacher, what good must I do to have eternal life?"

---

2. Karol Wojtyla, *Love and Responsibility*, trans. H. Willetts (New York: Farrar, Straus and Giroux, 1981; reprinted Ignatius Press, 1993), 41.

3. Ibid., 40.

(Matt. 19:16), shows that its answer can be found "only by turning one's mind and heart to the 'One' who is good. . . . *Only God can answer the question about what is good, because he is the Good itself*" (par. 9; cf. pars. 11, 12).[4] He continues by saying, "God has already given an answer to this question: he did so *by creating man and ordering him* with wisdom and love to his final end, through the law which is inscribed in his heart (cf. Romans 2:15), the 'natural law.' . . . He also did so *in the history of Israel*, particularly in the 'ten words,' the *commandments of Sinai*" (par. 12). John Paul II next reminds us that our Lord then told the young man: "If you wish to enter into life, keep the commandments" (Matt. 19:17). He says that Jesus, by speaking in this way, makes clear "the close connection . . . *between eternal life and obedience to God's commandments* [which] . . . show man the path of life and lead to it" (par. 12). The first three of the commandments of the Decalogue call "us to acknowledge God as the one Lord of all and to worship him alone for his infinite holiness" (par. 11). But the young man, replying to Jesus' declaration that he must keep the commandments if he wishes to enter eternal life, demands to know "which ones" (Matt. 18:19). John Paul II says, "he asks what he must do in life in order to show that he acknowledges God's holiness" (par. 13). In answering this question, Jesus reminds the young man of the Decalogue's precepts regarding our neighbor. "From the very lips of Jesus, man is once more given the commandments of the Decalogue" (par. 12). These Ten Commandments are based on the commandment that we are to love our neighbor as ourselves, a commandment expressing "*the singular dignity of the human person*, 'the only creature that God has wanted for its own sake'" (par. 13, with an internal citation from *Gaudium et spes*, n. 24).

What is the relationship between the primordial moral command to love our neighbor as ourselves and the quite specific commandments of the second tablet of the Decalogue? John Paul's answer is that we can love our neighbor and respect his or her dignity as a person *only* by cherishing the *real goods* perfective of him and by refusing to damage, destroy, or impede these goods. Appealing to the words of Jesus, John Paul II emphasizes that

> the different commandments of the Decalogue are really only so many reflections on the one commandment about the good of the person, at the level of the many different goods which characterize his identity as a spiritual and bodily being in relationship with God, with his neighbor, and with the material world. . . . The commandments of which Jesus reminds the young man are meant to safeguard *the good* of the person, the image of God, by protecting his *goods*." (par. 13)

The negative precepts of the Decalogue—"You shall not kill; You shall not commit adultery; You shall not steal; You shall not bear false witness"—"express with particular force the ever urgent need to protect human life, the communion of persons in marriage," and so on (par. 13). These negative precepts of the

---

4. John Paul II, *The Splendor of Truth: Veritatis Splendor, Encyclical Letter* (Boston: St. Paul Books & Media, 1993). It is also available at http://www.vatican.va/holy_father/john_paul_ii/encyclicals/documents/hf_jp-ii_enc_06081993_veritatis-splendor_en.html. Italics reflect the style of the original.

Decalogue, which protect the good of human persons by protecting the goods perfective of them, are among the universal and immutable moral absolutes proscribing intrinsically human acts, the teaching representing the "central theme" of the encyclical.

John Paul regards the precepts of the Decalogue as moral absolutes proscribing intrinsically evil *acts*. The truth of these moral absolutes is rooted in the primordial principle of natural law requiring us to love our neighbors—beings who, like ourselves, are persons made in the image of God and who, consequently, have an inviolable dignity. These moral absolutes, required by the love commandment, protect this dignity precisely by protecting the real goods perfective of human persons. These norms "represent the unshakable foundation and solid guarantee of a just and peaceful human coexistence, and hence of genuine democracy, which can come into being and develop only on the basis of the equality of all its members, who possess common rights and duties. *When it is a matter of moral norms prohibiting intrinsic evil, there are no privileges or exceptions for anyone*" (par. 96).

John Paul recognizes "the cost of suffering and grave sacrifice . . . which fidelity to the moral order can demand" (par. 93). He emphasizes that the Church "seeks, with great love, to help all the faithful to form a moral conscience which will make judgments and lead to decisions in accordance with the truth," ultimately with the truth revealed in Jesus. For it is "*in the Crucified Christ that the Church finds the answer*" to the question as to why we must obey "universal and unchanging moral norms" (par. 85). These norms are absolutely binding precisely because they protect the inviolable dignity of human persons, whom we are to love with the love of Christ, a self-sacrificial love ready to suffer evil rather than do it.

These absolute moral norms, which admit of *no* exceptions, point the way to fulfillment in Christ, the Crucified One, who "fully discloses man to himself and unfolds his noble calling by revealing the mystery of the Father and the Father's love" (par. 2, with a citation from *Gaudium et spes*, n. 22). "*The Crucified Christ*"—who gives to us the final answer why we must, if we are to be fully the beings God wants us to be, forbear doing the evil prohibited by absolute moral norms—"*reveals the authentic meaning of freedom: he lives it fully in the total gift of himself* and calls his disciples to share in his freedom" (par. 85).

As Jesus reveals to us, "freedom is acquired in *love*, that is, in the *gift of self* . . . the gift of self *in service to God and one's brethren*" (par. 87). This is the ultimate truth meant to guide free choices: to love, even as we have been and are loved by God in Christ, whose "crucified flesh fully reveals the unbreakable bond between freedom and truth, just as his Resurrection from the dead is the supreme exaltation of the fruitfulness and saving power of a freedom lived out in truth" (par. 87).

In our struggle to live worthily as beings made in God's image and called to communion with him we are not alone. We can live as God wills us to because he is ever ready to help us with his grace: the natural law is fulfilled, perfected, completed by the law of grace. God never commands the impossible: "Temptations can be overcome, sins can be avoided, because together with the commandments the Lord gives us the possibility of keeping them" (par. 102).

Catecheses on the Theology of the Body

John Paul's catecheses on the body began on September 5, 1979 and ended over five years later on November 28, 1984. Their length and their place as John Paul II's first teaching project as pope show how fundamental they are in his thought. Michael Waldstein has demonstrated that Karol Wojtyla had written the catecheses "Theology of the Body" (hereafter TOB) to be published as a book titled *Man and Woman He Created Them*.[5] Its publication was interrupted by Wotylya's election as pope on October 16, 1978. Sometime after his election, John Paul II personally adapted his manuscript for the Wednesday audience format.

A key idea of TOB, developed by John Paul II in the "catecheses" (=audiences) devoted to profound reflection the two accounts of creation found in Genesis 1 (the chronologically later account attributed to the Priestly and Elohist sources) and Genesis 2 (the chronologically older account attributed to the Yahwist source), is that the human body reveals the human person. A second key idea is that the human body, insofar as it is the body either of a male or female human person, has a "spousal" or "nuptial" meaning, that is, that the male body, precisely in its masculinity, is a sign that the male person is meant to be a "gift" to the female person, precisely in her femininity. This has ethical significance: a man ought never look at the body of a woman with a desire to "consume" her as a product but ought always to view her body as that of a person to be loved, and vice versa for a woman. All this John Paul sees confirmed in the fact that the second creation narrative stresses that the man and the woman were naked and were not ashamed. They were not ashamed because their naked bodies revealed them to each other as persons who are to be loved, not things to be used or consumed.

But Genesis 3, which stems from the same source as Genesis 2, tells the story of Adam's sin in eating the fruit from the tree of knowledge of good and evil that Eve, after yielding to the serpent's temptation, gave to him to eat. Then the eyes of both were opened; they were naked and were "ashamed." They were ashamed because concupiscence had entered the human heart and had veiled or obscured the spousal meaning of the body.

John Paul probes deeply into the effect of concupiscence both in subsequent catecheses on the text of Genesis and in those on our Lord's Sermon on the Mount and the teaching of Paul on purity of heart. I will focus on his reflections

---

5. On this see Waldstein's introduction to John Paul II, *Man and Woman He Created Them: A Theology of the Body*, introduction, translation, and index by Michael Waldstein (Boston: Pauline Books and Media, 2006), 7–11. All translations of TOB will be taken from this source. References will be made to the number of the audience (133 are given in the new translation), the paragraph number of that audience, and the page on which it appears in the new translation. Thus TOB 4.3, p. 143 refers to audience 4, paragraph 3, page 143 of the Waldstein translation.

on the Lord's Sermon on the Mount and Paul's teaching where he shows that precisely because of Christ's redemptive love we can, in union with him, recover the spousal meaning of the body and absorb concupiscence in love.

In the Sermon on the Mount Jesus deepens the meaning of the commandment "Do not commit adultery" by revealing the ethical meaning of the commandment (36.1, p. 271). Christ speaks of "adultery in the heart." If the fundamental meaning of adultery is that of a sin of the body, how can what a man does in his heart also count as adultery? "The man of whom Christ speaks in the Sermon on the Mount—the man who looks 'to desire'—is without doubt the man of concupiscence" (38.2, p. 279). But to see why he must be regarded as committing adultery we must recognize the ethical and anthropological significance of the "look to desire" or "lustful look."

The look expresses what is in the heart. The look, I would say, expresses what man is as a whole" (39.4, p. 285). Continuing, he says,

> . . . "looking to desire" indicates an experience of the value of the body in which its spousal meaning ceases to be spousal precisely because of concupiscence. What also ceases is its procreative meaning. . . . So then, when man "desires" and "looks to desire" . . . he *experiences* more or less explicitly *the detachment from that meaning of the body* which . . . stands at the basis of the communion of persons (39.5, pp. 285–86).
>
> Although society does not regard the exterior act of genital union between a married man and his own wife as "adultery" (42.5, p. 295), we conclude that . . . in *understanding* "adultery in the heart," Christ takes into consideration not only the real juridical state of life of the man and the woman in question. Christ makes the moral evaluation of "desire" depend above all *on the personal dignity itself of the man and the woman;* and this is important both in the case of unmarried persons and—perhaps even more so—in the case of spouses, husband and wife (42.7, p. 297).
>
> Adultery "in the heart" is not committed only because man "looks" in this way at a woman who is not his wife, but *precisely because he looks in this way at a woman. Even* if he were to look in this way at the woman who is his wife, he would commit the same adultery "in the heart." (43.2, p. 298)

But by union with Christ man can rediscover the "spousal meaning" of the body as it was "in the 'beginning.'" He can do so because Christ has won for us the redemption of the body. The pope develops this idea in his reflections on our Lord's Sermon on the Mount (Matt. 5). Jesus' words, "But I say to you, everyone who looks at a woman to desire her has already committed adultery with her in his heart" (cited in TOB 46.1, pp. 309–10),

> do not allow us to stop at the accusation of the human heart and to cast it into a state of continual suspicion, but that they must be understood and interpreted as an appeal to the heart. *This derives from the very nature of the ethos of redemption. . . .* Redemption is a truth . . . in the name of which man must feel called, and "called with effectiveness." He must become aware of this call also through Christ's words . . . reread in the full context of the revelation of the body. Man *must feel himself called to rediscover,* or

even better, to realize the spousal meaning of the body and to express in this way the interior freedom of the gift, that is, of that spiritual state and that power that derive from mastery over the concupiscence of the flesh. (46.4, p. 312–13)

Christ's words "testify that *the original power* (thus also the grace) *of the mystery of creation becomes* for each of them [man and woman] *the power* (that is, the grace) *of the mystery of redemption*. This concerns the very 'nature,' the very substrate of the humanity of the person, the deepest impulses of the 'heart'" (46.5, p. 313). We must realize that eros must not be equated with lust. For Plato eros "represents the inner that draws man toward all that is good, true, and beautiful" (47.2, p. 316). It refers also to the natural and hence "good" desire experienced in the attraction of men for women and vice versa. However "erotic" desire is often identified with lust (47.3, p. 317). A proper interpretation of the Sermon on the Mount, taking into account the multiple meanings of "eros," allows us "to find room for that ethos, for those ethical and indirectly also theological contents that have been drawn in the course of our analyses from Christ's appeal to the human heart in the Sermon on the Mount" (47.4, p. 317). Christ's appeal is

> . . . the category proper to the ethos of redemption. The call to what is true, good, and beautiful means, at the same time, in the ethos of redemption, the necessity of overcoming what derives from the threefold concupiscence . . . If the words of Matthew 5.27–28 represent such a call, then this means that, in the erotic sphere, "eros" and "ethos" do not diverge, are not opposed to each other, but are *called to meet in the human heart and to bear fruit in this meeting*. (47.5, p. 318)

Ethos must become the "constituent form" of eros. "Mere desire" is quite different from a "noble pleasure," and "when sexual desire is connected with a noble pleasure, it differs from desire pure and simple" (48.4, p. 320). Only through self-control can human beings attain "*that deeper and more mature spontaneity* with which his 'heart,' by mastering the instincts, rediscovers the spiritual beauty of the sign constituted by the human body in its masculinity and femininity" (48.5, p. 321).

John Paul further develops the truth that Christ has won the redemption of the body in his reflections on the teaching of Paul. Paul's horizons are the "beginning" in the sense of the first sin from which "life according to the flesh" originated and the final victory over sin and death of which Christ's resurrection is the sign. The "justification" we have through faith in Christ "is *a real power at work in man that reveals and affirms itself in his actions*" (51.4, p. 333). After contrasting Paul's opposition between the "works of the flesh" (e.g., fornication, enmity, anger) and works "of the Spirit" (e.g., love, joy, peace, self-control) (cf. Gal. 5:19–21), John Paul II affirms, "behind each of these realizations [i.e., the "works of the Spirit"], these ways of behaving, these moral virtues, stands a *specific choice*, that is, an effort of the will, a fruit of the human spirit permeated by the Spirit of God, which is manifested in choosing good." Among the fruits of the Spirit Paul includes "self-control" (51.6, pp. 334–35). John Paul stresses that when Paul speaks of putting to death the deeds of the body with the Spirit's help, he expresses the same thing Christ did in his Sermon on the Mount when he appealed to the heart and urged it to control lustful looks.

Mastery of *"putting to death the deeds of the body by the Spirit" is an indispensable condition of "life according to the Spirit,"* that is, the "life" that is the antithesis of the "death" about which he [Paul] speaks in the same context. . . . The term "death," therefore, does not signify only bodily death, but also the sin that theology was to call mortal" (52.4, p. 337).

However, "since by 'purity' must be understood the correct way of treating the sexual sphere according to one's personal state (and not necessarily absolute abstention from sexual life), such 'purity' is doubtlessly included in the Pauline concept of 'mastery' or *enkrateia.*" (53.5, p. 345).

Paul describes this purity in 1 Thessalonians 4:3–5 as follows: "For this is the will of God, your sanctification: that you abstain from unchastity, that each one of you knows how to keep his own body with holiness and reverence, not as the object of lustful passions." Someone manifests the self-control, the "purity" that Paul demands when "he knows how to control his own body with holiness and reverence, not as the object of lustful passions" (54.2, p. 342). Purity requires both "abstention" (from unchaste behavior) and "control" over one's own body "in holiness and honor" (54.3, p. 343). John Paul then relates the Pauline meaning of "honor" to his teaching on purity:

> To understand the Pauline teaching on purity, one must enter deeply into the meaning of "reverence," obviously understood here as a power belonging to the spiritual order. It is precisely this interior power that gives full dimension to purity as a virtue, that is, the ability to act in that whole sphere in which man discovers, in his own innermost [being], the many impulses of "lustful passions" and at times, for various reasons, surrenders to them. (54.4, p. 344)

Paul's teaching on respect for the sanctity of the human body, central to the Thessalonian text, is deepened in 1 Corinthians 12:18, 22–25, which states:

> God arranged the members of the body, each one of them, as he willed. . . . [T]he members of the body that seem weaker are more necessary, and those members of the body that we think less honorable we clothe with greater reverence, and our unpresentable members are treated with greater modesty, whereas our more presentable members do not need this. But God has so arranged the body, giving the greater honor to the member that lacked it, so that there may be no disunion in the body, but the members may have care for one another. (54.5, p. 344)

Commenting on this text, the pope says:

> Although the topic of the text just quoted is the theology of the Church
> as the Body of Christ, one can nevertheless note in the margin of this pas-
> sage that with his great ecclesiological analogy . . . Paul contributes . . . *to
> a deeper understanding of the theology of the body.* While in 1 Thessalonians
> he writes about keeping the body "with holiness and reverence," in the pas-
> sage just quoted from 1 Corinthians he wants to show this human body as
> deserving reverence or respect; one could say that he wants the recipients
> of his Letter to have the right understanding of the human body. Thus,
> the Pauline description of the human body in 1 Corinthians seems to be
> strictly tied to the recommendations of 1 Thessalonians. . . . This is an
> important line of thought, perhaps the essential one, of the Pauline doc-
> trine on purity. (54.6, pp. 344–45)

He then links all of this to the phenomenon of shame:

> In Paul's expressions about the "unpresentable members" of the human
> body, as well as about those "that seem to be weaker" or those "that we
> think less honorable," we find . . . *the testimony of the same shame* that the
> first human beings, male and female, had experienced after original sin.
> This shame impressed itself on them and on all the generations of "his-
> torical" man as the fruit of the threefold concupiscence (with particular
> reference to the concupiscence of the flesh). And what impressed itself at
> the same time . . . is a certain "echo" of man's original innocence itself: a
> "negative," as it were, of the image whose "positive" had been precisely
> original innocence. (55.4, pp. 346–47)

Paul ties his description of the human body to the state of "historical" man, at
whose threshold in history there is the experience of shame connected with "dis-
cord in the body." "Paul also indicates *the way* that leads (precisely on the basis of
the sense of shame) to the transformation of this [historical] state, to the *gradual
victory over that 'disunion in the body,'* a victory which can and should be realized
in the human heart. This is precisely the way to purity . . ." (55.7, p. 348). For
Paul purity has both a moral dimension as a virtue and a charismatic dimension as a gift, a fruit of life "according to the Spirit." In 1 Corinthians 6:19 Paul
writes: "Do you not know that your body is a temple of the Holy Spirit within
you, which you have from God? You are not your own." He says this only after
warning the Corinthians about the grave moral requirements of purity: "Shun
immorality. Every other sin which a man commits is outside the body; but the
immoral man sins against his own body" (1 Cor. 6:18). Such sins therefore "profane" the body, depriving a the body of a man or woman "of the reverence that
is its due because of the dignity of the person" and (much more so) due to "the
supernatural reality of the indwelling and continuous presence of the Holy Spirit
in man—in his soul and body—as the fruit of the redemption accomplished by
Christ" (56.3, p. 350). Moreover, our redemption came at a price, that of Christ's
death (1 Cor. 6:20). Thus the human body "is not meant for immorality, but for
the Lord, and the Lord for the body" (1 Cor. 6:13).

Thus in 1 Corinthians 6:15–17 Paul makes it clear that a Christian, who has become one body with Christ, not only commits an immoral sexual act by joining his body to a prostitute but also profanes the whole body of Christ. Because the human body, redeemed by Christ, is so supernaturally holy, Christians have a special duty to "keep" their bodies "with holiness and reverence" (56.5, p. 351).

Conclusion: John Paul II's Teaching on the Ten Commandments

Pope John Paul II, following the Catholic tradition,[6] firmly teaches that the precepts of the second tablet of the Decalogue (Commandments Four through Ten) are absolute moral norms that admit of no exceptions. Significantly, his encyclical *Veritatis Splendor,* which was addressed to all the bishops of the Catholic Church and condemned the teleological, consequentialist moral methodology of theologians who denied the existence of moral absolutes and intrinsically evil acts, includes the following passage in its final part:

> Each of us [bishops] knows how important is the teaching which represents the central theme of this Encyclical and which is today being restated with the authority of the Successor of Peter. Each of us can see the seriousness of what is involved, not only for individuals but also for the whole of society, with the *reaffirmation of the universality and immutability of the moral commandments,* particularly those, which prohibit always and without exception *intrinsically evil acts.*" (par. 115)

What has this to do with the Ten Commandments? The answer is a great deal. Pope John Paul II, along with the entire Catholic tradition as articulated by the magisterium of the church—for instance in the celebrated Roman Catechism or Catechism of the Council of Trent—and in the more recent *Catechism of the Catholic Church*—holds as a truth of Catholic Faith that the Commandments are integrally included in the natural law and that the Catholic Church has the God-given authority to interpret both the divine law and the natural law.

THE TEACHING OF JOSEPH RATZINGER / POPE BENEDICT XVI

Two major essays by Cardinal Joseph Ratzinger, highly critical of the views of those contemporary Catholic theologians who dissent from the Church's teaching

---

6. The Catholic Tradition, as set forth in the thought of Thomas Aquinas in his *Summa theologiae,* 1–2, q.100, a.8 and in the section of the *Roman Catechism* or *Catechism of the Council of Trent* on the Ten Commandments, strongly affirmed that the precepts of the second tablet of the Decalogue (Commandments 4 through 10 in the Catholic numbering) were absolute moral norms that admitted of no exceptions. Some contemporary authors cite certain texts of Aquinas outside of their context to defend dissent from this teaching. An excellent source defending it and showing the errors of dissenting theologians is Patrick Lee, "Permanence of the Ten Commandments: St. Thomas and His Modern Commentators," *Theological Studies* 42, no. 3 (Sept., 1981), 422–443. The same is true of the new *Catechism of the Catholic Church,* as Pope Benedict has noted.

on the absoluteness of the precepts of the Decalogue, are "The Church's Teaching Authority-Faith-Morals," published originally in German in 1979,[7] and "Handing on the Faith and the Sources of the Faith," published in French in 1983.[8] In both these essays his major concern is to affirm that God has entrusted to the magisterium of the Catholic Church, vested in the pope, the successor of Peter and bishops in union with him, the authority to give the authentic interpretation of Scripture. In each of these essays one of his principal concerns is to defend the teaching of the Roman Catechism or Catechism of the Council of Trent, that the norms set forth in the Fourth through Tenth Commandments admit of no exceptions as understood and taught by the church. While still a Cardinal he strongly affirmed the same regarding the teaching of the new *Catechism of the Catholic Church*.[9]

"The Church's Teaching Authority"

This essay is an important source for Ratzinger's moral thought. It is divided as follows: (1) an outline of the problem (pp. 47–52); (2) an initial response (pp. 52–55); (3) three examples of the interrelationship of faith and morals (pp. 55–65), which is subdivided into the Ten Commandments [pp. 55–58]; the name "Christian" [pp. 58–61]; and the apostolic exhortation [pp. 62–65]; and (4) faith-morals-teaching authority (pp. 66–73).

In (1) Ratzinger contrasts the focus on orthopraxis versus the focus on orthodoxy. In (2) he emphasizes that

> The originality of Christianity does not consist in the number of propositions for which no parallel can be found elsewhere (if there *are* such propositions, which is highly questionable). It is impossible to distill out what is specifically Christian by excluding everything that has come about though contact with other milieu. Christianity's originality consists rather in a new total form into which human searching and striving have been forged under the guidance of faith in the God of Abraham, the God of Jesus Christ. The fact that the Bible's moral pronouncements can be traced to other cultures . . . in no way implies that morality is a function of mere reason. . . . What is important . . . is the particular position they have or do not have in the spiritual edifice of Christianity. . . . it is incorrect to say that biblical faith simply adopted the morality of the surrounding world. . . . What we find is that, guided by Israel's perception of Yahweh, an often dramatic struggle took place between those elements of the surrounding legal and moral tradition that could be assimilated by Israel and those that Israel was bound to reject. (p. 53–54)

7. This essay was published in *Prinzipien Christlicher Moral* (Einsiedeln: Johannes-Verlag, 1975); English translation, *Principles of Christian Morality*, trans. Graham Harrison (San Francisco: Ignatius Press, 1986), 13–40.

8. This essay was originally published as *Transmettre la Foi au'jourdhui* in 1983; English translation in *Handing on the Faith in an Age of Disbelief*, trans. Michael J. Miller (San Francisco: Ignatius Press, 2006), 13–40.

9. Joseph Cardinal Ratzinger, "Current Doctrinal Relevance of the Catechism of the Catholic Church," 9 Oct. 2002; section on "Christian Moral Teaching in the Catechism" is accessible at http://www.vatican.va/roman_curia/congregations/cfaith/doc_rat_index.htm.

In (3), "three examples of the interrelationship of faith and morals," he begins with the Ten Commandments.

> The "Ten Words" show in practical terms what it means to believe in Yahweh, to accept the covenant with Yahweh. At the same time they define the figure of God himself, whose nature is manifested through them. This situates the Ten Commandments in the context of God's decisive self-revelation in Exodus 3, for there too God's self-portrayal is expressed in practical terms by setting forth his moral will: he has heard the groaning of the oppressed and come to liberate them . . . for Israel, the Ten Commandments are part of the concept of God . . . they show who this God is . . . Connected with this is the concept of the "holy" as it has developed in the religion of the Bible . . . through the "Ten Words" it becomes clear . . . that Yahweh's total otherness, his "holiness," is a moral dimension; to it corresponds man's moral action in accord with the "Ten Words" . . . the concept of the "holy" as the specific category of the divine has already coalesced with the concept of the moral; that is what is new and unique about this God and his holiness, and it is also what imparts a new status to the category of the "moral" [anticipating] Jesus' own picture of God. (pp. 55–57)

He then meditates on the name "Christian."

> In Roman Law . . . the *christiani* were members of Christ's band of conspirators; from the time of Hadrian, therefore, bearing the name "Christian" was a crime . . . for the pagan. The word *christianus* meant a conspirator . . . In response Ignatius of Antioch uses words that came to have a long history in Christian apologetics. In Greek phonetics, the word *chrestos* ("good") was, and is, pronounced *Christos*. Ignatius seizes on this. . . . The conspiracy of the Christians is a conspiracy of those who are *chrestos*, a conspiracy of goodness. . . . Here the link we found in the Ten Commandments between the concept of the moral idea is repeated on a most sublime and exacting level in the Christian context: the name "Christian" implies fellowship with Christ, and hence the readiness to take upon oneself martyrdom in the cause of goodness. (p. 61)

Finally, he considers *the apostolic exhortation* clearly expressed in 1 Thessalonians 4:11 and following. "As you learned from us how you ought to live. . . . For you know what instructions we gave you through the Lord Jesus." Ratzinger says,

> No doubt it is correct that here as elsewhere [e.g., in Phil. 4:8] Paul is referring to the moral awareness that conscience has awakened among the pagans, and that he identifies this awareness with the true law of God, according to the principles developed in Romans 2.15. . . . Conscience, as such, uncovers what is constant and thus necessarily leads to the "mind of Christ". . . . [But] anyone who reads the Pauline letters carefully will see that the apostolic exhortation is not some moralizing appendix with a variable content but a very practical setting forth of what faith means; hence, it is inseparable from faith's core. (p. 65)

In (4), his treatment of faith-morals-teaching authority, he emphasizes, the Church's official teaching does not end with the age of the apostles. It is a permanent gift to the Church ... the authentic followers of the apostles bear responsibility to see that the Church abides in the teaching of the apostles ... (p. 69)

it is manifest that the fundamental content of apostolic succession consists primarily in the authority to preserve apostolic faith; also that the plenitude of teaching authority that goes with this includes the task of making concrete the moral demands of grace and of working them out in detail with regard to the contemporary situation. (pp. 69–70)

Today this office is indispensable. Those who fundamentally deny that it has any competence to make detailed and practical decisions for or against an interpretation on the morality that springs from grace are trying to overturn the very basic form of apostolic tradition. (p. 73)

"Handing on the Faith and the Sources of the Faith"

Ratzinger's second major essay related to our theme has two major parts: (I) The Crisis of Catechesis and the Problem of Sources and (II) Toward Overcoming the Crisis. Part I is subdivided into (1) General Description of the Crisis and (2) Catechesis, the Bible, and Dogma. Part II is subdivided into (1) What Is Faith? (2) What Are Sources? and (3) The Structure of Catechesis.

In I.1, The Crisis of Catechesis and the Problem of the Sources, Ratzinger first considers contemporary culture, which is a-metaphysical and technological wherein morality is identified as social acceptability, as a major contributor to this crisis. As a result "the whole world view is mirrored ... in the news media ... and nourished by them. To a great extent, the representation of the world and of events in the media today makes more of an impression on people's awareness than their own experience of reality" (p. 14). He then shows that "an initial and momentous error down this road [of catechetics trying to find new ways to cope with the cultural situation] was doing away with the catechism and declaring in general that the category 'catechism' was outmoded" (p. 15). This happened because partly as a "pedagogical development that was characterized by a hypertrophy of method as opposed to content. The method became the measure of the content and was no longer the vehicle for it. In this way the actual potential of the faith to be an agent of change was crippled. Catechetics now understood itself, no longer as a continuation and concretization of dogmatic theology or systematic theology, but rather as a self-sufficient standard" (p. 15–16).

Going deeper we discover that "catechists no longer dared to present the faith as an organic whole, on its own terms, but only piecemeal, in excerpts that reflected individual anthropological experiences." This was "ultimately due to the fact that they no longer had confidence in that whole. It was due to a crisis of faith, or, more precisely, to a crisis of the faith shared *with* the Church of all ages ... dogma was largely left out of catechesis, and teachers tried to construct the faith right out of the Bible" (p. 17).

Here we come to the heart of the matter, "the status of the 'sources' in the process of handing on the faith. A form of catechesis that expounded the faith single-handedly, so to speak, directly from the Bible. However, "the Scriptures cannot be separated from the living community, the only context in which they are 'Scripture' in the first place" (p. 18).

The section called "Toward Overcoming the Crisis" is subdivided into "What Is Faith?" (pp. 23–28), "What Are 'Sources'?" (pp. 29–32), and "The Structure of Catechesis" (pp. 33–40). Regarding the first issue, faith must not be dissolved into theory. "The baptismal faith does not have to prove itself in theory, but rather theory must prove itself in reality, to the 'knowledge' of the truth that is given in the baptismal profession of faith" (p. 24). After quoting 1 John 2:27 Ratzinger says,

> Here, in the name of the apostolic authority of the disciple who had touched the Word-made-flesh, the faithful are challenged to resist the disintegration of their faith into theories, which are undertaken in the name of the authority of the intellect. This says to Christians that their authority, their "court of appeal" of the Church's faith, is higher than the authority of theological theory, because their faith expresses the Church's life, which has a higher standing than theological explanations. (pp. 24–25)

Ratzinger says that we must clarify what is understood by faith and what a "source of faith" actually is.

> The most important Catholic catechism [as of 1983], the *Roman Catechism* published during the reign of Pope Pius V following the Council of Trent, comments on the purpose and content of catechesis, noting that the sum total of Christian knowledge is expressed in the saying of the Redeemer that John has handed down: "This is eternal life, that they know you, the only true God, and Jesus Christ, whom you have sent." (John 17.3) (p. 25)

Ratzinger affirms "faith is life because it is relationship; a knowledge that becomes love and love that comes from knowledge and leads to knowledge . . . Hence the essential task of catechesis is to lead to the knowledge of God and of the One whom he has sent, or, as the *Roman Catechism* advisedly says, to remind people of this knowledge, for it is written in the deepest part of each and every one of us" (pp. 26–27).

But we find another essential aspect in the First Epistle of John.

> The very first verse describes the Apostle's experience as a seeing and touching of the Word that is life and that became tangible because it became flesh. From this resulted the Apostle's task of passing on what he had seen and heard (cf. 1 John 1:1–4). Faith, therefore, is not only directed frontally toward the "Thou" of God and Christ; this contact, rather, which is inaccessible for man by himself, is revealed in communion with those to whom he has communicated himself. This communion . . . is the gift of the Holy Spirit . . . Faith, therefore, has not only an "I" and a "Thou," but also a "We"; in this "We" lives every memory that enables us to recover what has

been forgotten: God and the One whom he has sent . . . In other words, there is no faith without the Church. (p. 27)

Concerning "Sources," he refers to how revelation was understood in the thirteenth century. Theologians, then, did not use either "revelation" or "source" to refer to the Bible "but the respect for it was much more unconditional" than it is today. For them theology

> can and should be nothing other than interpretation of Scripture. But their concept of the harmony between what is written and what is lived out was different from contemporary notions . . . the term 'revelation' was applied only, on the one hand, to that ineffable act which can never be adequately expressed in human words, in which God makes himself known to his creatures, and, on the other hand, to that act of reception in which this gracious condescension of God dawns upon man and becomes revelation. Everything that can be grasped in words, and thus Scripture, too, is then testimony to that revelation but is not revelation itself. And only revelation itself is also a 'source' in the strict sense, the source by which Scripture is nourished. (p. 29)

> When one views the Bible merely as a source in the [historical-critical method] then the only competence for interpreting it is that of the historian . . . If . . . the Bible is the precipitate (or product) of a much greater . . . inexhaustible process of revelation . . . this does not diminish the Bible's importance, but . . . fundamentally transforms the question about competency in interpreting it . . . the Bible is part of a referential context in which the living God communicates himself in Christ through the Holy Spirit . . . it is the expression and instrument of that communion, in which the "I" of God and the "Thou" in man come into contact within the "We" of the Church that Christ has inaugurated. [The Bible] is then part of a living organism . . . that holds the "copyright" to the Bible and can speak of it as its very own. (pp. 30–31)

> If the foregoing description is correct, then in catechesis historical sources necessarily have to be viewed at all times in connection with the real source, namely, with the God who acts in Christ. This source . . . can be accessed only within that living organism which created it and continually keeps it alive. In this organism the books of Sacred Scripture and the declarations of the Church's faith that explains them are not dead witnesses of past things; rather, they are the sustaining elements of a common life. Here they have never ceased being a living reality at the same time delimiting the present; inasmuch as they bring us together with the One who holds time in his hands, they also make the boundaries between the ages permeable. The past and the future touch one another in the today of the faith. (pp. 31–32)

In the section on the structure of catechesis, Ratzinger says that the framework of catechesis

> . . . follows from the fundamental events in the life of the Church, which correspond to the essential dimensions of Christian life. Thus in the earliest period a catechetical structure developed that goes back to the origins

of the Church, a structure as old as or even older than the canon of biblical writings . . . it was a question . . . of a simple arrangement of the requisite memorized material of the faith: the Apostles' Creed, the sacraments, the *Ten Commandments* and the Lord's Prayer. These four classical "principal divisions" of catechesis have sufficed over the centuries as organizational subdivisions and collecting points for catechetical instruction and have simultaneously opened the way into the Bible as well as into the living Church. (pp. 32–33, emphasis added)

This was the structure of the Roman Catechism—and in 1993 in the *Catechism of the Catholic Church* published in 1993.]

From this we can see how deeply Ratzinger valued the Ten Commandments. He has as pope consistently urged use of the *Catechism of the Catholic Church*, whose third part, on the moral life, takes up the Decalogue in detail with a teaching fully in line with the Roman Catechism, which Benedict, as a theologian, regarded so highly.

Scripture Index

Name and Subject Index